Contemporary Criminal Justice Careers

Contemporary Criminal Justice Careers

A Comprehensive Guide

Matthew J. Sheridan
Thomas J. Lalka

ROWMAN & LITTLEFIELD
Lanham • Boulder • New York • London

Published by Rowman & Littlefield
An imprint of The Rowman & Littlefield Publishing Group, Inc.
4501 Forbes Boulevard, Suite 200, Lanham, Maryland 20706
www.rowman.com

86-90 Paul Street, London EC2A 4NE, United Kingdom

British Library Cataloguing in Publication Information Available

Library of Congress Cataloging-in-Publication Data

Names: Sheridan, Matthew J., 1948-author. | Lalka, Thomas J., 1953- author. | Rainville, Raymond R.,1948-Exploring and understanding careers in criminal justice.
Title: Contemporary criminal justice careers: a comprehensive guide / Matthew J. Sheridan, Thomas J. Lalka.
Description: Lanham: Rowman & Littlefield, [2022] | Completely revised edition of: Exploring and understanding careers in criminal justice: a comprehensive guide, first published in 2016. | Includes bibliographical references and index. | Summary: "Picking up where Exploring and Understanding Careers in Criminal Justice, left off, this book provides an updated guide for the novice and professional alike, full of essential information from entrance into the profession, through career development, occupational refocus, professional options, to retirement preparation"—Provided by publisher.
Identifiers: LCCN 2022005711 (print) | LCCN 2022005712 (ebook) | ISBN 9781538168103 (cloth; alk. paper) | ISBN 9781538168127 (paperback; alk. paper) | ISBN 9781538168110 (epub)
Subjects: LCSH: Criminal justice, Administration of—Vocational guidance—United States. | Law enforcement—Vocational guidance—United States.
Classification: LCC HV9950 .S545 2022 (print) | LCC HV9950 (ebook) | DDC 364.973023—dc23/eng/20220228
LC record available at https://lccn.loc.gov/2022005711
LC ebook record available at https://lccn.loc.gov/2022005712

™ The paper used in this publication meets the minimum requirements of American National Standard for Information Sciences—Permanence of Paper for Printed Library Materials, ANSI/NISO Z39.48-1992.

Matthew J. Sheridan

For Mom; Lynda, my wife; and McKenzie, my daughter, who have provided love, encouragement, and support. For my father, who would have loved to have seen this. Since the publication of the first edition of Exploring and Understanding Careers in Criminal Justice, *my friend, my writing partner, and the greatest colleague Raymond R. Rainville passed away. His writings have been an inspiration, and his contribution to the first edition are preserved.* Contemporary Criminal Justice Careers: A Comprehensive Guide *is dedicated to the memory of Raymond R. Rainville, scholar, husband, father, and educator. Finally, this book is dedicated to every student who sat before me and taught me what they needed to know. Hopefully, every student who now reads this book will be helped toward a successful career.*

Thomas J. Lalka

This work is dedicated to my parents, Stanley and Stephanie Lalka, may their souls rest in peace. They have taught all our family that "Education is something that no one can take from you." This work is also dedicated to Wakako Takasaki, my wife. I could never have completed this task without her patience, encouragement, understanding, and love. Since the publication of the first edition of Exploring and Understanding Careers in Criminal Justice, *Raymond R. Rainville passed away. While not knowing Ray, his scholarship is an inspiration, hence my contributions to this book are dedicated to his memory.*

Contents

Foreword

WHAT TO EXPECT

If you are considering a career in the criminal justice field, it is essential that you base your decisions on the information in this book. You will not only need a description of the job, but also the availability of positions, opportunities for advancement, educational requirements (language and computer skills), and the respect accorded the professionals in the field. You will have to consider the sources of stress associated with the careers that you have chosen such as physical danger at one extreme and shift work at the other. Potential income and benefits are also important factors.

In order to evaluate the information in this book, it is important that you know something about the authors. For example, I have known Dr. Matthew J. Sheridan for 24 years.

DR. MATTHEW J. SHERIDAN

In 1990, the State of New Jersey established the guidelines for the position of Licensed Professional Counselor. Those of us in the addictions field had already planned to develop a 60-credit Master of Arts program to train people to be professional counselors. Having spent nine years at Integrity House, a well-respected drug therapeutic community (TC) in Newark, New Jersey, I was aware of the need for such a program. The basic courses covered counseling theories, the history of the addictions field, developmental issues, social and community factors, behavioral research, tests and measurements and program planning and evaluation techniques. Students were also required to have an internship experience. In addition, there were special topics. Dr. Sheridan's course, "Addictions Counseling in Criminal Justice," was the most popular of these special courses. I met Dr. Sheridan at the annual conference for counselors and administrators in New Jersey. He was the keynote speaker. I was so impressed by his presentation that I decided to hire him to teach an advanced graduate course in addictions and the criminal justice system. That course was designed to incorporate the special vocabulary in the field (See Dr. Sheridan's dictionary: *Historical Dictionary of American Criminal Justice*) as well as the experience of incarceration.

Over the years, I have followed many of our graduates, especially those who have become responsible administrators and program planners. When I asked what they remembered most about the master's degree courses, they invariably refer to Dr. Sheridan's class. Not only were they able to communicate using the vocabulary of the field, but they were also able to understand the experiences that they might not have faced previously. They also laughed when they heard a clinical psychologist state that he had never had an alcoholic or addict as a patient. They felt that he wouldn't have recognized the telltale signs. One also needs to know the questions to ask and the behaviors to analyze.

What was most challenging for the program was the makeup of the student body. Most of them had been counselors in such therapeutic communities as Integrity House, CURA (the Hispanic Program), and Daytop, their adolescent facility in Mendham, New Jersey. Many of these experienced counselors (Dr. Sheridan's students) were also administrators. One of the students was a lawyer with expertise in compulsive gambling as well as addictions. The TC counselors were in recovery. Given their backgrounds, they felt comfortable in challenging our expertise. One course that they did not criticize was Dr. Sheridan's criminal justice class. Since the students were also working, they commented that their skills were greatly improved, especially their ability to communicate with many of their colleagues and with their clients. Despite the fact that they had to travel for the program and spend hard earned time and money for a 60-credit degree, they felt the effort was more than justified. The program also attracted law enforcement officers who felt that they understood the experience of incarceration better than they had before Dr. Sheridan's class.

THERAPEUTIC COMMUNITIES

Essentially, therapeutic communities are run by counselors who are graduates of such a program and who are in recovery. For those of you who are not familiar with the concepts associated with TCs, most programs include "members of the family" or "students" as they are variously called as well as injured athletes, former military personnel, recovering gamblers, drug dealers, patients exposed to pain medications, and youth exposed to drugs in school. Both men and women are vulnerable to drug addiction. The members of the community are young and old, from every race, educational level, and economic background. A former governor of New Jersey was a member of Integrity House. All the counselors have one factor in common. They have accomplished a difficult recovery process and can act as role models. I was first introduced to Integrity House when they needed a researcher to evaluate their projects. The reason that I included this section is because their opinions are valuable as the information from Dr. Sheridan has influenced and improved their careers.

DR. THOMAS J. LALKA

The co-author of this book is Dr. Thomas J. Lalka from Missouri Western State University where he teaches statistics and management courses. He has had more than 18 years of career counseling both in the United States and abroad during his time teaching in Japan. His focus in this book includes interviewing techniques, researching jobs, and writing effective resumes. He has defined what it means to be a professional in the criminal justice field and how to establish career goals. Furthermore, he has identified those who are appropriate references, multicultural issues, internships, virtual learning opportunities, career transitions, and privatized criminal justice programs including security, risk management, and asset protection. Asset protection refers to such issues as shoplifting and employee theft, sabotage, and cybersecurity which includes protecting the internet, clearly a growing threat. Tom Lalka has had more than five years as a corporate executive addressing credit card fraud. The challenges, mentioned above, are generating new skills and careers in the criminal justice field.

It is clear that this contemporary guide to so many diverse careers will provide the reader with information that has not been available previously.

Judith A. Waters, PhD, LPC
Professor Emeritus of Psychology and Counseling
Fairleigh Dickinson University

Preface

COVID-19 and Criminal Justice

Contemporary Criminal Justice Careers: A Comprehensive Guide was originally considered to be a second edition to *Understanding and Exploring Careers in Criminal Justice* which had been under consideration for some time. In early 2020, the world was struck with COVID-19. In March 2020, my interns lost their positions, and my courses went virtual. Criminal justice agencies went to greater use of virtual technology, such as courtroom procedures, and to facilitate staff working from home.

Shortly after, law enforcement was challenged as never before with accusation of excessive force, officers were suspended, fired, others were criminally charged, and one, to date, has been convicted of second-degree murder. The Black Lives Matter (BLM) movement went worldwide with demands for change which included the abolition of police, the abolition of prisons, and the removal of symbols of racism. New legislation was proposed which would definitively alter the manner police would or could do their jobs. Large numbers of police officers resigned from their jobs and some tragically committed suicide, thus ending their careers in law enforcement.

The phrase "The New Normal" entered our language, although (and at the time of this writing) there was no conclusive definition of what "The New Normal" would be. Life and lifestyle adjustments were not only life-changing but if not made became life-threatening. Part of "The New Normal" for both the immediate and the long term required a critical assessment followed by a methodological adjustment for preparing students for a career in criminal justice. All components of the criminal justice system and its staff underwent change for which many, if not most, had little preparation.

Normally, we can obtain information that has the qualities of being satisfying or at the other extreme overwhelming. In the beginning, we did not know where the pandemic originated. Quickly, and even though information was often contradictory, there was no denying its deadly nature. In less than a years' time the death toll exceeded more than half a million people, new variations of the disease emerged, vaccinations appeared critical for both personal safety and as a means of gaining some control over the virus.

Officers, correctional personnel, and others contracted COVID-19. On the state and national level, a debate raged over whether COVID-19 was a real disease or simply the flu as infections and deaths skyrocketed. The Federal Bureau of Prisons reported that more than 70 percent of the inmates had contracted COVID-19.[1] The environment of the prison is a petri dish for diseases and is now the hottest of spots for the pandemic which has complicated the release and transition of convicts to the community. Despite the condition in prisons, there was the emergency early release of convicts touted to diminish the threat inside prisons. The release, however, then threatened the community with additional disease, spiking infections, and the potential for more death. A lack of services almost certainly ensured for many a return to addiction. The infection rate of correctional workers increased and there were daily reports of staff succumbing to the disease.

The financial circumstances of many became precipitous if not disastrous because of loss of jobs and shuttered businesses. Those venturing out to perform essential tasks, such as obtaining groceries, now became potentially life-threatening. Soon, it seemed that everyone personally knew or knew of those affected by the virus or who had died. Nevertheless, there was hope, albeit false, that the changes would be short lived while the peaks and valleys of infections and death rose and fell.

The magnitude of the social and political turmoil which became daily events found many students, for the first time, questioning what had been their careers objectives, such as law enforcement specifically, and more generally whether criminal justice represented a viable career path. Unfortunately, the uncertainty of the times, compounded by contested values, caused some students to change their majors in hopes of achieving a successful career elsewhere—criminal justice as a profession had become personally threatening as reflected nationally in the decreased enrollment in undergraduate criminal justice degree programs.

In addition, many immutable concepts of justice, such as due process and police presence for public safety, were challenged at their core. Many questioned whether those concepts would or could be maintained when a "normalcy" once more returned.

Criminal justice revolves around

> Laws, procedures, institutions, and policies at play before, during, and after the commission of a crime. As a modern concept, criminal justice expresses two central ideas. The first is that criminals and victims of crime have certain rights,

while the second is that criminal conduct should be prosecuted and punished by the state following set laws.[2]

The purpose of the criminal justice system, among other things, is to provide order, keep people safe, and to achieve a sound standard of justice. Criminal justice evolves as law is written, courts, and especially the U.S. Supreme Court, create holdings of constitutional merit, causing procedures and practices to be amended to guide and regulate the components of the system.

Many people who perform the duties of law enforcement, the courts, and corrections, both public and private, require different degrees of education, training, certification, specialization, and more to adequately perform their jobs with high degrees of skill.

The new material brought to *Contemporary Criminal Justice Careers: A Comprehensive Guide* was influenced by COVID-19, recent social events, and the changes to the criminal justice system which affected preparing people to work in the profession of criminal justice. A new book seemed required to meet the exigencies of the times.

Some of the changes are quite apparent as courses went virtual and in-person internships, externships, service learning, volunteering, visiting, and opportunities to observe such as law-enforcement agencies, courtrooms, and correctional, as well as community correctional agencies would no longer accept requests. However, formerly lesser-used modalities provided expanded possibilities such as zooming into the classroom for a guest appearance and courtrooms for adjudications.

Contemporary Criminal Justice Careers: A Comprehensive Guide takes all of this and more into consideration and offers alternatives and suggestions which will help the inquiring student and others to overcome the deficits caused by the pandemic. The opportunities are not the same. However, a reader following the guidance offered in the new book will result in a well-informed person about careers in criminal justice, possessing the tools with which to seek a career.

NEW TO *CONTEMPORARY CRIMINAL JUSTICE CAREERS: A COMPREHENSIVE GUIDE*

Ironically and sadly, many of the "new" challenges now facing students seeking careers in criminal justice were not addressed the first edition. The current crises could not have been anticipated. Several sections from the first edition have been expanded to include the importance of courses, internships, and interviewing which shifted into a virtual mode. In other cases, we have attempted to clarify subjects, such as criminal justice ethics, to address the social issues of Black Lives Matter (BLM) or law enforcement use of force. In addition, there is a discussion of career advancement, career conflicts, and current social issues, and civilian and law enforcement interaction.

The preparation of students for the transition from academia to careers in criminal justice assumed new dimensions of curriculum adjustment and course content adaptations. At the beginning of the pandemic, a search for virtual internships in criminal justice revealed they were not available. Out of need, some did appear quickly. Host agencies, nevertheless, had enough on their plate dealing with the disease and no time for new projects with students. Students also expressed their reluctance to take on virtual internships and raised concern about the tasks they would be asked to perform and whether the experience would have transfer value into real world jobs. This book takes the approach that many virtual internships will not approach the quality of on-site and in-person internships. However, virtual internships properly developed can fulfill some of the experiential learning and provide unique skill development. Virtual opportunities may exceed expectations and expand experiences such as internships in other states and countries. A new section has been added about virtual internships—how to obtain them and how to maximize value from them.

Preparing a new book to meet the challenges described above meant that all chapters had to be reviewed and consideration given for the effects of the pandemic on careers and the preparation for careers and for students to achieve goal fulfillment especially when "hands-on" experiences are not possible. For example, many students are technologically savvy and are already aware of its potential for creating resumes and cover letters. However, utilizing technology such as Zoom and Webex professionally is another matter. The issues of dress, posture, and language are raised to another level. This book has added content for conducting job and internship searches such as the virtual career fair and how to prepare for a virtual interview.

The new book raised the challenge of whether there should be new career discussions. The result is new material on private criminal justice and risk management. While it was not neglected in the first edition, we felt that it could be given much greater emphasis for involvement during and after a career. New profiles have been added for the reader to review and consider how those profiled managed successful careers during trying times.

Updates to the new book include that all salaries have been reviewed and the median salary noted. For instructors, a website has been listed which provides charts with various heading which differentiate salaries throughout the country.

Contemporary Criminal Justice Careers: A Comprehensive Guide is more than career explanations. An intention has been to discuss functions within the criminal justice system as they apply to careers.

Another new section is a glossary. The glossary is not intended to be all-inclusive of criminal justice terms. The glossary primarily describes terms related to careers. Other new or expanded ideas include expungements, 401ks, and paying for college.

We hope the students who will use *Contemporary Criminal Justice Careers: A Comprehensive Guide* will find it advantageous as they prepare for careers in "The New Normal."

Acknowledgments

We are only as successful as those who support us. Family represents our strength and motivation. Students are our beacons of light. Criminal justice is affected by events and outcomes which guide our organizations. Circumstances such as those experienced during the pandemic (demonstrations, actions taken by criminal justice professionals, politicians, and others) provide guidance to the advice we offer to students. We hope that those seeking careers in this profession will have a greater base of knowledge from which to be successful—choosing, advancing, and looking back with a sense of accomplishment.

A special acknowledgment is extended to Dr. Judith A. Waters who hired me many years ago to teach a graduate course, Addictions Counseling in Criminal Justice. She knew her students needed criminal justice career information for competent counseling. And I began to learn about helping future professionals excel in their careers.

We thank our colleagues at Rowman & Littlefield beginning with Kathryn Knigge who recognized the potential of the first edition which exceeded our expectations, and Becca Rohde Beurer who understood and supported the idea of a new book as timely and necessary given the tenor of the times. Becca supported *Contemporary Criminal Justice Careers: A Comprehensive Guide* to advance the original ideas and incorporate new ideas for students and others seeking careers in criminal justice. We would be remiss if we did not also mention our production editor, Megan DeLancey, who patiently worked with us and diligently ensured that all was correctly constructed. We know there are many others at Rowman & Littlefield who reviewed material and ensured it was in the possible format for publication. We thank you all.

We also acknowledge our late colleague Raymond R. Rainville for his wonderful ideas and perseverance to produce *Exploring and Understanding Careers in Criminal Justice: A Comprehensive Guide.*

Acronyms

Criminal justice as a profession relies upon a broad spectrum of acronyms and some are unique to specific agencies. The listing of acronyms is extensive but not inclusive and has been limited to those contained in this book and those which we believe the job seeker may encounter while exploring criminal justice as a profession. The acronyms listed are sources of criminal justice information and the agencies which they represent as possible sites for job exploration. Some of these acronyms and their references may be important for your use during interviews.

a. you might be asked about them
b. you may wish to bring one or more up in response to a question.

While many of the listed acronyms should become familiar to the job candidate, the other acronyms and more will become very familiar upon starting a career in criminal justice. Caution: Many acronyms are like other acronyms and some agencies share the same acronym—be careful—correct terminology is important.

ABA: American Bar Association
ACA: American Correctional Association
ACE: American Council on Education
ACJS: Academy of Criminal Justice Sciences
ADA: American with Disabilities Act
ADHD: Attention-Deficit/Hyperactivity Disorder
AFIS: Automated Fingerprint Identification System
AJA: American Jail Association
APICS: American Production and Inventory Control Society
APPA: American Probation and Parole Association
ASC: American Society of Criminology
BATF: Bureau of Alcohol, Tobacco, Firearms and Explosives
BJA: Bureau of Justice Assistance

BJS: Bureau of Justice Statistics
BOP: (Federal) Bureau of Prisons
CAC: Commission on Accreditation for Corrections
CALEA: Commission on Accreditation for Law Enforcement Agencies
CCAS: Center for Coordinated Assistance to States
CCM: Certified Correctional Manager
CEILE: Council of Educational Institutions for Law Enforcement
CIA: Central Intelligence Agency
CIO: Chief Information Officer
CISM: Critical Incident Stress Management
CJCA: Council of Juvenile Correctional Administrators
CJIS: Criminal Justice Information System
CJJ: Coalition for Juvenile Justice
CMS: Case Management System
CO: Correctional Officer
COLA: Cost of Living Adjustment
COPS: Community Oriented Policing Services
COSTEP: Senior Commissioned Officer Student Training and Extern Program
CUNY: City University of New York
CWLA: Child Welfare League of America
DA: District Attorney
DARE: Drug Abuse Resistance Education
DEA: Drug Enforcement Administration
DHS: Department of Homeland Security
DOD: Department of Defense
DOE: Department of Energy
DOI: Department of the Interior
DOJ: Department of Justice
DOL: Department of Labor
DOT: Department of Transportation
DSW: Director of Social Work
DUI/DWI: Driving Under the Influence/Driving While Intoxicated
EEO/AA: Equal Employment Opportunity/Affirmative Action
eGov: Electronic Government
EM: Electronic Monitoring
EPA: Environmental Protection Agency
FAA: Federal Aviation Administration
FBA: Federal Bar Association
FBI: Federal Bureau of Investigation
FCI: Federal Correctional Institution
FDA: Food and Drug Administration

FDU: Fairleigh Dickinson University
FEMA: Federal Emergency Management Agency
FFL: Federal Firearm Licensees
FLETC: Federal Law Enforcement Training Center
FOIA: Freedom of Information Act
GAO: General Accounting Office
GED: General Education Diploma
HHS: (Department of) Health and Human Services
HUD: (Department of) Housing and Urban Development
IACA: International Association of Crime Analysts
IACP: International Association of Chiefs of Police
IAFIS: Integrated Automated Fingerprint Identification System
IBET: Integrated Border Enforcement Team
ICCA: International Community Corrections Association
ICE: Immigration and Customs Enforcement
INS: Immigration and Naturalization Service
INTERPOL: International Criminal Police Organization
IRS: Internal Revenue Service
ISP: Intensive Supervision Program (Parole or Probation)
IT: Information Technology
IVC: Institution Volunteer Coordinator
JDAI: Juvenile Detention Alternatives Initiative
JJDP: Juvenile Justice Delinquency Prevention
JTTF: Joint Terrorism Task Force
K-9: Canine Operations
KSAs: Knowledge, Skills and Abilities
LCADC: Licensed Clinical Alcohol and Drug Counselor
LCSW: Licensed Clinical Social Worker
LEAA: Law Enforcement Assistance Administration
LEEP: Law Enforcement Education Program
LLB: Bachelor of Laws or Legal Laws Baccalaureate
MOU: Memorandum of Understanding
NCCD: National Council on Crime and Delinquency
NCIA: National Correctional Industries Association
NCIC: National Crime Information Center
NCJA: National Criminal Justice Association
NDAA: National District Attorneys' Association
NIC: National Institute of Corrections
NICS: National Instant Criminal Background Check System
NIJ: National Institute of Justice
NJACOP: New Jersey Association of Chiefs of Police
NJSP: New Jersey State Police

NOBLE: National Organization of Black Law Enforcement Executives
NRRC/CCETAC: National Reentry Resource Center/Corrections and Community Engagement Technical Assistance Center
NSA: National Security Agency
NSA: National Sheriffs' Association
OJJDP: Office of Juvenile Justice and Delinquency Prevention
PHS: Public Health Service
POST: Peace Officer Training and Standards
PREA: Prison Rape Elimination Act
QPR: Question, Persuade, and Refer
RCRP: Residential Community Reentry Programs
RFA: Request for Application
RFP: Request for Proposal
RICO: Racketeer Influenced and Corrupt Organizations
SAC: Special Agent in Charge
SAGs: State Advisory Groups
SEC: Securities and Exchange Commission
SIFI: Student in Field Instruction
SME: Subject Matter Expert
SSA: Social Security Administration
STATE: United States Department of State
SWACJ: Southwest Association of Criminal Justice
TC: Therapeutic Community
TRO: Temporary Restraining Order
TSA: Transportation Security Agency
UCR: Uniform Crime Report
UMDNJ/UBHC: University of Medicine and Dentistry/ University Behavioral Healthcare
USAF: United States Air Force
USCG: United Sates Coast Guard
USCS: United States Customs Service
USMS: United States Marshals Service
USPC: United States Parole Commission
YSC: Youth Services Commission

Introduction

Why Another Book on Criminal Justice Careers?

The concentrations of criminology, criminal justice, police science, and private criminal justice (often called security) are among the most popular college programs at the two year, four year, and university levels. A few statistics illustrate the desirability of these programs. Keep in mind that the databases do not cleanly break down the data in the specific fields mentioned above. Nevertheless, the numbers do indicate some idea of the number of students enrolling in and graduating from CJ programs. In fact, the numbers may be greater if all fields were clearly defined in databases for enrollment and degrees conferred in the specific concentrations of criminology, CJ, police science, and private CJ.

Butterfield reported in 1995 that 350,000 students majored in CJ.[1] In contrast, the Digest of Educational Statistics notes that for 2003–2004, 452,000 were enrolled, and another 78,000 in CJ and security.[2] Finally, CJ and corrections degrees awarded in 2019 totaled 122,741.[3] The popularity of CJ and added benchmarks of eligibility standards have increased the competitive nature of employment. The events of the pandemic diminished the ranks of police and corrections. As we write, this has now changed with increased demand for law enforcement and correctional officers. The seeker of CJ employment can meet that in one word—*preparation. Contemporary Criminal Justice Careers: A Comprehensive Guide* maintains the emphasis on preparation from the first edition and has greatly improved on it to provide the reader with the most comprehensive advice and information to achieve a job which will develop into a career.

Crime and criminals intrigue and capture our attention and our imagination. Newspapers, TV, and radio reporting typically begin with the latest and most graphic, sensational criminal event. The more extraordinary the crime, the sooner someone writes a book about it, and the names of the judge, the cop, the prosecutor, or the offender become household names. Some of the more popular TV shows today are centered on crimes and criminals. One show has a serial killer solving other crimes by serial killers; others are about criminal profiling, and one is even about probability theory used to solve and prevent crime. Of course, forensics, homeland security, and terrorism have grabbed their share of viewers' attention, as well, and have become all the rage. New college courses and majors have appeared in colleges and universities centered around featured professions such as federal marshals, crime scene investigators, medical examiners, forensic scientists, FBI agents, criminal profilers, and others.

Many interested in CJ were glued to their televisions, waiting to see what secrets would be revealed when Geraldo Rivera opened the lost vault of Al Capone. Viewers were equally disappointed to see that it was empty. Many of the better actors, from Humphrey Bogart and Jimmy Cagney to Clint Eastwood, Robert DeNiro, Al Pacino, and Denzel Washington, have cemented their reputations by starring in criminal roles that depict someone, real or fictional, in the field of CJ. Literature, both adult and juvenile, from Sherlock Holmes to the Hardy Boys and Nancy Drew to the novels of James Patterson, are rife with crime, crime-solving, and superior criminals sought after by even more superior crime solvers.

Offenders, victims, wardens, correctional officers, judges, police officers, federal agents, and medical examiners have written their personal stories of their experiences within the CJ field. College and university CJ programs became and remain the fastest-expanding programs and the largest departments on their respective college campuses. New majors, such as homeland security, appear regularly to keep pace with events and demands in the CJ profession.

Criminal justice is a vast industry that for prisons alone has a combined national annual budget that "eclipses the GDP [Gross Domestic Product] of 133 nations." Estimates of the national cost of prisons are above $74 billion.[4] However, that figure may underestimate the real cost of prisons, for example, when we take into account the cost of California prisons at $7.9 billion,[5] Texas at $3.3 billion,[6] and Michigan at about $2 billion.[7] Those three states total more than 13 billion dollars. These figures do not take into account the cost of municipal and county jails or other costs that are subsumed by departments other than the departments of corrections. New Jersey serves as an example. The cost of vehicles for the New Jersey Department of Corrections is found in the Department of Treasury budget.

This information suggests that the cost of incarceration in the United States exceeds $100 billion.

Some of the industry which caters to the CJ field is even listed on the New York Stock Exchange. Crime has gone public. State and federal governments and private companies manage CJ operations. For-profit corporations and nonprofit agencies operate private prisons, halfway houses, and day reporting centers. They also manage the medical, psychological, and social service needs of both convicts and ex-convicts and provide for technology (including upgrades and maintenance), food for the prisons, and more.

The U.S. Congress and each of the state legislatures have committees that specifically address crime and crime control issues. Prisons are purposely located and built where they will improve the economic situation of local communities. Daily, new legislation is passed that affects the CJ system which generates jobs and products. The point is that CJ is always undergoing change.

THERE IS SO MUCH INFORMATION AVAILABLE, WHY ANOTHER BOOK?

Students tend to see the CJ system through rose-colored glasses and are often myopic as they plan their futures for a specific field. The authors have each been career-oriented professionals. One was a correctional practitioner for more than thirty years and the other built a career as a business professional. Each has also been in academics for more than thirty years, beginning while they were working and continuing after retirement from their careers. As practitioners, they became painfully aware of the lack of preparation new employees brought to their respective fields. As members of the academic community, they became more painfully aware that students had been poorly and even inappropriately advised about career opportunities. In addition, there is the recognition that students oftentimes rely upon faculty, who in a former life were practitioners, to gain knowledge about jobs and careers.

There is, perhaps, no one more influential to a student than a dynamic professor who has had a fulfilling and involved career. However, that wonderful professor may be speaking about his/her specific niche in the CJ field while unsuspectingly overlooking not only other aspects of the field, such as business, but also what it takes to be successful in the CJ field overall, or unfortunately, what might be a better fit for a student asking questions about a career.

The intrigue of the CJ profession, the depth of potential employment, and the multitude of career opportunities cannot be adequately covered in any one course. Some colleges and universities now offer courses that specifically address jobs in the CJ profession. Professors teaching these courses rely on texts that have been developed for other courses. *Contemporary Criminal Justice Careers: A Comprehensive Guide* will serve as a text for these courses as well as a resource for the administrators of CJ programs as they guide students to meet their goals through their undergraduate studies in academic tracks.

The arrival of the COVID-19 virus has possibly affected CJ like no other single event. Social unrest and political turmoil added fuel and turned the fire into a raging inferno. All components of CJ were affected as were higher education, and vocational training for careers. The new normal (once more undefined) has not arrived and seems likely to endure a prolonged period of fluctuations. Career preparation, we suggest, must now more than ever prepare the future career-oriented person for uncertainties and change.

There is no single book or site that lays out the breadth and depth of working in the CJ field, and too little is included in CJ curriculums to describe all the career opportunities in CJ. Furthermore, there is little to no guidance that explains how an individual is to conduct himself or herself in the profession in terms of advancing one's career or changing careers. A person's career is a journey. Bo Orichowsky (see profile in appendix A) is an excellent example of someone who broke into the CJ profession, took advantage of opportunities to advance, and then landed a position that provided him with career satisfaction. Then there is the end of the career to consider—retirement.

Retirement and the future are barely mentioned, thought of, or consequently planned for in the early career stages. The early days of a career are potentially the most productive time during which to begin planning for retirement and one's personal economic future well-being. The past decade has seen severe challenges to retirement plans and medical benefits. A successful retirement requires early planning.

A common theme from those who have generously supplied their profiles for this book is what they would have done differently if they could go back to the beginning of their careers. This book will not ameliorate those issues, but hopefully, it will at least minimally address them so that students and even those employed in the profession can begin to think about improving how they manage their careers—from the moment of hiring to their separation from the job.

TV shows and movies serve to glorify the CJ field, television commercials for private technical schools play up the personal benefits of working in the field. They advertise that their courses of study will provide students with the training they need to qualify. In reality, such training may actually be of little use. The CJ profession has its own training academies, and especially for those vocations in law enforcement. The specialized law enforcement academies are rigorous. Generally, students know little about how to prepare for the academy of their choice. Therefore, academy preparation is included in this book.

CAREER PROFILES

Career profiles (which have been expanded for *Contemporary Criminal Justice Careers: A Comprehensive Guide* to provide exposure to other potential career pursuits) are a special feature of this book and have been collected from many professionals in the CJ field. Each professional has shared what he or she has thought to be important about their career and has attempted to highlight not only what has made them successful but also what enabled them to develop as a professional. Perhaps they, too, serve to glamorize the field. However, they represent a sampling of the breadth and depth of experiences that are to be found in CJ careers. These successful practitioners attempt to highlight both the opportunities they were fortunate to have taken advantage of and the missteps that interfered with their entrance into the CJ field.

This book was written for those who wish to have a career in the CJ field. The authors are acutely aware of the effect of the pandemic on careers and the preparation for careers. The social events and tragedies which occurred challenged not only professors who prepare students but also students to consider if a career in CJ remains most important to them. *Contemporary Criminal Justice Careers: A Comprehensive Guide* takes the issues seriously and has tried to offer guidance for students to make decisions which will be best for them. High school and college counselors who guide students about career opportunities in CJ will also find *Contemporary Criminal Justice Careers: A Comprehensive Guide* a valuable resource.

Finally, there are those who are curious about CJ and have relied upon the media for guidance. Unfortunately, the media's primary purpose is entertainment and not accurate information. This book provides a better understanding of the field of CJ and how its components relate to one another. There are many who do not know which questions should be asked, simply because they lack knowledge about the depth and breadth of the profession. The uniqueness of *Contemporary Criminal Justice Careers: A Comprehensive Guide* is that it anticipates the concerns that are commonly expressed, and others less commonly expressed. Please use the expanded subject index as you explore your career choice for the inclusion of information about topics that can be found in other chapters. Many questions of students and others will require a broader treatment than would be possible for the scope of this book. To help resolve this deficiency, a bibliography of suggested readings and websites has been included in the appendixes. Specific questions about the components that comprise the CJ field may be more appropriately answered in courses such as Introduction to Criminal Justice, Policing, The Courts, Corrections, Juvenile Justice, or Criminology. Nevertheless, as a career in CJ is considered, your ability to explore personal questions and obtain appropriate answers to your questions is critical. This book will provide greater clarity about the pursuit of a career in CJ and what may be the more appropriate career choice for you.

THE INDEX

You may wish to use the index as you consider whether you are clear about the answers to your questions. That is, the index provides a reference to other places in the book where such information may additionally be discussed. For example, examine the following questions. They have begun to be addressed in this chapter, and the questions are more completely answered in other chapters. Some important questions that may be asked are:

- What are the three primary areas of CJ in which there are career opportunities?
- What are the differences between the three principal components of the CJ field?
- Are the job requirements different in federal, state, and local employment?
- What are the benefits of a career in criminal justice?
- What are the risks of a career in criminal justice?
- What are the ethical issues to consider in a criminal justice career?
  - Is there a minimum or maximum age to start employment in a criminal justice career?
- Is there a maximum age at which you must terminate your employment?
  - What are the maximum number of years you can work in a specific career in criminal justice?
- What options are available upon retirement from a career in criminal justice?
- Does age affect which pension system you can join?
- Does age affect when you can retire?

And now we add one more question: how do unexpected events such as a pandemic, social upheaval, and political unrest affect career trajectories?

Perhaps these questions have already entered your mind. Perhaps you now have additional questions. You should develop your own questions (and we suggest that you write them down—questions not preserved get forgotten quickly) as you read through *Contemporary Criminal Justice Careers: A Comprehensive Guide*. When those questions arise, you need to get answers. Speak with a professor or an advisor. This book cannot answer all possible questions about the field of CJ, but it will serve as a guide to discovering satisfactory answers to many questions.

THE APPENDIX

To further assist career exploration, and particularly if you are investigating a career that is less commonly discussed, you will find websites listed in the back of the book which will help you achieve a comprehensive understanding of your choice of career. In addition, there are sections in the appendixes that provide guidance including such items as sample résumés, a networking guide, civil service exam preparation materials, and interview advice which have been expanded for *Contemporary Criminal Justice Careers: A Comprehensive Guide*. More interviews are conducted virtually than ever before, thus the focus on interviews now emphasizes this preparation.

BIBLIOGRAPHY OF REFERENCES AND SUGGESTED READINGS

The bibliography has been formatted into nine informational segments to provide a broad range of sources from which to pick and choose to learn about potential profession. All professions have a downside as well as an upside. Students should not ignore the downside when selecting a chosen profession in which they are likely to spend twenty, twenty-five, thirty, or more years. For example, under policing, *Serpico* is referenced. The author, Frank Serpico, was a New York City police officer who helped to uncover massive corruption in the police force. Under corrections, the student may wish to read *Newjack* by Ted Conover or *The Green Wall* by D. J. Vodicka. Conover was an investigative reporter who was denied access to a corrections training academy. He discusses his application process, his academy training experience, and his assignment to Sing Sing Correctional Facility. Vodicka, a well-intentioned prison guard, gets caught up in a corrupt prison system. Other books on the list cover the careers of ministers, educators, correction officers, and wardens.

The number of and type of positions in the CJ field constantly changes to meet needs. The likelihood is that CJ will require different specializations because of the burgeoning numbers, the pandemic, increased attention to racism, unacceptable failure rates, other social issues, and the necessity to change because the cost has become intolerable. In addition, new and improved technology is being implemented. For example, in the past decade we have seen such innovations as day reporting centers added to the area of community corrections and increased use of electronic monitoring. Nevertheless, CJ will remain a large field of employment which requires a well-educated, well-trained, and well-informed workforce. Good luck in your search for a successful career path and in your understanding of what that career entails.

This primer has been expanded to provide the most informed source of material for those aspiring to a CJ career. We invite students, counselors, and career professionals alike to provide us with their comments and suggestions to make *Contemporary Criminal Justice Careers: A Comprehensive Guide* a valuable resource for all. Feel free to contact the authors with your experiences and questions.

Some information is repeated in different sections, as it applies to information in that section. We do not wish to be repetitive, but we recognize that some will not read the entire book. Therefore, we have repeated certain information so that important details relative to a specific topic are not missed.

Chapter 1

Exploring Careers in Criminal Justice

A BRIEF REVIEW OF THE CRIMINAL JUSTICE SYSTEM

The criminal justice system is comprised of three components: law enforcement, corrections, and the courts. Generally, but not always, they operate separately from each other. In addition, there are distinctions in operations from state to state, and there may be jurisdictional issues between federal government agencies and the states as well as within state agencies at both the state and local levels. Together, they represent a complex array of agencies that may or may not interact with one another. In addition, the operations and responsibilities of state and federal agencies often overlap, and they may come into conflict with each other as they attempt to determine jurisdiction.

CAREERS AND PROFESSIONALS

There is a wide breadth of careers in criminal justice; however, not all careers require that the individual be a professional, have a college degree, or be involved in law enforcement. Some careers are more professional than others, and some have specific law enforcement requirements. Within the field of criminal justice, career paths intersect, and they work together, for success and accomplishment within the field. Of course, when they fail to cooperate, then there are breakdowns in operations and even failure to successfully complete some assignments.

THE CRIMINAL JUSTICE ENVIRONMENT

Each component of the criminal justice system has unique situational or geographic factors which should be considered by the student or job seeker. The CJ environment is distinctive because of its daily interactions with those who have violated the law or are suspected of violating the law, as well as tragic events and problems that often lack acceptable solutions. Similarly, each position in the CJ field has the upside potential of making contributions to society (most commonly defined as "making society safer") and unraveling the specific challenges to discover "what works."[1] At times, some of the more problematic circumstances, such as domestic violence or ensuring the care and well-being of children, are best served when persons from the criminal justice field and others from different career paths, such as social services, work together to find acceptable solutions. The current hot topic, terrorism, helps to illustrate criminal justice professions at their best when it comes to working together. The 9/11 tragedy saw professionals from many CJ career paths come together to provide assistance, comfort, counseling, reassurance, and more to help a nation overcome great loss. A more recent notable example was the cooperation between many law enforcement agencies to resolve the bombing incident that occurred during the Boston Marathon of 2013. However, the changes which intended to provide improved communication and cooperation between agencies once more broke down on January 6, 2021, during a riot at the Capital. Criminal justice is not different than other systems and agencies and requires the regulated review of policies and procedures to ensure that interagency cooperation is maintained.

Negotiating problems and developing solutions require good people skills, being well-trained, anticipating difficulties, developing good organizational skills, and thinking outside the box. To be sure, jobs in criminal justice require the successful employee to look at problems and situations differently to discover unconventional problem-solving approaches. Often, employees will only discover how successful they may be when they are on the job facing real-life circumstances. Some discussion of the environments in which criminal justice personnel work will be helpful to the prospective employee to understand the value of introspection and soul searching to discover whether their personality and skills match the job. Obviously, a quality education with an emphasis on criminal justice is the first step to making an appropriate career decision.

THE COURTS

Courts, apart from the juvenile court, are open to public scrutiny. Juvenile courts operate behind closed doors to preserve confidentiality for the accused juvenile. Many court cases are routine, and the daily operation of the court is a management chore. However, the higher profile the case, the greater the media and social attention paid to it. The nature of the case—whether it involves issues of wealth (Bernie Madoff), impropriety (Barry Bonds), race (O. J. Simpson), celebrity (Martha Stewart), or politics (Rod Blagojevich)—influences the audience. In addition, the nature of the case is important, and each mentioned defendant has caught the attention of different facets of the criminal justice profession. These cases add to the confusion, controversy, and uncertainty which exist about the role of the courts in modern society.

High-profile court cases have considerable social implications that may then be reflected in changes of legislation (Megan's Law) and rules (testing for steroids), considerations for legal representation (Johnnie Cochran's declaration that "if the glove don't fit, you must acquit"), or selection for recognition (Pete Rose's lifetime ban from baseball for gambling following his conviction and prison time).[2]

The focus on the actors in high-profile cases has resulted in considerable controversy. Heretofore, there was little challenge to the competency of a judge, prosecutor, defense attorney, or others in specific criminal justice capacities. (Some examples include Judge Ito's rulings in the O. J. Simpson trial and Marcia Clark's change of appearance for the courtroom cameras, or Mark Fuhrman's neglect of protocol in handling the evidence.) The majority of cases brought before the court are ordinary and even mundane, involving circumstances in which the primary actors follow procedures, day in and day out, from which there is little deviation.

The actors in the courtroom play roles and assume duties that, to the untrained observer, may seem to contradict what is in the best interest of the public. For example, public defenders and defense attorneys may appear to be helping obviously guilty parties to avoid penalties for their actions (such as making motions for dismissal because of improper procedures followed by law enforcement in obtaining evidence or a confession). Overzealous prosecutors may seem to be acting in the best interest of the public safety by bending the rules (such as by withholding evidence from defense attorneys) to ensure a guilty determination and thus remove an offender from the streets. And judges may seem to ignore important issues, prevent testimony or evidence from being presented, or instruct juries to ignore evidence that has been presented that would ensure a successful prosecution. These are examples of denial of due process.

The point is that each actor in the criminal justice system must follow certain rules in their specific roles to maintain the integrity of the criminal justice system. Defense attorneys are there to protect the rights of the accused, even if that protection means a supposedly guilty party is found not guilty. Prosecutors who violate constitutional protections (such as by submitting dry-labbing evidence)[3] are denying rights guaranteed to all citizens. Judges, on the other hand, are to act as referees who interpret constitutional issues to ensure and enforce the upholding of the rights of all defendants. They are not to support the actions of defense attorneys or prosecutors except as they fail to act in accordance with the rules of the court and the constitution.

LAW ENFORCEMENT

Law enforcement officers are depended upon to provide protection and safety, both on and off duty. Police work is dangerous and results in frequent injuries. Stress is common to the profession and contributes to illness and at times bad judgment. Policemen and women are exposed daily to potential dangers, whether from those who would break the law or from other circumstances. Subsequently, law enforcement officers must maintain a heightened state of awareness and vigilance to respond to threatening or dangerous situations. Frequent injuries and death are associated with the daily routines of law enforcement (such as when they encounter accidents or respond to criminal events). Of course, among the more tragic and unfortunate events associated with on-the-job stress is the occurrence of suicide, divorce, and substance abuse. Careers in law enforcement are well-known for their negative effects on police officers and their personal lives. (Note: See Cop 2 Cop for a helping agency that responds to police stress in New Jersey.[4] Also see the profile of William Ussery, the founder of Cop 2 Cop in profile appendix A.)

The work of law enforcement is generally scheduled around a forty-hour workweek, but there is the necessity for frequent overtime which is often the result of required written reports on the day's activities, the need for more police coverage at an event or incident, or the need to continue work because of having already responded to an incident. The more complex the incident, the more hours of overtime will be required. Investigations require extended hours of labor and complex arrangements of support to ensure not only the successful completion of the investigation but also the protection and well-being of those involved. Police work is shift work, but duties must be performed around the clock, seven days a week. The officer just emerging from the academy will undoubtedly pull the least desirable shifts—nights, weekends, and holiday duty—and often the least desirable locations to patrol.

Federal enforcement agents encounter different obstacles that obstruct a normal lifestyle. They are called upon with little or no notice to travel. Travel may include protective services (especially for U.S. Marshals and Secret Service personnel), such as guarding judges during high-profile cases, or even the president of the United States; and investigations (especially for CIA, FBI, or U.S. Treasury agents); or after receiving promotions in rank, such as assuming administrative duties in different locations with the BOP or the U.S. Parks Service. Some positions involve periodic transfers that may occur several times during the course of a career. And to be sure, some postings and responses to incidents can place officers in the harsh conditions of inclement weather and other hazardous situations, such as the events of September 11, 2001, and January 6, 2021.

The bulk of police work comes under the heading of "patrol," which involves the performance of a variety of routine tasks during daily assignments, many of which vary little from when they were initiated by Sir Robert Peel in London in 1829. Patrol primarily accomplishes three tasks:

1. Maintaining a police presence,
2. Providing availability for emergencies, and
3. Detecting and solving crimes.[5]

The face of law enforcement has undergone many changes since its humble beginnings. Great mystery stories, terrific movies, and TV episodes with intricate plots are filled with accounts of men and women who have a career in law enforcement or others who have left official law enforcement careers to pursue it privately. The plots are intense (find the kidnapped girl before she dies), dramatic (discover the shooter before he shoots you), exciting (breathtaking car chases with outrageous crashes, from which everyone inexplicably walks away), and filled with great lines, such as "Was it five shots or was it six?" that stimulate the imagination. While these images, made possible through the lens of the camera, are titillating, they are also exceptional and do not bear much resemblance to the everyday work of law enforcement personnel.

Unfortunately, law enforcement itself has also had its share of unsavory incidents, such as Abner Louima, Rodney King, and George Floyd becoming the victims of police brutality, Mark Fuhrman's inappropriate actions in the O. J. Simpson case, and the scandalous corruption made known through *Serpico*. These incidents have all contributed to public perceptions of police officers acting at odds with the public good. Nevertheless, there are confused perceptions of the manner in which law enforcement must operate or be considered soft that has been promoted in novels and films such as *Dirty Harry*, in which the end justifies the means; that is, police officers must do whatever is necessary to apprehend the criminal, even if it involves committing crimes themselves or violating the constitutional rights of citizens.

Police officers have bemoaned U.S. Supreme Court decisions such as *Miranda v. Arizona*, which upheld the principle that suspects must be read their rights. At first, law enforcement considered this a hindrance to their ability to catch criminals, thinking it would lead to fewer convictions, but instead more effective police work has resulted in a sharp increase in convictions and fewer cases lost on appeal. Fortunately, the unsavory incidents that detail human failings are not characteristic of all who do the job. Unfortunately, however, such incidents do reflect negatively on all who perform the job of law enforcement.

The changing face of law enforcement has brought with it increased responsibility and expanded involvement for professionals from an assortment of disciplines. The police psychologist,[6] for example, was once a dreaded or even scorned professional, but has in recent times emerged to play an ever-increasingly valuable role. The role of the psychologist was once limited to the examination of new recruits for fitness that could eliminate them from law enforcement. That function now includes that they conduct follow-up sessions with police officers after critical incidents that could relegate them to desk duty or relieve them from duty altogether. The psychologist is now seen as providing a beneficial and supportive role that might salvage a career or even a reputation. The psychologist, as often seen on television shows such as *Bones*, may also be critical to an investigation by providing advice about suspects or by developing a profile that leads to the apprehension of an offender.

CORRECTIONS

Corrections is probably the least understood and the more confusing of the three components of criminal justice professions. Its operations are hidden by the tall walls that shield its actions from outsiders. In addition, corrections officers, by far, receive the greatest press and the most mention in textbooks and other sources. These sources almost entirely ignore civilians who work in such occupations as administrators, social workers, psychologists, human resources personnel, teachers, counselors, fiscal management counselors, public relations workers, grant managers, doctors, nurses, researchers, and other managers.

Corrections may be the environment that is the most potentially hazardous. Ted Conover,[7] an investigative reporter and the author of *Newjack*, could not gain access to the New York Correction Officers Academy, yet he could apply for, gain acceptance to, and advance through the academy to become a correctional officer himself. Conover explored the manner that corrections officers are trained and then how they fulfill their job assignments. Through Conover, we get a glimpse into the conflicting if not confusing or contradictory expectations of the corrections business generally, and the work and environments of the correctional officer specifically.

The history of corrections has shown itself to exist in a capricious manner through its constantly shifting philosophical position from the humane intention to the retributive posture and the repetitive struggle to instill meaningful reforms. The environment is caught up in the dilemma of whether to punish or to treat—a debate that gains strong emotionally charged supporters for each side. All too often, the contrasting and conflicting goals of the penal sanction (retribution, incapacitation, rehabilitation, and deterrence—terms not always easily understood) are confounded by startling revelations that leave even the more conservative or liberal observers wondering about the role that prisons should play to punish offenders and safeguard society. COVID-19 has created different considerations and brought to the forefront new questions about the need and use of prison systems, pushing existing boundaries, including the call to abolish prisons.

Extreme, extraordinary, and unusual events, such as shootings in California prisons,[8] the Attica[9] and New Mexico riots,[10] abusive Arkansas prison farms,[11] the mistreatment of prisoners in Abu Ghraib, the medical experiments in Holmesburg, and the case of Willie Horton, who absconded from prison and committed a terrible crime—capture the headlines because of notoriety. They seem to be soon forgotten until the next tragedy occurs. These circumstances raise questions about ethical and appropriate conduct that challenge the purpose of the prison as a social institution and the roles that correctional officers, professional employees, and administrators are to serve.

Criminal justice environments are subject to constant scrutiny by the media and the legislature. The nature of the work is difficult to manage on a day-to-day basis and the nature of the client may require day-to-day adjustments. Correctional intentions, problems, administrative needs, and staff demeanors call into play complex decision making that often exceeds the ability of the best trained person. There have been sharp reactions (media, legislative, watchdog groups, and others) to serious improper incidents which have received inappropriate and unquestioning support (from government, administrators, and unions), leading to suspicion about conduct and disbelief about the occupational work of being in a helping profession.

CIVILIAN VERSUS LAW ENFORCEMENT

Choosing to pursue a career in criminal justice is only the first step to landing that first position. There are three distinct career paths in criminal justice. There is the civilian track, the law enforcement route, and the private path. Your choice of the law enforcement, the civilian, or the private path will affect your preparation process. Your personal aspirations will help you determine the strengths and weaknesses for each career path.

Careers in law enforcement, and primarily those in state and federal agencies, seem to attract the greater attention. After all, they are more likely to be the subject of media attention, as well as featured in TV shows and movies. However, civilian careers are much greater in number and cater to a notable diversity of skills. Some civilian career paths include administration, social work, psychology, human resources, teaching (both academic and vocational), counseling, fiscal management, public relations, grant management, doctors, nurses, researchers, and overall management. The choice of whether to pursue a sworn or a civilian position is personal and should be based on your own interests, your abilities, and the available means for preparation. Something to be kept in mind for career preparation is that there are those who do switch from the law enforcement side to the civilian side or the private side and vice versa. Career changes and advancement occur over many years, perhaps even several decades. See the profiles of Lenny Ward (who went from parole officer to administrator) and Bo Orichowsky (who went from social worker to parole officer, see profile appendix A). Warden Bob Hood (see profile appendix A), to be sure, provides one of the more interesting career profiles, as he advanced from a prison teacher to become the warden of the Alcatraz of the Rockies—ADX, the federal supermax prison.

There are some common means of preparation for each position. A most interesting thing about preparation is that students discover more about the criminal justice profession than they ever imagined and will begin to discover which may be the better personal career choice and how many options are available. There is also the likelihood that what begins as a desire to work on one side may change after exposure to other types of criminal justice careers. That is, what initially interested you may lose ground to other aspirations that have greater potential for personal satisfaction and achievement as you explore the field and discover the variety of available positions in the criminal justice field. As your experiences with criminal justice professionals and the components of the criminal justice profession increase, your choice of a career path may become more complex as you realize the depth of possible career opportunities and the requirements for each. The person interested in the criminal justice field owes it to themselves to understand the many opportunities that are available. That also includes inquiring about limitations or the downsides to one profession as opposed to another. Visiting criminal justice websites (see appendix J) and reviewing requirements for jobs will help you with this exploration.

THE ROAD TO CAREER SELECTION

Many aspects of the criminal justice system are readily available for review by interested persons. A productive activity is to explore websites available for each agency that has an appeal. Write down questions and take notes of strong features on each website. Your questions and your notes will be a guide for other activities such as making a phone call to an agency that will help you to arrange a visit. When a phone call will not work, a professor may be able to open a door. Treat the visit like a field trip by adequately preparing yourself. Think about what questions you need to have answered and review what you believe to be strong points. Ask your professors what you should look for and what questions they suggest you might ask.

Hopefully, the visit will permit you to carry a notebook which lists your questions and where you will record the answers and your observations. You can later compare your notes from each visit to confirm the strengths and weaknesses of a specific career choice. Plan to dress professionally, and afterward send a thank-you note. First impressions are always important, and they should never be ignored. Similarly, good manners are recommended and will be remembered by your host.

COLLEGE COURSES

While college may not be for everyone, neither is it a necessary requirement for all careers in criminal justice. However, a college degree in criminal justice will provide greater exposure to many facets of the criminal justice field. A college degree will also help prepare you for career advancement and possible changes in your career. Nevertheless, college courses, and specifically introductory courses, will provide overviews to many career possibilities while removing some myths and misunderstandings that develop as a result of media portrayals. Many college criminal justice programs are staffed by professors who have already completed a career in the criminal justice profession. See the profile of Dr. Robert Louden (provided in appendix A), who went from New York City police officer with the rank of the commander of the detective squad and hostage negotiator, to college professor, and finally to university criminal justice program director. During a college program you will have the opportunity to meet men and women who have served in both law enforcement and civilian careers. They represent not only informed persons but also role models of success.

Certainly, one of the values of taking courses taught by experienced professionals is that they can pull a less certain student under their wing to guide them and make suggestions that lead to a better, more informed decision about a career path—they can answer questions that are of specific concerns to students. More importantly, they can provide introductions to professionals in the field with whom the student may serve internships, volunteer, or simply ask questions.

College courses, such as Introduction to Criminal Justice, Criminology, or Corrections, provide background information such as the structure of the courts; more specialized subject matter, such as crime scene investigation; and theoretical foundations, such as victimization.

Oftentimes, the course selection will be influenced by what the student perceives their career choice to be. As the student becomes more certain of a potential career path, then a heavier concentration of courses in that area may be more appropriate. There are more courses available that are part of the required curriculum. They are called electives and are available for students to do additional exploration in specialized fields of study. College courses are inclusive of all areas of criminal justice, but they are not inclusive of all work in criminal justice. For example, traditional undergraduate courses may not discuss the role of a psychologist in law enforcement or in corrections, or that of a business manager. To be sure, the role of the food service supervisor will be even further removed from the instructional curriculum. However, college courses will provide students with the opportunity to explore their personal interests in criminal justice and thus consider what may become their ultimate career choice.

A SAMPLE COLLEGE CURRICULUM

Undergraduate programs, and specifically two-year college degree programs, are generally more focused on the practitioner's functions in the criminal justice profession. Oftentimes, college departments will offer what are called tracks, options, certificate programs, or specializations, in which the courses are even more sharply focused on the specific profession. The examples below provide a track for law enforcement and another for corrections.

THE LAW ENFORCEMENT CURRICULUM

- Introduction to the Criminal Justice System
- Police in the Community
- Criminal Law
- Police Administration
- English Composition I and II
- History of Western Civilization I or II
- Concepts of Health and Fitness
- Introduction to Psychology
- Introduction to Sociology or Social Problems
- Computer Concepts
- Criminology
- Human Communication or Public Speaking
- History elective
- Political Science elective
- Mathematics elective
- Laboratory Science elective
- Criminal Justice elective
- Criminal Justice Internship
- Free electives

CORRECTIONS CURRICULUM

- Introduction to the Criminal Justice System
- Introduction to Corrections
- Community Corrections
- Juvenile Justice
- English Composition I and II
- History of Western Civilization I and II
- Concepts of Health and Fitness
- Introduction to Psychology
- Computer Concepts
- Introduction to Sociology
- Introduction to Social Problems
- Multiculturalism
- Criminology
- History elective
- Mathematics elective
- Political Science elective

- Laboratory Science elective
- Human Communication or Public Speaking
- Criminal Justice Internship
- Free electives

This is in sharp contrast to four-year colleges or university degrees that begin with introductory courses and then progress to more theory-based or criminological studies. An example is provided below. The prospective student will note that in each case there are standard course offerings, such as English and math. These courses seek to round out a student's education and should not be neglected—they will be needed on the job. Free electives provide students with opportunities to take courses, such as psychology or social work, that are outside their primary field of inquiry. Students would be well-advised not to neglect these opportunities with which they can explore other interests or even take a minor (as discussed below).

FOUR-YEAR DEGREE AND UNIVERSITY STUDY

- Introduction to Criminal Justice
- Criminology
- Police Work
- Correctional History and Philosophy
- Crime and Public Policy
- Criminal Procedure
- Law and Politics
- Criminal Justice Research Methods
- Introduction to Political Science Methods
- Quantitative Methods in Psychology
- Introduction to Social Research
- Computer Analysis of Social Science Data
- Introductory Statistics for Business
- Ethics
- Social Deviance
- Independent Study
- Internship

Coursework provides opportunities for research. Research may cover literature searches—explorations of what others have done in a specific area. Research may also include opportunities to interview persons in the criminal justice field—excellent occasions to ask those questions that have not yet been answered in the course material. Interviews are a great opportunity to ask questions and obtain answers from someone who is doing the actual work. In addition, a more exciting prospect would be the opportunity to visit sites where work in the criminal justice field is taking place, such as a local or state police station, a courthouse, or a correctional facility. Students would be well advised, prior to interviewing or visiting a site, to search its specific web page for background information about the site to be visited. Visiting the website is more important than ever with limitations for visits due to the pandemic. There is uncertainty when allowance for visiting sites will reopen. Of course, for the student more inclined toward the criminology side of the criminal justice curriculum, the four-year college or university may offer greater opportunities for hands-on criminological research currently being conducted by professors.

Students will find themselves more directed to enroll in and take online courses. While this is beneficial for colleges, the student may not find them as beneficial for meeting their goals. Please see appendix F and chapter 6, in which the benefits and downsides of online education in a criminal justice career are discussed.

We live in a rapidly changing world and the field of criminal justice is also changing. For example, since the tragedy of 9/11 many colleges now offer undergraduate majors and graduate degrees in homeland security and forensics. Another growth area in criminal justice is that of private security (see appendix K) for which a new section has been developed for this edition. The complexity of corporations, especially of those involved with technology, has required them to develop their own in-house private security components, which are not only responsible for site protection but also for the welfare of scientists and other workers. These highly skilled professionals develop cutting-edge technological advances that must be guarded and protected from such events as cybercrime, otherwise the corporation risks losing billions of dollars.

College offers the opportunity for students to specialize in a major, and to select a minor course of study. The value of a minor cannot be understated, it will provide a different perspective about areas of interest and expand versatility in the workplace by increasing opportunities for promotions or a change from one area of criminal justice to another. The minor may also provide the way to a new career or perhaps an avocational interest either during or upon retirement from a career. Some minors, such as sociology, psychology, chemistry, and others, combine nicely with the field of criminal justice. A minor may also provide the student with the opportunity to pursue a personal interest such as cooking or archaeology. College preparation does not have to be limiting; instead, it may be the means to explore and master some other personal interest or skill.

There are several ways that career exploration can be undertaken proactively. The professional criminal justice career will require a well-educated, well-trained individual. The better-educated and the better-trained worker will make wiser choices and be more qualified for advancement. Three primary avenues to gain exposure to the criminal justice profession include college and other educational courses, internships, and volunteering. Each has its own advantages.

YOUR SELECTION OF COLLEGE COURSES AND THE INTERNSHIP

Many college courses are required and thus preselected according to your curriculum; that is, you have no choice about taking them. However, degree curriculums also leave room for electives and minor courses of study. College courses frequently excite and stimulate interest for students in many areas, and the internship may be *the stuff* that ultimately cements for the student the fact that they are making the right decision. Of course, there is also the possibility that the internship may show a side of a profession that dissuades students from further consideration of that job for a career. This may seem terrible—as if the career aspirant has just had their hopes and dreams crushed. But the better news is that this is an opportunity. Now that the student has been exposed to what their career would really have been like, he or she can refocus their goal; that is, make different choices for a successful and rewarding career for themselves. While internships are generally limited to second-year students at a community college, or to third-and fourth-year students at four-year colleges and universities, another means of field exploration is available to the curious student prior to that time—volunteering.

CAREER GOALS

Selecting a career and preparing for it are only the first steps to a career. A student should make some preliminary decisions about how to advance in a career and what to do as the career comes to a close. College is an excellent time to prepare for a life course. See Twenty-Five Year Plan (see chapter 10). You can devise a five-year plan, a ten-year plan, and a twenty-year plan. This does not suggest that once you have made these choices, you are stuck with them. Just like the initial preparation, you are beginning to determine where, or to put it another way, how far you might go. This preparation will prevent stagnation, that is, remaining forever in one position. Preparation begun early will set you up to be organized and ready to take the next steps when opportunities, such as eligibility for promotion, present themselves.

One important preparation you can make at this time is to understand the requirements for promotions. Once you have identified those promotions, you can begin to explore the means to achieve them. Career advancement requires more than doing a good job. You can anticipate changes in departments, and you can prepare yourself through ongoing personal development.

You may think that any consideration of graduate school is somewhat premature at this point. But graduate school is an investment. Graduate school degrees can be the deciding factors when it comes to promotions. You should not ignore the fact that a graduate degree can open doors for other opportunities, such as teaching at a training academy. There is one last thing to consider about when to start work on a graduate degree—in a word, you should start *immediately*. We often hear from students that they want a break after completing their undergraduate degree, or that they are tired of school and will soon return. Unfortunately, life can and will get in the way. Taking a job can mean facing a transfer, and more serious life events such as marriage and children which alter the way we think about everything. We would suggest that if you can, do not delay—go get your graduate degree as soon as possible.

CIVILIAN AND LAW ENFORCEMENT INTERACTION

Law enforcement has greater daily interaction with civilians than either of the other criminal justice components. Corrections, in many ways, discourages civilian access to prisons to maintain custody and security. The rules of the courts specify what involvement civilians may have, and in the case of the juvenile courts, civilians may not observe the proceedings unless they have some direct connection to the case under consideration. On another level, the job functions of civilian employees in the criminal justice system may complement or conflict with law enforcement functions. In some cases, civilians report directly to law enforcement personnel, and in other cases law enforcement may report to or be accountable to civilians.

SUMMARY

Contemporary Criminal Justice Careers: A Comprehensive Guide will help you to realize the depth of the criminal justice field. Generally, the more correct the initial career choice is, the more likely it will be that you will enjoy success in your career because you have been able to prepare properly. Related to that, the more successful you are in your career, the more opportunities you will have during your career, and this will create greater opportunities in retirement. Whether you are still in your career or you have completed it, you want to have achieved satisfaction. Looking ahead and asking, “What else is possible?” and, “What do I need to do?” will assist you to achieve that status. There are many avenues with which to explore and prepare yourself for employment. Your future is in your hands.

Chapter 2

Careers in Law Enforcement

Entrance into the law enforcement profession is a formal complex process that has become more rigorous in its requirements. This chapter will be concerned with the law enforcement as it exists on the state level, in local policing, the state police or highway patrol, and for the sheriff's officers.

The aspiring officer should search their state's websites to assess all agencies which employ police officers in that state. The point is to find an agency that is hiring, for which you have/can meet the requirements, and that does the work or has a position that interests you. If that sounds a little complicated, perhaps what follows will help to explain.

Police officer Michael Di Lieto's book, *How to Become a New Jersey Police Officer or State Trooper*,[1] examines his personal struggle to become a police officer and what he learned in order to be successful in that effort. While his book is specific to New Jersey, there are many helpful suggestions that may be generalized to policing anywhere. He lists the "13 things you can do to be the best candidate" for a position as a police officer:

1. Have a college degree.
2. Have a specialization from a vocational school.
3. Be fluent in a foreign language (Spanish is usually an agency's preferred choice).
4. Have alternate route certification.
5. Become a police officer special II.
6. Become a police officer special I.
7. Become a county deputy sheriff.
8. Become an auxiliary police officer.
9. Have experience in police dispatching.
10. Have experience with police explorers.
11. Have certification in first aid and an EMT-B.
12. Have experience as a firefighter.
13. Become a charity or community group volunteer.

Officer Di Lieto explains the importance of each position, and in some cases, he provides accompanying information that further emphasizes the value to be obtained at each step.

New Jersey has more than 550 law enforcement agencies which range from municipal to college and university police departments. If you anticipate an interview with a department (see appendix C for "A Guide to Interview Questions"), learn as much as possible about the specific agency and the areas of responsibility for the position. Most police agencies have their own websites, and this would be a good place to familiarize yourself with the history and philosophy of a specific agency. Some basic questions for exploring a website would include: How large is the local population that it serves? How large is the geographic (jurisdiction) territory? How many departments (sometimes called "bureaus") does it have? What are its specialized units, such as public morals (vice), narcotics, juvenile, detective, and patrol divisions, as well as public/community relations? What are the starting salaries? Do they have their own training academy, or is there a county academy? Who pays for academy training? What impresses you the most about the department?

New Jersey law enforcement agencies deliver diversity in programs and policing activities. There is a similarity in requirements for each. The hiring methods may be different (civil service versus municipal positions) and may be specialized to the local department which has jurisdiction. Small departments often have what is referred to as a "chief's test," specific to the local community. All law enforcement personnel in New Jersey are governed by the New Jersey Statutes Annotated (N.J.S.A.) 52:17B-98, which established the Criminal Justice Act of 1970. A careful review of the Criminal Justice Act of 1970 for New Jersey, therefore, would be informative. Other states have promulgated criminal justice legislation to regulate law enforcement.

JOB POSTINGS FOR LAW ENFORCEMENT OFFICERS

Openings for police officer positions may be found in police department websites, the state department of personnel listings, newspapers, postings placed on bulletin boards at the local college, and unemployment agencies. Check several sources regularly for these positions. Oftentimes, postings are listed for a specific time period, which means there is a cutoff date after which no more applications will be accepted. When you see a posting, carefully review the hiring requirements to ensure you meet the minimum standards—take action to meet the minimum requirements before the vacancy is posted again.

The Application Process

Once you have begun to make decisions about where and which departments you will focus on for law enforcement officer employment, prepare yourself for the application process. There are several steps to take. The next sections will briefly describe the steps of preparation.

Documentation: The Application Portfolio

Assemble all original documents into a single file (see the Document Portfolio Checklist in appendix G). These should minimally include a birth certificate, Social Security card, high school diploma, certificates of training, college or graduate school degree(s), skill certifications, driver's license, health insurance card, voter registration card, passport, military ID, Selective Service registration ID, firearms ID, awards received, and other pertinent documentation. Hopefully, the departments with which you will file applications will have websites that list the required documentation, as well as other suggested documentation. Do not assume that a listed document or certification is minor and thus irrelevant. Such documents may include certifications for lifeguarding, scuba diving, EMT training, completion of training to operate a motorboat, CPR, or first aid. These documents may also be helpful in the pursuit of a college degree, which will be explained later.

Once the documentation is assembled, make a minimum of two copies. The point is to never send or give away an *original* document. Whenever possible give copies to the requesting agency. However, to complete some applications you may have to appear in person with the original document/record for the department to copy. *Always make sure that your documents are returned!* Once the documents are returned, place them in the appropriate file.

REFERENCES

References require careful consideration. (See chapter 6 for additional reference information.) Draft a preliminary list of potential references. Write a short summary describing why each reference is important and the capacity in which they can provide a reference. Review the list and organize it from most to least important. Many hiring applications will require three references. Your personal list should be longer and have a minimum of 10 from which to choose from when they are requested. You may not have 10 at this time but build your list carefully.

Speak to each person on the list to determine what each will say about you. For example, you received an A in a course from a dynamic professor who had a distinguished career in law enforcement. This, in your opinion, is someone who has name recognition and would give you an excellent reference because of your grade. The reality is that when someone gives a reference, they are extending their own reputation to the one for whom they give the recommendation.

A college course typically lasts fifteen weeks, and interactions with professors are often quite limited. While the professor may attest to your grade or that you turned in an excellent paper, they may be unwilling to say much more about you. The time period for which they have known you is short and because of class size, the professor may not remember you. Many professors teach classes with more than 125 students which leave little opportunity to interact with and remember individual students. However, this not the time for you to take a shot in the dark; be certain of what your reference will say and that they can attest to special characteristics such as timeliness, attention to detail, and more. It can and will affect the image you portray to prospective employers.

Let's tackle one more example with the same potential reference. This time the professor knows you well. The problem in this case is something different: is the reference in good standing with the department to which you are applying? During careers, we encounter situations and persons with whom we have had difficult relationships. A reference may have had an unfortunate circumstance occur with the chief of the department to which you are applying. Your reference, because of that circumstance, is either unwilling to write a letter to that department, or if they write a letter on your behalf, it has little meaning because of the bad circumstance, which had nothing to do with you. You are then caught in the middle. It would be in your best interest not to include this person as a reference. Return to your list and select another. This should help explain why it is important to talk to your reference prior to submitting their name on an application.

Always ask to be provided with a copy of the reference letter. This eliminates surprises if the letter is brought up during an interview. Importantly, if you know what is in the letter, you can prepare responses for the interview to cover points made in the letter. You may wish to make this part of your "ten-point preparation," discussed in appendix C, "A Guide to Interview Questions."

THE INTERVIEW

You can and should thoroughly prepare for your interview. While your résumé and application will get you in the door, the interview is the time to sell yourself. Begin by asking yourself, *What do I have to sell? What makes me special? What do I have to contribute?* These may be simple questions, but there are others that are not so simple. One of the toughest questions to answer is, "What do you see as your two weakest points?"

The question seeks to discover whether there is sufficient self-reflection, awareness of your weakest points; in other words, how well do you know yourself? However, when someone is asked about a second weak point, this may be the interviewer's attempt to discover how well you think on your feet. Your preparation is to reflect on the question and plan a response: write out responses to such potential questions before interviews. A common behavioral interview is based on the STAR Interview Method.

The STAR method stands for Situation, Task, Action, Results. This behavioral interview process is used by employers to assess candidate's ability to act in certain situations on the job based on their past experiences. The job applicant will explain a particular circumstance, explain the task to be undertaken, the action(s) they would take, and what they foresee as the outcome.

Many years ago, I appeared on a television show that had listeners call in to ask questions or make comments. While I think well on my feet, I was prepared with "My Ten Points," generic answers to a variety of questions. Such preparation means that you will not be stumbling around to think about the best answer before responding. A little hesitation during an interview is good and suggests you are reflective. However, a longer period of dead air indicates that perhaps you do not know the subject matter or are not adequately prepared. Remember, the questions you are asked are also the questions other interviewees are asked. (See the section in appendix C titled, "A Guide to Interview Questions." This guide discusses in some detail the preparation of the "My Ten Points." You can begin to develop your Ten Points on the chart at the end of this section.)

PANDEMIC AND POST-PANDEMIC

Virtual interviews began before the pandemic, have become more common, and will likely continue long after some "new normalcy" is in place. Do not think that the camera is kind. The camera sees beyond you into your surroundings. Prepare extra carefully for the virtual interview. Some clothing and some colors appear better than others. Experiment with your wardrobe on Zoom or other video applications to choose the best selection. Look at your environment and correct what you can. For example, the source of light should be in front and never behind you. From behind you appear in the dark. Environments are difficult to control but there are ways to appear at your best. For example, choose an appropriate backdrop which can be provided through several websites. Go to google and type in images for Zoom backdrop. Have fun choosing but think how the interviewer will react to your choice. A word of caution, social distancing and isolation has resulted in some students coming to class in pajamas or attending while lying on their bed. An interview is not the time to be comfortable—look professional. Lying on a bed is not professional and an employer will not want you working on a bed if you are working from home.

TESTS, REQUIREMENTS, AND OTHER QUALIFICATIONS

The process of entering a career in law enforcement requires the applicant to pass tests and meet other requirements. Minimally, the applicant must meet the age and education requirements and be a U.S. citizen. Some jurisdictions require a residency; that is, the applicant will have to establish a state or local residence. Generally, the minimum age requirement is eighteen, and the maximum age is thirty-five. In some cases, the applicant may register for tests or submit an application prior to their eighteenth birthday, as long as the applicant turns eighteen by the date of hire. A critical piece of information to keep in mind is that states which require civil service tests may offer the test sporadically or on a less-than-annual basis. Review the state's personnel or human resources sites for testing dates. You may be able to apply before you reach your eighteenth birthday.

Among the examinations will likely be a written test, a physical assessment, including vision and hearing tests, and tests of agility and stamina. (To review samples of test packages, a list of prep manuals is in appendix H.) The applicant will be examined for physical abnormalities or other characteristics that could render them unable to bear up to the strenuous duties of police work. There will be a psychological evaluation (often both written and oral), a criminal and personal background check, a drug test, a polygraph test, a B-PAD (Behavioral Personnel Assessment Device) test, and perhaps an oral board exam. The B-PAD test is sometimes referred to as the Video Simulation Exercise, and it is used by law enforcement to enhance its hiring practices. It is a standardized test. This may be its sole source of detraction because there are those who simply do not test well. Otherwise, it is well recognized for its fairness. In many cases, it has replaced the oral board because of its reported reliability. Among the strengths of the B-PAD test are that it:

- Assesses individual ethical determination.
- Assesses the ability to work effectively with the public.
- Assesses problem-solving abilities; and

- Assesses interpersonal skills.

See websites for information about the B-PAD and test-taking tips to help obtain a higher score. The websites provide test scenarios and advice, such as using a logical sequence of answers for a higher score. Visit the listed websites for many helpful suggestions for taking the B-PAD.

The information in the previous paragraph applies to one specific test. There are many available books or manuals that can help you plan a regimen for test-taking and academy preparation. See the recommended readings at the end of this book for some of these book titles and manuals.

ACCESS TO ACADEMY TRAINING

There are more than 600 police training academies in the U.S. plus training alternatives. Check your state's approved/accredited alternatives to police training. The first step is to be hired by a police department. This is the more financially attractive option to official academy training. The hiring police department may pay the cost for the academy and pay you a salary at the same time.

An alternative is to pay for academy training prior to acceptance by a police agency. However, many academies only accept official candidates for law enforcement positions. In addition, prior academy training may not be helpful. Some hiring agencies will not accept prior academy or private training and require the completion of their "academy training." Often, there must be a certificate of completion from the private entity if a police department is to accept alternate training. Academy training in one state may not be accepted in another state. This also applies if the applicant has prior experience as a police officer in a different state—the applicant may be required to complete the academy training for the new state.

Police officer jobs are highly prized, and generally there are more applications than there are openings. The applicant should not be discouraged by their position on a hiring or civil service list. Applicants tend to advance quickly on lists. Every academy session shortens it, and some applicants may not wait and will accept other employment. Those who accept other jobs will then skip academy training because they now have a different job. Some will not pass the psychological examination or cannot meet the physical requirements. Some will (believe it or not) fail the drug tests or have acquired a criminal conviction that renders them ineligible. Of course, there are also those who will not pass the academy tests or realize through the academy training that law enforcement is not for them. The point is that the list *will* shorten, and if you are serious about gaining a position in law enforcement, be patient and your turn will come.

EDUCATION REQUIREMENTS

Education requirements for law enforcement varies from state to state and from locality to locality. Almost all police agencies require a minimum of a high school diploma, and others require one or two years of college or even the completion of a bachelor's degree. Nevertheless, there are departments that may hire you even without meeting the degree requirement. In this case, the department may require that you complete the degree requirement in a specified time.

We cannot emphasize strongly enough the value of a criminal justice degree from a college or university. The course work provides knowledge about the interconnectedness of the criminal justice components, police/law enforcement history, legal issues, and technological applications to police work and more, which increases the general knowledge base. Internships provide exposure and experience which links theoretical concepts to police practice. To be sure, persons who have attained a criminal justice degree almost always do better on civil service/law enforcement examinations.

All agencies do not require a degree; however, it is recommended. The law enforcement profession has become more complex with greater technical expertise to conduct modern operations. The social unrest, highlighted by the many charges of excessive force, have fostered new legislation. The consequences of that legislation either for police operations or for training is not yet determined.

A criminal justice degree will provide general knowledge about many aspects of the field, including the courts and corrections, specific information about performance expectations, and a theoretical foundation in law enforcement. Those who have completed academy training but have not achieved a degree have the advantage of the academy training courses being evaluated for credits toward a degree. Some colleges assess academy training and award a specific number of credits. In addition, many colleges offer reduced tuition for members of law enforcement and those who have served in the military and are seeking employment in law enforcement.

Some states give extra credit on exams or in the civil service application process for having completed the criminal justice degree. In many cases, the degree need not be in criminal justice or law enforcement; other fields of study are acceptable. The degree may also be of assistance to obtain other positions in law enforcement once you are hired. For example, you may be asked to teach in the academy. The degree may be a means to transition to larger police departments or to a federal agency such as the FBI, DEA, or other specialized lines of policing employment.

Physical fitness is a necessity for entering the law enforcement profession. The inclusion of physical education and sports participation during college is an affirmation of physical ability. Fitness activities will help prepare you for your academy training by increasing your stamina, flexibility, and competitiveness, and be an indication that you are a team player. Sports participation can be listed on your résumé where you describe your degree and major.

Academy training includes daily physical fitness activities and requires demonstrated fitness by passing prescribed requirements essential to job performance. There are differences in the physical fitness requirements for men and women (see appendix M for a specific example—the Vermont Police Training Academy). A review of these standards will help the law enforcement applicant to prepare for the academy.

The ability to write well cannot be overemphasized. Law enforcement officers are required to write many reports which are official documents and can become court records. The reports are critical for court testimony. Oftentimes, court testimony comes long after an arrest and the charges are filed. The report is an official record of the events, and report accuracy is essential. A well-written report is crucial when the case comes to court—sometimes months in the future. The report is a tool to stimulate recall for testimony before the court. Poorly documented information or any indication that the officer is confused about his testimony can damage the court case.

ACADEMY TRAINING

Classes for academy training are routinely scheduled to fill vacancies for qualified police personnel. Occasionally, academy classes are scheduled when unusual circumstances present a greater need for sworn law enforcement officers. Depending upon the specific requirements for an agency, applicants are required to remain at the academy and mandated to adhere to the rules and regulations of the academy for the duration of training which may range from as few as four weeks to more than six months.

The training curriculum is a well-thought-out experience of academic and physical tests designed to transform the recruit into a well-rounded officer competently prepared to fulfill the duties of law enforcement. In 1970, the Commission on Accreditation for Law Enforcement Agencies (CALEA) was established to accredit police departments, and in 2002 to accredit training academies. CALEA establishes standards and ensures consistency of training requirements established by state agencies. CALEA accreditation provides quality assurance to the administration of the academies and for the police departments for whom it trains its personnel.

The curriculum is generally a legislatively mandated requirement overseen and developed by an agency such as the Peace Officer Standards and Training (POST) Councils. In New Jersey, the Police Training Commission approves curriculum, reviews course content for consistency with changes in law or practice, and mandates changes to the curriculum to maintain legal currency. Many police academies include very specific ethics training because of legal challenges and court rulings. Officers must stay current with changes in the law, and the academy trains officers to come into compliance with new legislation and court holdings.

A case in point was Miranda v. Arizona, which produced the Miranda warning. The Miranda warning was seen as an impediment to police work because it was the means for a defendant to avoid questioning. That is, the suspect, upon realizing that they might be charged with a crime, could request an attorney, which meant the investigating officer had to terminate questioning until an attorney was provided. This gives the appearance of hampering an investigation and causing delays. However, the Miranda warning resulted in better, more conscientious police work that produced both increased convictions and fewer reversals upon appeal.

Police academy training is divided into classroom experiences and on-the-job training, in which the officer-to-be or recruit job-shadows a sworn officer. This allows the recruit to see firsthand the distinctions between training in the academy and the realities of the job.

Academy trainers are generally active-duty police officers and civilians of specific expertise who have passed additional training that certifies them as academy trainers and subject matter experts (SME). For example, New Jersey's Police Training Commission requires Methods of Instruction (MOI) training to ensure that instructors are prepared to deliver high-quality classroom instruction. That is, the instructor, through MOI certification, has shown that he or she is competent at teaching others the skills needed to be an accomplished police officer. During the training session, recruits are also subject to a variety of guest speakers, such as persons from the prosecutor's office, experts on ethics from the attorney general's office, representatives from drug enforcement, and others from the gang identification and management unit. Recruits will also get an introduction to their union representatives.

Completion of academy training is a cause for celebration. The recruit has successfully passed each phase of training and demonstrated competence to perform law enforcement duties and the responsibilities that accompany the badge. The applicant will be certified or sworn in as a law enforcement officer. A longstanding tradition is the pinning of the badge on the recruit by a family member or other sworn law enforcement person who has had a strong influence in the life of the recruit. Depending upon the state and the jurisdiction, the certification may have a lifetime status or it may have to be renewed periodically. The swearing-in ceremony and the tossing of the hat is not the completion of training. Now comes on-the-job training (OJT), learning of the practical side of the job. The newly sworn officer will be paired up with a veteran who will augment the academy training with actual life experiences of being a police officer.

The portrayal of becoming a police officer has included illustrations that the recruit may place their senior partner in jeopardy. *Dirty Harry* movies suggest that the recruit hampers the seasoned veteran, which can result in their own death. In other renderings, the recruit is not respected because they are "new" and lack practical know-how. However, recruits are not just thrown into the mix; the on-the-job training is designed to teach them how to best perform on the job and how to stay safe. Oftentimes, recruits will bring to the job certain specializations that they have acquired elsewhere, such as in the military, through university training, or through some other source of instruction. In the best of all possible worlds, the employing police department will be aware of individual special talents and call upon that person when circumstances require that proficiency.

CAREERS, BLACK LIVES MATTER, EXCESSIVE FORCE, AND POLITICAL AND SOCIAL UNREST

Recent events regarding law enforcement (in addition to the threat of COVID-19) include Black Lives Matter, excessive force, and political and social unrest. There have been calls for the abolition of police, an old and repetitious discussion which is not likely to happen. A few cities have acted to affect some forms of abolition of police including Camden, New Jersey, and Baltimore, Maryland (long identified as violent cities), and Minneapolis, Minnesota (which will require approval through a popular vote in November 2021). These cities did not abandon the idea of policing but restructured it and changed the training curriculum to be more racially conscious, judicious in their use of force, and instituted greater access to civil forms of redress. Legislation was created to change or add to training. Finally, some police departments have seen defunding and cuts to the police budget.

There are minimally two career related concerns to recent incidents: whether a student should pursue a career in law enforcement and how these events affect training and performance on the job. Headlines should not determine career choice. A different perspective is proposed. This is a book about preparation for a career. While the occupation of police officer will be affected, career preparation can be an opportunity to manage changes effectively. Recent events which include the Derek Chauvin trial and conviction and others charged with criminal malfeasance appear to threaten law enforcement. However, like previous changes of law which have impacted police performance, the trained police officer will find the opportunity to rise above the threat.

The opportunity is to alter the paradigm, recognize problems, and seek solutions. Cameras record the events fostering concern, and other technology is protective. The *Executive Order on Safe Policing for Safe Communities* called for creating an independent credentialing authority to lead training curriculum revisions and job qualifications. Additional grant funding will be available for implementation. These are enhancements, not setbacks, to police performance; to better serve all—police and the citizens they serve. Be well informed and review the website https://ballotpedia.org/Changes_to_policing_policy_in_the_states_and_100_largest_cities,_2020 for changes in legislation—what is changed in one state may also lead to change in another state.

THE BENEFITS OF LAW ENFORCEMENT

There are benefits to work in law enforcement. The first is satisfaction derived from worthwhile work safeguarding communities and ensuring quality of life. Salaries are comparatively good, with a potential for increases. However, the starting salary for many police officers coming out from the academy may appear comparatively low. Low salaries can be offset by overtime for staff shortages, special events, and other off-duty policing needs in the private sector. A college degree is a plus for attaining many higher level off-duty work assignments (which usually pay better). If you pursue graduate school, a master's or doctorate degree can open doors for promotions or to lecture as an adjunct professor or program director/chair in a college. This will be discussed in chapter 9. (See appendix A, the profile of Dr. Robert Louden.)

While working as a police officer or in another law enforcement capacity, inquire with local colleges whether they will provide credit for completed academy and other specialized training, as well as on-the-job experience. Some colleges provide law enforcement personnel with generous credit allowances and reduced tuition as an incentive to complete a degree. Credit allowances may include graduate studies. In many cases, law enforcement agencies will provide monetary assistance for college. Generally, these grants require that you receive grades above a C and maintain a certain grade-point average. The granting agencies may require that you remain in service for a specified period of time as payback for the monetary assistance. In instances when a specific grade is not achieved or the grade-point average drops below the set standard, funding may be discontinued, or reimbursement may not be approved. Education is a benefit with great potential. While most who enter policing are young and the notion of retirement seems too far off to require immediate action, nothing could be further from the truth. The right undergraduate degree or an advanced degree can help supplement your pension. More importantly, the degree or an advanced degree frequently sets the individual up for satisfying activity in retirement. This is discussed in greater detail in chapter 9.

Law enforcement need not be static employment. There are many opportunities for promotions and transfers either within departments or to other departments. Law enforcement is becoming more and more specialized, and opportunities are available for those who have the credentials.

The day of the average cop who just walks a beat on patrol may have come to a close. Specialized areas of expertise are in demand and the generalist may be reduced to an almost irrelevant status. While those assigned to patrol are more likely to arrive on the scene first, they may have little to do except to contain and protect the integrity of the crime scene. Television shows portray the more graphic and elaborate degrees of specialization, but they do not mention all. Some of the more forgotten or ignored of these, which would be utilized in larger police departments, include the public information officer, who responds to the press and/or limits the dispersal of information while satisfying the right of the public to know. Another specialization often neglected in these discussions is the range officer. While all officers need to demonstrate proficiency with weapons, the range officer must requalify all officers with their weapons at least annually if not more often. The range officer is an expert in weaponry and its uses, and he ensures that the many functions to take place at the range are satisfactorily completed. First, he makes sure that police officers qualify, that is, know how to use their weapons proficiently. In addition, this officer is responsible for range safety and the suitability of the weapon.

There is a diverse assortment of weapons available to law enforcement. Many are only to be utilized in the most unusual of circumstances. In such cases, only those qualified in the use of a specialized weapon will be allowed to engage it. Of course, the range officer is also responsible for the paperwork that certifies each officer as qualified in the use of weapons.

Specializations allow the officer to utilize skills in which the officer is already proficient, scuba diving or computer programming for example. The vast array of specialized training now taken advantage of by police agencies, whether on a state or federal level, allows the officer to explore personal interests that heretofore were unavailable. For example, the officer may wish to learn forensics. Once certified, those talents will likely be utilized by the police department and, in times of emergency, by other departments.

There are specialties in policing that may cater to your interests. Those specialties include domestic violence, organized crime, electronic surveillance, cybercrime, juvenile crime, internal affairs, homeland security, SWAT teams, hostage negotiations (see Bob Louden's profile in appendix A), and many others.

THE POLICE BENEVOLENT ASSOCIATION (PBA) AND THE FRATERNAL ORDER OF POLICE (FOP)

The PBA and the FOP are national organizations (or, unions) that represent police officers. Every police department elects some of its members to serve as union representatives. The unions are supported by the dues that are paid by the police officers. The PBA and FOP organizations work tirelessly to ensure that officers are adequately compensated, are fairly represented in disciplinary and court proceedings, and they will file suit when officers are unfairly treated. Unfortunately, the risks of the profession sometimes become a reality, and in times of loss, they help to provide support to officers' families and dependents. Some of the local and national organizations also offer scholarships for officers and their dependents. Do not neglect to inquire upon hiring whether the local PBA will assist you to finance additional education.

MEDICAL AND RETIREMENT BENEFITS FOR LAW ENFORCEMENT

When choosing the law enforcement profession, do not ignore medical and retirement benefits. There are excellent health benefits that provide coverage for the officer and his or her family. Benefits, in addition to medical insurance, may include dental and vision coverage. Generally, earlier retirement is allowed than what is available in other professions, along with a generous pension, and medical benefits. There are other retirement opportunities such as deferred compensation plans. In some cases, eligibility for retirement comes after only twenty years on the job. However, early retirement means that you need to be prepared to live a productive life for the many decades to come after your career in law enforcement.

MULTICULTURALISM IN LAW ENFORCEMENT

Multiculturalism is receiving greater emphasis in law enforcement. Many serious incidents have received national attention since the beginning of the pandemic and have increased the focus on multiculturalism[2] in law enforcement. Officers do not get to choose their assignments and with whom they will interact. A more diverse police force which reflects the cultural and racial makeup of the community it serves will better serve that community. Anyone considering a career in law enforcement will benefit from a course in multiculturalism and diversity.

There are two perspectives to keep in mind to avoid confusion regarding arguments about multiculturalism. The first is the concept of fairness. An oversimplification of explanation is to hire more minorities to create a more racially diverse police force. The second is to hire those best qualified to do the job. The perspectives seemingly both compete and conflict. The answer seems to lie somewhere in the middle and possibly hinges on recruitment practices. That is, seek out the best candidates through a broader spectrum of recruitment which reaches for a deeper pool of applicants which reflect the community's racial and cultural makeup. Providing that the recruitment practice is inclusive, there is greater likelihood to ensure that not only will the police force be diverse but also is represented by highly qualified personnel.

"Creating a Multicultural Law Enforcement Agency: An Intentional Priority"[3] is an excellent article discussing these concerns. The author, Patrick Oliver, PhD and retired Chief of Police, does a thorough job discussing the issues.

A SECOND LANGUAGE

Proficiency in a second language, both verbal and written, is a valued specialty and will improve the likelihood of greater sensitivity. A second language is a plus in a diverse community and if you have aspirations of entering the federal service, then it is definitely a positive point on a résumé. Another benefit of proficiency in a second language is your personal safety. Knowing a language may help you better understand the intentions of those with whom you must interact. That is, when they speak to another person in their native language, you can hear and understand what is being said. If harm is intended, you are more likely to be able to remove yourself from harm's way. Conversely, if you do not know a language, you cannot interpret the intentions of others and will not be forewarned if they have dangerous intentions.

ON THE JOB

The job of law enforcement seldom entails a forty-hour, nine-to-five workweek. Initially you should plan on afternoon, night, weekend, and holiday duty. As you gain seniority and promotions, this will change, and more favorable shifts will become available.

A NOTE ABOUT THE MILITARY POLICE

The men and women who serve as our military police are in many ways similar to those who serve in law enforcement—they protect and serve. Their service is usually the enforcement of military laws and regulations regarding army personnel and property. They also perform duties similar to civilian police forces which include patrol, traffic control, and writing tickets. And there are the tougher tasks of policing, such as crime scene investigation, interrogation, interviewing witnesses, arrest and charging of suspects, and coming to the aid of those in need.

Military policing dates its history back to 1775 and the War for Independence. The rich and noble history of the U.S. Army Military Police Corps is preserved in the Regimental Museum located at Fort Leonard Wood, Missouri. The museum is open to the public. Fort Leonard Wood serves as the U.S. Army Military Police School.

There are many benefits to being a member of the Military Police Corps. Many of the required training courses that prepare and qualify a soldier as military police are certified by the American Council on Education (ACE) for college credits (undergraduate and graduate). In addition, during active duty in the military, college courses can be taken toward a degree. The military will provide full tuition, payment toward books and fees, payment of existing college loans, and a stipend for living expenses. In addition, there is the GI Bill, which supports education after your service is completed.

Military police training is similar to the preparation given to civilian police, and thus it has great transfer value from the service to civilian police. Many civilian police agencies will credit time served in the military police and recognize the importance of military police training. The website http://www.wood.army.mil/usamps/MissionVision/MP Disciplines.PDF provides a list of both general and advanced training in the military police corps.

Anyone interested in a career in law enforcement will benefit from the military police corps website: http://www.goarmy.com/careers-and-jobs/browse-career-and-job-categories/legal-andlawenforcement/military-police.html.[4]

Brigadier General Mark Spindler, retired, was the Deputy Provost Marshal General of the Army Commanding General, United States Army Criminal Investigation Command, and Army Corrections Command had a distinguished and decorated career in the U.S. Army. He was a graduate of basic and advanced military police training. He prepared a recommended reading list[5] for those interested in service as a member of the military police corps.

There are many positive points to consider when advancing from the military to civilian law enforcement. Military police seeking to transition into the law enforcement profession have several advantages over regular applicants. The applications of servicemen and women may be fast-tracked, or there is incentive pay and points added to civil service or municipal applications. Military service time can count toward retirement. Do not neglect time served in the military. The purchase of retirement credit later in your career can become very expensive. The person with military experience has had valuable experience and training desired by police departments; a disciplined officer who is well-trained to follow orders, familiar with weapons, and familiar with high-stress and dangerous surroundings is a valued asset for any law enforcement agency. Military personnel possess skills and experiences that the average new police recruit lacks.

SUMMARY

Law enforcement offers many career opportunities. The career may remain rooted in one department and has the potential to allow the officer to expand their interests and assume different roles as their skills and training increase. The law enforcement officer, in many ways, is only as limited as they fail to see themselves in other roles. Law enforcement officers have the ability to train, adapt, and prepare for other opportunities. The benefits of the law enforcement career are excellent and extend beyond early retirement, pension, and medical benefits. The law enforcement career can transition into a second career and the fulfillment of personal interests.

Obviously, any detailed discussion of the extensive nature of police work is much too involved for this writing. The interested student should refer to the bibliography of suggested readings for a more in-depth understanding of police work.

Chapter 3

Careers in Corrections

The fifty states, the District of Columbia, and other U.S. territories are responsible for more than 1,800 correctional facilities[1] and another 3,200 local and county jails.[2] Prison systems continue to expand, and few prisons ever close. That number does not include juvenile or federal prisons, nor private prisons, or private nonprofit community corrections centers.

"An estimated 6,899,000 persons were under the supervision of adult correctional systems at year-end 2013."[3] About 2.2 million convicts[4] are in some form of confinement, and the remainder are supervised in some form of community corrections. The number of people under correctional supervision is not likely to decrease, although the ratio between confinement in prisons and jails and community corrections may experience a shift. Legislators recognize that reliance on prisons and other forms of confinement has proven much too costly and ineffective.[5] Corrections have failed to serve the needs of offenders and society to provide long-term public safety. This failure is expressed as recidivism, or the crime rate (see UCR—Uniform Crime Report).[6] Recidivism[7] has not decreased, and despite a booming prison population, neither has the crime rate been reduced as has been projected that it would during the past forty-five years of rapid prison expansion.

A career in corrections is comprised of both civilian and law enforcement positions at the federal, state, and local levels. Private correctional enterprises, which include armed security, are also expanding. The increase of the incarceration rates in the past forty-five years has caused the ranks of correctional officers and parole officers (law enforcement) to expand beyond 474,000[8] positions nationally. Similarly, the ranks of civilian employees have likewise expanded to meet the needs of the increased correctional population. In addition, the increase of private companies that operate private prisons also includes community corrections centers such as halfway houses, day reporting centers, resource centers, and other agencies. The current focus on the potential of community corrections has increased and will likely see the additional need for those centers to achieve more positive results in reduced recidivism and a diminished crime rate.

This chapter cannot answer all your questions. However, many answers can be found in college courses and are also available from such sources as the internet, textbooks, and professionals who work in the field. Write your questions down and then ask them of knowledgeable experts in the field! Your questions are your guide to answers for your anticipated career path.

INSTITUTIONAL CORRECTIONS

The correctional officer median salary is $46,313, an increase of almost 20 percent since 2016.[9] The posted salary for correctional officers will be different than what is posted because of several variables including a daily stipend for shift overlap—one shift officer cannot leave until the next shift officer is in place—this is referred to as the shift differential, about fifteen minutes of overtime per day. Correctional officers' contracts include different rates of compensation for overtime; for example, a larger amount if he/she is required or has a mandatory assignment to work more than two shifts in a row. This may occur because a shift is shorthanded or because of emergency circumstances. Those who work holidays may receive an increased daily wage, and if there is overtime on a holiday, then the compensation is larger than the normal rate for overtime. Therefore, correctional officers are guaranteed to earn more than the stated base salary.

LAW ENFORCEMENT

The law enforcement side of corrections includes correctional officers, juvenile correctional officers, sheriff officers, or deputy sheriff officers (titles change by jurisdiction), parole, and probation officers. Some states have granted probation officers status as law enforcement officers which permits them to be armed and sworn as law enforcement personnel. Correctional officers, juvenile correctional officers, and sheriff officers operate federal and state prisons, county jails, and juvenile detention centers. Parole officers and probation officers provide community supervision of ex-convicts, offenders placed on probation, and juvenile offenders who are released from confinement or have noncustodial sentences from the court.

Are They Guards or Correctional Officers?

Correctional officers have been called a keeper, a night keeper, a jailer, a hack, a screw, a guard, and a turnkey, among other terms. These terms are antiquated or derogatory, depending upon who is saying them and the context in which they are used. Stinchcomb and Fox help to clarify the difference between a guard and a correctional officer:

> A "guard" is one who watches over, protects, and prevents escapes, etc., but more than that, a "guard" is a technician trained to do a rather specific task, maintain security/custody. On the other hand, an "officer," by definition, is one who . . . is called "to minister," to serve. Specifically, a corrections officer is one who serves other people in a holistic way, concerned about the total person . . . and the surrounding environment. They learn how to care for the physical health of a person, how to promote mental/emotional well-being, and how to lift the spirit by promoting self-esteem. They learn how to provide a safe and secure environment. Above all, they are respecters of persons, individuals, and their rights.[10]

Correctional officer is the more recent term and is considered a professional title distinguished from the other terms by training and standards of conduct both on and off the job. Correctional officers are sworn members of the law enforcement community trained to carry weapons and uphold the law, and in some jurisdictions, they are dual-certified so that they can report to a patrol position if needed.

The prospective employee will apply to take a test and be placed on a civil service or appointment list that can number in the hundreds of applicants. As mentioned in the previous chapter, the list of applicants will shorten quickly for many reasons. Those reasons include:

- Some candidates will not wait and will take other jobs.
- Some test-takers will not pass the physical, psychological, or drug tests.
- Some applicants will not pass the academy.
- Some individuals will realize in the academy or shortly thereafter that they do not wish to work in corrections and will resign.
- Some applicants will commit felonies and be ineligible for law enforcement positions.
- Correctional officer ranks experience high turnover rates.

Departures from careers occur for many reasons. Some officers cannot handle the stress and others leave for civilian positions. There will be terminations for incompetence and inappropriate, unethical, and illegal conduct—criminal behavior, on and off the job, will result in dismissals. Injury on the job will cause others to leave. And, there are many who complete their service and honorably retire. Correctional facilities must be staffed 24 hours a day, seven days a week, and vacancies must be filled. Academy classes will be scheduled to fill the ranks of officers leaving and to fill new positions or other correctional jobs. New recruits who graduate from the academy will enable correctional facilities to operate at required staffing levels, also known as "post tricks."

Once on the employment list, the applicant will move up quickly, perhaps even sooner than anticipated, and receive a letter to report to the academy. This is when the real work begins, and the applicant will be challenged to earn the privilege to be called a correctional officer.

RISING THROUGH THE RANKS

The correctional officer's career provides opportunities for promotions, assignment changes, and transfers to sometimes less desirable, or perhaps more desirable duty. After a specified time period, an officer may qualify for a promotion. Often a test must be taken to qualify for a new position to advance through the ranks from officer to sergeant to lieutenant, then to captain, and perhaps to chief. Depending upon the jurisdiction, the actual correctional titles may vary.

New Jersey is an example of changing job assignments. When a position becomes available, it is posted. Eligible officers may bid for the job. Eligibility is based on seniority, or other requirements such as education, special skills, or the possession of a Methods of Instruction (MOI) certification. The advantage of seniority is that officers will gain more desirable shifts and assignments. Officers usually begin their service on second or third shifts, that is, from 2 p.m. to 10 p.m. or from 10 p.m. to 6 a.m. These shifts are also likely to include weekends and holidays (and overtime pay) for the recruit.

The needs of a corrections department might mean that openings in other institutions become available. These openings may be closer to home or have more desirable work hours. In other cases, there may be openings in different divisions of the department that would permit the officer to transfer. These may include a move from a correctional institution to parole, which is often viewed as a more attractive duty since it removes officers from the prison environment and direct contact with convicts. The role of a correctional officer is seldom a static assignment and offers many opportunities for change and growth.

The Federal Bureau of Prisons offers an example of advancement from the custody ranks to civilian status. In this case, promotions are usually from within, and an officer may advance to become a warden. If there is an exception to this process, it is for the medical doctor or a hard-to-fill position. Warden Bob Hood (profiled in appendix A) has emphasized that retirement is mandatory at 57 and comes with "a nice twenty-year retirement package."

Promotions are the result of experience and preparation. There is a minimum time that must be spent in rank to qualify for a promotion. And then there is the test. The smart officer (or other correctional employee) should be aware that there is often a civil service test requirement, and the scores determine an officer's placement on a list. The exception is the person who has served in the armed forces and has "veteran's status" and moves to the top of the list. The final step for promotion is the interview. (See appendixes B and H for preparation guides for tests and interviews.) There are companies, for a fee, that provide assistance with preparation for promotional tests through classroom instruction, books, and sample tests.

THE BENEFITS OF CORRECTIONAL EMPLOYMENT

There are tremendous benefits to working in corrections. Law enforcement and civilian employees are provided similar benefits. New Jersey, for example, provides the following benefit package for correctional employees:

- Twelve vacation days per year
- Fifteen sick days per year
- Three administrative leave days per year
- Vision care reimbursement
- Health and dental benefits
- Prescription drug plan
- Retirement plan
- Deferred compensation plan
- Life insurance
- Paid leave for annual military training

A difference between law enforcement and civilian is the number of years required to qualify for pension benefits. Some law enforcement officers can retire in 20 or 25 years with 65 percent of their salary, while civilian employees have a somewhat lower salary percentage. The scale is based on a combination of age and years in service. These benefits are under current review and may see revisions in the upcoming years due to fiscal considerations. Nevertheless, these benefits will remain generous when compared to benefits in other, non-correctional employment.

CORRECTIONAL OFFICER JOB DUTIES AND RESPONSIBILITIES

Correctional officers are responsible for performing many tasks such as working the tiers or galleries of cells. (The language of prisons changes slightly from state to state.) This assignment is usually worked regularly and may last a long time. The advantages to having officers regularly assigned to cell blocks is that they get to know the convicts and the convicts get to know them, each comes to learn what they can expect from the other. For the prison administrator, this means consistency as well as a more intimate knowledge of the convicts, which helps the administrator to anticipate and prevent trouble. Similarly, should a convict have a problem, he knows the working officer and may turn to him in time of need. While the correctional officer will argue that he is not a social worker, he may need to refer convicts to medical, social, or psychological staff to manage problems. This helps the prison to maintain conformity and improves the custody and security of the prison. Many convicts will not request such a referral, and only when the officers know those confined will they have a sense of trouble that they can act on and thus prevent possible disturbances or other unforeseen problematic occurrences.

Prisons may be likened to small contained cities because of the number of persons and the diversity of work, such as work a mailroom, supervise visits, oversee kitchen duty, perform intake of new convicts, work roving patrol around the perimeter of the prison, have yard duty, perform laundry services, and transport convicts to court, or to other prisons. Some assignments place the correctional officer in contact with the convicts or with the public. A few assignments place the officer in an isolated circumstance—the lonely assignment, working the tower. Assignment to the training academy generally means a more reduced contact with the prison population. The career of the correctional officer is filled with a diversity of job assignments.

Advancement in rank has advantages and disadvantages with career implications. A supervising officer may feel relief that they are no longer working the cell blocks but be disappointed if the new assignment places them in an office pushing papers. Prisons operate with bureaucracy which includes the headcounts taken and recorded several times a day, incidents to be written up and investigated. Disciplinary matters begin with a charge, proceed to an investigation, and culminate in a hearing with assigned corrective action. Training never stops. There are policies and standard operating procedures to be reviewed and implemented and adapted to the working environment.

A crucial duty of supervision is maintaining consistency of the staffing pattern. Recruits, fresh out of the academy, must transition from the ideal to the practical, and understand that interactions in the prison world are vastly different from those in the civilian world. It is important to remember that convicts are still people with real needs and real concerns just like everyone else. The recruit, the "newjack," must learn the ropes and acquire the hands-on skills that allow prisons to operate with minimal difficulty.

INTERNAL AFFAIRS

Television and movies portray internal affairs as the bad guy of law enforcement who goes after their own. Internal affairs performs vital law enforcement functions including background checks. These checks are made for new hires (both civilian and law enforcement), volunteers, contract workers, and others who would enter into the correctional field. Background checks ensure that persons with inappropriate histories, including criminal histories, are made known to the hiring authorities to determine suitability for employment. A criminal history may exclude someone from the sworn law enforcement positions, but not for many civilian, volunteer, or other positions.

Internal affairs conduct a variety of investigatory functions such as allegations of unethical or criminal conduct by staff or misconduct by those in custody positions. The investigations maintain the integrity of the organization, ensure that allegations are valid or invalid, advise the administration of the need for reviews of standard operating procedures (SOPs), and prepare and refer cases to the prosecutor when the actions of the correctional employee are determined to be criminal. Corrections, like other areas of law enforcement, has been severely criticized for ethical breaches, cover-ups, and other inappropriate actions.

Internal Affairs conducts investigations of disciplinary charges filed against convicts to determine if breaches of discipline are processed within the prison or to refer it for prosecution. A well-run internal affairs office helps to maintain the integrity of the correctional organization by ensuring that all persons, both staff and those in custody, are not in violation of correctional laws, procedures, and other functions. (See chapter 9, "Criminal Justice Ethics.")

THE SHERIFF AND DEPUTY SHERIFF

The median salaries for sheriff careers have increased approximately 10 percent since 2016:

- Sheriff: $100,512,[11]
- Deputy sheriff: $44,973,[12] and

- Sheriff's officer: $58,000.[13]

The idea of a sheriff may call to mind such characters as the sheriff of Nottingham from the Robin Hood tales; Sheriff John Stone from the Beach Boys' song "The Sloop John B"; Sheriff Andy Taylor of Mayberry; or the man who may be the most famous, albeit controversial, modern sheriff, the self-proclaimed *America's Toughest Sheriff* (his book title), Joe Arpaio.[14]

The history and the exploits of sheriffs generally make for good reading because of the exciting adventures and myths that have developed through interactions with famous outlaws. An exploration of the position, as it developed in the United States, will extol its virtues as key to the establishment of order and civility in the Old West, but at the same time, there were some, due to a lack of accountability, who used the badge and the position to be nefarious and threatening to public safety. Some famous names associated in this regard were Bat Masterson and Wild Bill Hickok. George Washington was the first president but what is not often recognized is that his father held the office of sheriff.

The position of sheriff is unique. It is the original law enforcement officer not operating in a military capacity. While almost all sheriffs are elected,[15] they are not required to have prior experience in law enforcement, and they may not have been through academy training. However, after being elected sheriff, there is a necessity to complete firearms training. The position requires the sheriff to carry a firearm. Sheriff's deputies and officers do receive academy training.

The position of sheriff originated in England prior to the tenth century and was called a *shire reeve*. The first part refers to a geographic area and the second part loosely translates into "guardian." In time, the sheriff's duties increased from providing protective services to include the collection of taxes, delivering orders from the king, and keeping the suspect in jail until a sentence would be handed down by the court.

The American sheriff evolved to serve and protect and to mete out punishment, including executions, public shaming, and whippings, which are now banned. The English sheriff responded to the king, whereas the American sheriff became more responsible to the citizens.

The duties of the sheriff and his subordinates (sheriff officer, or deputy sheriff) are perhaps the widest ranging of any law enforcement position. The duties can be separated into two categories: general and special. There are inconsistencies in the duties to be performed because the duties are determined by the state in which the sheriff will operate. General duties more closely resemble the responsibilities of a police officer. The sheriff officer/deputy sheriff officer's duties include:

- Executing warrants,
- Providing chaplain services,
- Responding to emergencies,
- Providing courtroom security,
- Investigating complaints,
- Promoting homeland security,
- Collecting of delinquent taxes,
- Conducting the sale of property,
- Performing evictions, and
- Arresting suspects on bench warrants.

The special functions of the sheriff include:

- Maintaining the security of the jail and the courthouse,
- Supervising the prisoners,
- Providing transportation for inmates, witnesses, and others between the jail and the courthouse, and
- Providing protective services to the courthouse, including admittance to the courthouse security for the judge and those in attendance during a trial.

In accordance with courtroom functions, the sheriff will also serve warrants and execute civil actions, such as collecting delinquent taxes, serving evictions, and conducting sheriff's sales and repossessions. Officers also testify in court for both criminal and civil matters.

PAROLE AND PROBATION OFFICERS

Most states now require parole and probation officers to possess a bachelor's degree. In some states, there are specific degree requirements, such as a criminal justice/social science major. Students interested in careers in parole and probation should check their individual state's requirements for education. A parole officer's median salary is $58,867,[16] and a probation officer's median salary is $44,000.[17] Since 2016, the median salaries for parole and probation officers have increased about 20 percent.

PAROLE VERSUS PROBATION

Parole and probation officers are different positions with some similar duties and others that are unique to each position. In some jurisdictions, there is little or no difference between the positions. Probation is generally under the judiciary, and parole is generally within a state division such as corrections. Probation officers are more likely not to be armed, while parole officers are sworn law enforcement officers.

PAROLE OFFICERS

Parole officers (referred to as "agents" in some jurisdictions) were a late addition to the criminal justice profession. Parole officers work with convicts following their release from confinement. The requirements vary from state to state and the federal government. There are instances where the educational requirement is as minimal as a high school diploma, but other jurisdictions require a bachelor's degree, and in a few instances, a master's degree. A degree in criminal justice is often the required degree.

The specific jurisdiction defines the duties for the parole officer. In some instances, there is a separation between adult and juvenile officers. The adult officer has greater focus on the law enforcement function that ensures that the parolee maintains compliance with the conditions of their parole, while juvenile officers having an increased emphasis on rehabilitation, including social and educational services.

Employment prospects for parole officers remain positive through 2020. The U.S. Bureau of Labor Statistics for 2012–2013 Occupational Outlook Handbook[18] expects growth to remain steady at about 18 percent. Of course, as the parole officer starts out, he/she may expect to make considerably more than their starting salary due to overtime and holiday pay. In addition, parole officers receive the same excellent benefits as other members of the law enforcement profession.

PAROLE TRAINING

The parole officer receives extensive academy training that may last from a few weeks to as many as sixteen weeks. Possible courses in an academy curriculum would include:

- Supervision,
- Counseling (such as drug and alcohol addiction),
- Weapons Qualifications,
- Excessive Force,
- Investigation,
- Policy and Procedure,

- Computer Skills,
- Legal Issues Related to Parole,
- Physical Fitness and Defensive Tactics (such as verbal judo), and
- Procedures of Arrest, Filing Warrants, and Report Writing.

Training and accountability are an ongoing part of a parole officer's life, just as it is for other members of law enforcement. The officers must minimally requalify with weapons and be advised of and often trained and retrained in statutory additions and changes. Parole officers are required to keep current with changes in the law and in policies and procedures. In some cases, such as the Interstate Parole Compact, officers must remain current with other states' requirements.

THE WORK OF PAROLE

The parole officer supervises offenders released from prison on parole. Primary to the work of the officer is the maintenance of the caseload. Just as prisons have become overcrowded, parole officer caseloads have grown, which challenges appropriate levels of supervision and guidance.

Parolees released from prison have standard and special conditions which must be adhered to as part of their parole. The parole officer is responsible for accountability. Part of the parole officer's routine is to interview the parolee and assess willingness and openness to cooperate and to negotiate acceptance of available services following release. The purpose is to help the parolee establish stability upon return to their community.

A risk/needs assessment tool (such as the LSI, or Level of Service Inventory) may be administered to help prepare for the prisoner's release. These tools assess employment, education, medical, therapeutic, and other needs. These elements are referred to as *criminogenic factors* and are placed in two categories: static and dynamic. Static factors cannot be changed, such as an offender's age. Dynamic factors can be changed, such as the level of education which would make the offender more employable. The officer will identify resources as needed and stipulate that the offender complies with the provided services until such time as the adjustment is apparent.

Standard supervisory functions include increasing or decreasing the level of supervision for the offender. A parolee starting out may be required to report in every other week. In time, reporting may be decreased to monthly, bimonthly, semiannually, or annually depending upon the severity of the sentence, the length of time the person will be on parole, and the parolee's adjustment. The officer must be a conscientious bookkeeper, collecting debts and fines and keeping accurate records. The officer will also be required to follow up on job, school, or other program attendance. There will be checks of accountability, such as ascertaining that the offender is maintaining an assigned curfew, staying away from undesirable persons, and adhering to restraint orders. Officers may conduct drug and alcohol screenings, recommend discharge from parole supervision, make arrests when violations occur, and file for parole revocations. These are only a few of the duties performed by parole officers. More detailed examples of parole officer duties are discussed below.

ELECTRONIC MONITORING

Parole officers have several tools to help them work with offenders who are perceived as representing the greatest risk. Electronic monitoring devices are among the more recent innovations. Among the more frequently used devices are ankle or wrist bracelets. These devices are fairly simple to employ, and they rely on a telemetry signal that is sent to a central receiving station. In other cases, the parolee may be required to wear a backpack that has a programmable global positioning device (GPS) which reports the parolees' location or sets off an alarm if the parolee either goes beyond approved borders or enters an area that is prohibited. The system requires around-the-clock monitoring. Some drawbacks to GPS utilization include the high cost to implement and paying the salary of the person who does the monitoring. Parole officers currently monitor about 200,000[19] persons nationally on these instruments.

INTERSTATE PAROLE COMPACT

The Interstate Parole Compact is an area of specialization for a parole officer requiring special training in their state. The officer will attend national conferences/trainings to remain current with changes in the Interstate Compact. The contract involves the transfer of parole supervision from one state to another or to a U.S. territory other than that in which the person has been sentenced. The contract is made in accordance with the Interstate Commission for Adult Offender Supervision and other criminal justice concerns and is an agreement between the 50 states, the District of Columbia, Puerto Rico, and the Virgin Islands. At any one time, there are thousands of offenders involved in the Interstate Compact. (For more information about Interstate Compacts, including common myths, visit http://www.interstatecompact.org/.)

The parole officer in charge of administering the state's Interstate Compact will ensure that the offender meets the requirements of both the sending and the receiving state. Those requirements include such criteria as time under supervision, demonstrated compliance with parole conditions, and a supervision plan. The receiving state ensures that the offender will be able to comply with the receiving state's policies for supervision. The policies include that the person has a visible means of support, such as employment or a promise of employment, and is or has been a resident of that state or territory or has family with a residency.

Offenders do not have a right to transfer and may only be approved after the receiving state has investigated so that both the receiving and the sending state agree. The receiving state may impose special conditions that were not ordered in the sending state, thus changing the conditions of parole for the offender. Similarly, the sending state may also attach special conditions to the parole status of the offender going to the receiving state. For example, the sending state may stipulate that the offender not return to the sending state without permission of both states during the specified time that the offender is on parole.

THE PROBATION OFFICER

Probation officer work combines investigator, supervisor, social services coordinator, counselor, and enforcer. The officer has a distinct impact on the lives of those with whom they interact. An example of each will help illustrate how this happens and how it is important in the probationer's life, societal protection, and the reduction of criminality—all of which are intertwined.

The investigator determines suitability for a sentence of probation or a recommendation for incarceration. Presentence investigative reports examine the client's life, including school, family, work, societal involvement, the current offense, its impact on victims and others, and prior instances of legal violations.

The role of the supervising officer ensures that the client meets the conditions of probation as determined by the court. The supervisory/counselor role may result in independent action by the probation officer to assess need and determine other avenues of service to best help the probationer through his/her time of supervision. The probation officer maintains records of involvement with the probationer, including reporting, adhering to conditions of probation, attitude, payment of fines, and personal effort to demonstrate responsible citizenship. The probation officer can recommend termination of probation for failure to be compliant with the conditions of probation or recommend revocation for new criminal offenses. In such cases, the officer may become a witness before the court whose testimony and records will be critical to judicial decisions.[20]

About 4 million persons[21] are on probation at any given time for misdemeanors and felony offenses. More than half the states combine their probation and parole services into one agency. Probation is the most widely used sanction of the courts. The offenders' reporting schedule is determined by the probation officer. Probation services cost only a fraction of the cost of institutionalization. Nationally, the approximate cost of institutionalization per convict is more than $30,000 per year,[22] whereas probation only costs between $700 and $1,000 per year.[23]

Probation officers may or may not be sworn members of law enforcement. Generally, probation officers report directly to the court. Among the duties performed by probation officers are:

- Initial interviews with offenders,
- Investigation including presentence investigations,
- Supervision of offenders including enforcement of court orders,
- Holding offenders accountable for violations of probation conditions,
- Probation violations and reports,
- Probation revocation recommendations,
- Child custody and visitation reports,
- Counseling (family and personal),
- Financial planning,
- Case documentation,
- Collecting fines or other court-ordered costs,
- Screening for drug use,
- Electronic monitoring,
- Conducting risk/needs assessments,
- Arranging transportation and providing shelter and other subsistence,
- Evaluating offenders' progress and determining necessary courses of treatment, such as job training, educational opportunities, employment assistance, and special programs,
- Service referral and coordination, identifying offender treatment resources and services, and
- Meet with offenders and their family, and others who are directly involved with the offender.

Probation officers work with either adults or juveniles and are concerned with community safety to ensure that the offender does not represent a risk to the community. Pre-trial investigation seeks to determine whether a probationer represents a risk to the community. Probation officers present their reports to a judge with a written recommendation. Officers may also supervise those placed on bond awaiting trial or other adjudication.

The role of the probation officer has evolved. The officer may be thought of as a community treatment specialist or a case manager. In these capacities, officers will be concerned that probationers receive treatment, obtain employment, or perhaps return to school to complete their education as an enhancement for employment.

Probation officer caseloads vary in size. The American Probation and Parole Association (APPA) recommends a caseload of 50 cases per officer.[24] However, an officer may supervise several hundred persons in high-density urban areas, while in the rural area the caseload may be as few as 50. Frequently, an officer in a rural area will cover a larger geographic area, which will result in larger caseloads. Officers dealing with high-risk offenders or those who are assigned to special programs (drug court, domestic violence, sex offenders, etc.) may have reduced caseloads. Intensive supervision programs are often administered by the judiciary outside the regular probation divisions. These programs have small caseloads and more rigorous compliance, which, in turn, has a higher success rate than regular probation.

REQUIREMENTS FOR PROBATION OFFICER

Probation officer requirements are similar to other positions in criminal justice and include: a bachelor's degree; a record clear of criminal offenses; pass a written test (see appendix H for more information on civil service tests), a psychological test; a physical; and attend academy training. The duration of the academy training will be shorter than for other positions of law enforcement. There is a lower turnover rate of probation personnel than in other areas of criminal justice, although stress and burnout are not uncommon.

CIVILIAN CAREERS

The number of civilian staff members in all areas of criminal justice has increased greatly during the past three decades. This is especially true for corrections. Changes in programs and in treatment philosophy have been the primary forces that have pushed these increases. Salaries of civilian staff range from the mid-$30,000 range for entry-level positions to some well above $120,000 for administrators.[25]

There are any number of ways to classify the civilian workforce. A four-part breakdown of positions by work performed and their starting salaries would include:

- Coverage or client supervision ($51,765),[26]

- Treatment and counseling services ($44,445),[27]
- Support staff ($42,996),[28] and
- Management and administration ($105,680 and up).[29]

Other job descriptions include teachers, social workers, youth workers, business managers, accountants, administration/management personnel, classification officers, substance abuse treatment workers, public information specialists, ministers, human resource managers, nurses, doctors, psychologists and psychiatrists, food service coordinators (cooks, food preparers, and managers), storeroom managers, industry employees, architects, building compliance or code enforcement personnel, information technology experts, researchers, and grant managers.

Entrance into the civilian/professional ranks requires education ranging from a high school diploma to a graduate degree or a medical degree and/or possession of special certifications or credentials, such as substance abuse counselor or certified public accountant. Many positions are placed along career paths; that is, only certain titles fall into these categories, and to advance the employee must have previous experience in a lower title. One of the premier tools for employment and advancement is the civil service test. The good news is that the more often you take these tests, the better you tend to score. There are prep courses available for civil service examinations. Advancement or employment may be affected in several different ways. There are open tests for these positions, assuming the candidate meets the minimum qualifications. Then there are those position openings that fall under the heading of promotional examination. These are only open to those already in the career track who meet the qualifications. Of course, as part of your career planning, you will be considering what type of continuing education you should pursue that will best prepare you for promotional examinations and other opportunities to advance.

Civilian correctional positions can be found in institutions, community correctional centers, and private correctional enterprises, such as private prisons and halfway houses. As an example of the changing nature of the civilian profession, the correctional counselor has become an expanding career position. The correctional counselor may wear many different hats, including providing support to those having difficulty adjusting to institutional life, preparing convicts for release, performing risk/needs assessments, and providing assistance to those just released from institutions. The emphasis on community corrections has expanded from post-incarceration concerns to addressing the concerns the individual will face before leaving incarceration such as medical circumstances (e.g., an HIV-positive status). Some issues receive institutional focus, while others come from parole, and others yet come directly from the private and nonprofit community corrections providers. The reader is urged to explore the topic of reentry. Job seekers for civilian positions may find employment announcements posted in newspapers or in state personnel, human resource, or other publications, such as *Corrections Today* magazine (see appendix O), or online sites such as indeed.com.

PRIVATE PRISONS AND COMMUNITY CORRECTIONS

The first private prison was in Louisiana in 1844. The emergence and rapid expansion of private prisons has been driven by at least four factors: overcrowding, exorbitant costs, expanding government, and the avoidance of lawsuits. As private prisons have emerged, controversy about this phenomenon has also surfaced. In its July/August 2011 issue, *Correctional News* published several articles and detailed some of the pros and cons. Among the more crucial issues are whether private groups can really operate correctional facilities less expensively than state equivalents, whether private correctional facilities can be operated safely, whether needed services can be provided to clients, and whether private correctional facilities are effective. In each category, the results have been mixed. In some states, such as Arizona, the cost seems to be less than the state expenditures, while in other states, such as California, the cost is greater. California, four other states, and the federal Bureau of Prisons are considering doing away with private prisons. According to the Bureau of Justice Statistics (2001), the cost savings of private prisons have generally been less than what was projected.[30]

A number of issues that have come under scrutiny include the education and training of private prison employees, who are generally less well educated or credentialed, as well as being less well trained and consequently less well compensated. Among the more vocal critics of privatized prisons and the issues just mentioned are unions such as the PBA or CCPOA that represent state and federal employees. Among the union arguments are that private corrections jeopardize public safety, the safety of their own employees, its professionalism, and the safety, well-being, and rehabilitation of offenders. Privatized prisons have been a growth industry.

Perhaps the more discouraging employment note is that the turnover rate in private prisons exceeds that of state prisons.[31] These arguments are not to suggest that the prospective corrections employee ignore employment opportunities in this newer field. The field of private corrections provides opportunities that range from getting that first job, to having a second career, to providing consultation for experienced correctional employees.

One theme for this book has been that the criminal justice career aspirant must plan for the future, and that the planning should begin as soon as possible. Corporations and nonprofits that operate private correctional facilities rely heavily on retired correctional employees from correctional officers to administrators. There are several reasons for this. The career professional is trained and experienced with the environment, sound management practices, correctional problems, legal concerns, treatment issues, and more. Those retired from correctional administration have relationships with former colleagues and current correctional administrators who can help resolve issues between government and corporations. An additional incentive is that with a pension already secured, going to work for a corporation provides another good salary (that may exceed either the pension or the salary from the career position), among other benefits.

JOB STRESS

A discussion about work in the correctional field must include information about job-related stress. Positions inside prisons are probably more stressful than those working the street. That is not to suggest that positions outside of prison are not stressful or that other settings, such as community corrections, lack stress. Anyone can be susceptible to job stress. The employee, and especially the correctional officer, must be vigilant and protective of his/her personal condition. Stress can be caused by long hours on the job and especially overtime, working nights and holidays that interfere with home and family life, as well as social and confrontational interactions associated with the job. Stress may often come from outside the work environment and then be carried over to the worksite. The causes of stress may be financial, marital, or other life-affecting conditions, but any cause of stress should not be ignored.

The consequences of on-the-job stress are many and include alcohol and substance abuse, domestic violence, divorce, suicide, and other behavioral acts (including criminal acts) that have been identified as stress-related. Of course, stress also contributes to physical and mental illnesses such as depression.

Many correctional agencies provide various employee assistance programs that are confidential for the staff person seeking assistance. In addition, there are many other groups that offer assistance. In New Jersey, Cop 2 Cop (1-866-COP2COP [267-2267]) provides 24-hour-a-day assistance and is law enforcement at its best looking after its own. (See appendix A, the profile of Bill Usury.) One message that comes across loud and clear from the many articles published in recent years is that no one needs to be abandoned who needs help. Help is available, and lives and careers can be saved by asking for it.

COMMUNITY CORRECTIONS

Community-based corrections has evolved from its humble beginnings that include a Boston shoemaker volunteering to work with an offender who had a drinking problem: John Augustus—the father of probation. Community corrections consists of several types of operations: parole, probation, day reporting centers, halfway houses, assessment centers, information resource centers for ex-offenders, centers for substance abuse, and more. As the emphasis on community corrections continues to grow, we can expect to see more, and possibly different types of programming develop. One of the newer additions to the field of community corrections includes community or problem-solving courts. Drug Court is the better known of these courts. Service providers include both for-profit enterprises such as GEO corporation and nonprofit providers such as Volunteers of America. Many of these organizations are members of the International Community Corrections Association (ICCA), which promotes evidence-based practices.

Community-based corrections comprise an array of activities from pretrial diversion to intermediate punishments to post-incarceration supervision. In addition, there are treatment centers and others that provide education and job readiness preparation. Those involved in community corrections include individuals who have been charged with an offense and others who have been convicted.

Community Corrections is a combination of law enforcement activities such as those performed by parole and probation officers, and service provisions performed by social workers, substance abuse counselors, family counselors, and job readiness trainers. Each seeks to use the skills of their chosen profession to assist offenders with the complex and often daunting tasks of reentry and reacclimation to society.

Chapter 4

The Courts, Its Actors, and Its Functions

Covid-19 has unfortunately removed many opportunities for students to gain real-life experiences from the courts and attorney's offices. Internships, volunteering, and observing which have been utilized in many undergraduate courses such as Introduction to Criminal Justice are no longer available or have only been granted on a very selective basis. Hopefully, as the country begins to reopen these opportunities will return. However, they may be slow to return since they are not essential positions. Nevertheless, this is not a dead-end street for students. While what is available is not perfect, ingenuity and creativity will provide opportunities to learn and from which to help determine a career. The internet and websites are available. Many websites allow you to ask questions. We suggest that you write out your questions and reach out to law firms and the courts for answers. We strongly advise other agencies, which interact with attorneys such as probation and parole, are valuable sources of information. Many agencies maintain attorneys on their staff to provide legal reviews and creating statutory law and can provide guidance regarding the legal tasks performed for these agencies. Of course, professors may also provide contacts from which you can seek assistance. For example, one of my students recently reached out to me with a question and she was put in contact with an individual who has been a federal prosecutor, a state deputy attorney general, a sheriff, and who had also held a position as a high-ranking elected official. Former Lt. Governor Kim Guadagno met with the student who afterward decided that a career as an attorney was her career choice. A little more work was required to make determinations about career choices and the person who persists will be in a stronger position to make career choices and the choice which is best suited for them.

The primary figures of the courts are the judge, the prosecutor, and the defense attorney. However, many other persons perform a variety of roles that ensure the effective, efficient, and secure operation of the court. Judges, prosecutors, and defense attorneys require advanced degrees. The process for a career in law begins with the completion of an undergraduate degree (often in political science or criminal justice) and then to law school to obtain a JD, or Juris Doctor degree—the degree most common for persons serving in these capacities.

Court operations represent many opportunities for student internships. Internships for the courts provide students with exposure to special programs operated by the courts, the inner working of the courts and other agencies such as probation, and the complexities of a multifaceted arm of the criminal justice system. Internships with the courts are often viewed as prestigious in part because they are limited to students who have excelled, have excellent recommendations, and who possess interests and talents related to the work of the court.

The research for the *Contemporary Criminal Justice Careers: A Comprehensive Guide* has found that salaries have increased 10 percent or more since the 2016 publication of *Exploring and Understanding Careers in Criminal Justice*.

ATTORNEYS

Juris Doctor (JD)

The JD is a professional degree. While the JD takes about as much study or time in post-baccalaureate study as a master's or doctorate degree, there is no thesis requirement. JDs usually do not refer to themselves as doctors; instead, and upon passing the bar exam they will place *Esq.* or *Esquire* after their name. The first JD was proposed at Harvard University in 1902,[1] but it did not become popular until about thirty years ago, when it replaced the LLB (Legal Laws Baccalaureate), or what was essentially a second bachelor's degree.

Roles of Attorneys

There are three principal roles for attorneys in the courts—the judge, the prosecutor, and the public defender or defense attorney. Private attorneys have the potential to make an excellent living; however, this is not always the case for criminal attorneys. Criminal attorneys engage clients who are often destitute, cannot make bail, and are without support. The defendant's case, especially when it is more serious, such as murder, may desperately require investigatory and other work to support a viable defense. Supporting defendants can be expensive if the case is to be successful. Clients, unfortunately, may be indigent. To put that another way, criminal justice clients/defendants may have poor or no resources with which to support their cases. Indigents must rely on the courtroom skills of their attorney. More complicated cases, such as those involving the death penalty or, to provide a specific example, the O. J. Simpson case, require incredible amounts of adjunct work to support the defendant. The late Johnnie Cochran[2] became famous for his brilliant defense in the O. J. Simpson case. However, as he initially remarked, "This case . . . is a loser."[3] Of course, Cochran could not have anticipated the advantages provided by the prosecuting attorneys, and particularly the glove that resulted in Cochran's now-famous closing statement, "If the glove don't fit, then you must acquit." Cochran had seemingly done the background work. The prosecutors introduced the glove into evidence not knowing whether it would fit. They opened the door for the defense attorneys who assumedly did their homework and were aware that the glove would not fit on Simpson's hand. Simpson could not get the glove on his hand when so instructed.

Few criminal justice cases make it to trial. Almost all clients make a plea deal. The best hope for the client is that their public defender can make them a good deal.

Defense Attorneys

The defense attorney is an integral actor in the criminal justice process. The purpose of the defense attorney, whether public defender or private attorney, is to ensure that the defendant's rights are not violated, that the defendant gets a fair hearing before the court. Representation by a defense attorney is a constitutional right and has been upheld by the U.S. Supreme Court.[4]

Arrest, a criminal charge, and criminal prosecution are not guarantees of guilt. The defense attorney helps to ensure that someone receives due process and is not convicted for crimes of which they are innocent. Unfortunately, and despite constitutional guarantees, innocent persons are at times found guilty and, in some cases, have even been executed. In other cases, there have been travesties of the judicial process, such as the infamous prosecution and harm to the Scottsboro Boys.[5] Zealous work on the part of defense attorneys has helped to rectify some of the wrongdoing. A lesser-known case was detailed in John Grisham's book *An Innocent Man.*[6] In this case, a life was destroyed despite exoneration. The work of the defense attorney is arduous and fraught with the possibility of miscarriages of justice. However, everyone is entitled to be represented by competent defense counsel.

Prosecutors/District Attorneys

The prosecutor, also referred to as the district or state's attorney, is the second-most powerful actor in the courtroom. The prosecutor decides which cases to try for criminal offenses, determines the appropriateness of the plea bargain, and decides the degree to which the defendant will be prosecuted. In addition, the prosecutor will also make recommendations for the sentence. Prosecutors are most aware that their position is a political position that can allow them to advance to public office. New Jersey Governor Chris Christie made his reputation as a tough federal prosecutor who fought public corruption, and that became his platform when running for office. Chris Christie is an excellent example of advancement from attorney to federal prosecutor to chief of his federal office to governor of his state.

Other Roles for Attorneys

Other roles for attorneys in the court include the defense of the accused and convicted. Legal Aid, the American Civil Liberties Union, and the Innocence Project are three of the better-known efforts through which attorneys may voluntarily pursue support for indigents accused of crimes, subjected to violations of their rights, represented by incompetent counsel, or convicted, that is, the challenge to discover whether the defendant was accorded due process. More recently, every state has developed Innocence Projects.[7]

There has long been supposition that many persons are imprisoned for crimes they have not committed. The problem has always been how to prove innocence when there have not been issues of due-process violations. The advent of DNA[8] has proven itself to be invaluable in these efforts. Innocence Projects join attorneys and investigators to reexamine evidence, and in some cases, to search for evidence not available or that has become lost over time. Many of these cases are one, two, or more decades old. Innocence Projects seeks to have its clients exonerated, that is, to prove that they did not commit the crimes.

These do not, as the saying goes, turn someone loose on a constitutional technicality. There have been by-products of DNA analysis, such as affirming the guilt of someone or of discovering the person who committed the crime. Again, these are often the result of DNA analysis.

Innocence Projects teams are often comprised of a lead attorney, graduate students, and others. They reexamine cases and help search for evidence. Law school students practice their craft by filing motions, and other interested parties concerned in the pursuit of justice are engaged in the process of discovery.

JUDGES

The United States is a federal republic comprised of 50 states, the District of Columbia, and other areas of U.S. protection. There are many jurisdictions with its own set of rules. Accordingly, the rules for the election or appointment of judges and other public officials and those that govern the legal process differ state by state. In accordance with the U.S. Constitution, each state establishes its own court system as laid out in each specific state's constitution.

The courtroom is the setting for the adversarial confrontation between the prosecutor and the defense attorney moderated by the judge. Alan Dershowitz explains the position of the judge as "the weakest link in our system of justice, and they are also the most protected."[9]

At the conclusion of the confrontation, there is an expectation that some truth will emerge in the quest for justice.

The judge, in this formal, regimented environment, is referred to as "judge" or "your honor." There are other terms by which a judge might be referred, and these are generally the result of the jurisdiction in which the judge presides. For example, in the U.S. Supreme Court, judges are referred to more formally as "justices." In other instances, the term may be "surrogate," and in others as the "justice of the peace," magistrate, chancellor, arbitrator, or referee. In some special circumstances, the judge may be called a "master" or a "special master." In these cases, the "master" will be expected to review specific evidence, and his or her authority is determined by statute or the state or federal constitutions.

Curiously, not all judges are trained in law or are required to have a law degree. This is more common in situations where they are elected to the bench and are not career judges. While most judges in the United States are trained in law and are attorneys, those who are lay judges, nevertheless, are referred to as judges and have the same rights as judges who are trained as attorneys. These judges are often part-time, serving in courts of limited jurisdiction.[10] State constitutions determine whether state judges are elected or appointed. Some judges serve a term with the possibility for either reelection or reappointment.

Despite the quote from Dershowitz that introduced this section, the judge is the most powerful actor in the courtroom, and he or she must perform many functions. In many criminal matters and in civil matters, the judge may hear the case before him without a jury. In these instances, the judge must make determinations about the credibility of the evidence as well as the truthfulness or reliability of the witnesses. The proceedings are somewhat different when there is a jury. Primary to the role, the judge is expected to be impartial; to act without bias toward either side; to ensure that the rights of all are upheld; to ensure that defense attorneys and prosecutors follow rules of procedure; to instruct the jury on its duty; and to be the interpreter of the law or, to better illustrate the importance of the position, to interpret the constitutionality of the circumstances that are raised. The rulings become the law of the land. Of course, the more serious act in any case is when the judge passes sentence on the defendant. Sentences can range from fines and/or years in prison, or even the death penalty.

Federal judges are nominated by the president of the United States and confirmed by the Senate. Prior to Senate confirmation hearings, the nominee is subject to a background check by the FBI. The candidate is also subject to additional review by the Senate Judiciary Committee. Once the recommendation is passed on to the full Senate, only a simple majority, or 51 percent, of the Senate is required for the confirmation. There can be one small snag to what is otherwise a somewhat uncomplicated process, and that is a "filibuster."[11] In this case, to bring the filibuster to an end, "cloture"[12] is invoked, and 60 votes are required.

Five Basic Steps to a Career as a Judge

Step 1: Get an education: Generally, the minimum requirement is a bachelor's degree. Among the skills for success in this occupation include analysis, logical thinking, speech, and research. Skills for competent performance on the judicial bench can be acquired through the college curriculum, and more specifically courses that include public speaking, government, English, philosophy, and history.

Step 2: Become an attorney: A majority of federal, state, and municipal judges are required to have the degree of Juris Doctor (JD). In addition, anyone seeking to become a judge must pass the bar exam given by a specific state and acquire experience working in the legal system. Many attorneys are permitted to practice law in more than one state by passing the bar exam in each specific state.

Step 3: Apply your knowledge: All those aspiring to become a judge should determine which court they desire to work in, although appointment procedures will be different depending on the type and location of the court. When an opening in the chosen court is available, apply for a judgeship.

Step 4: Gain political support: An important part of this process is gaining political support. Individuals interested in becoming judges should be aware that this occupation is very competitive, and potential judges must be able to make a favorable impression on those who hold the power to place them in their desired positions. You will have to convince the nominating/appointing persons that you are worthy of the position.

Step 5: Get appointed or elected: Members of the Judicial Nominating Commission oversee appointing state judges. To become a judge of a different sort, however, partisan or nonpartisan, elections are held by the state.[13]

The U.S. Supreme Court

U.S. Supreme Court justices are nominated by the president, generally have prior court experience, and require approval by the Senate. Senate hearings for U.S. Supreme Court positions often have political overtones that expose and explore the judge's background, question previous judicial decisions, and query personal conduct. Judge Clarence Thomas[14] is an example. He was accused of sexual harassment two days before the Senate vote. Other federal court nominations are much less rigorous. Once confirmed by the Senate, federal judges serve for life. However, federal judges may be impeached for misconduct. Supreme Court Justice Abe Fortas[15] is the only example of a U.S. Supreme Court Justice being impeached,[16] and this serves to illustrate the rarity of impeachment. The salary for a federal court judge is currently $268,300[17] and may not be reduced during their time in office.

One of the more unique aspects of the Supreme Court is that anyone can become a justice. Curiously, when it comes to the U.S. Supreme Court, the nominee also does not have to be an attorney. As a matter of fact, there are no education requirements at all for the position. The primary requirement is a nomination by the president followed by Senate confirmation (see Article 2, Section 2, Clause 2 of the U.S. Constitution). There are no education or experience requirements. There is no bar examination to be passed. However, should someone wish to pursue this career path, they would have to exhibit very special qualities and convince some powerful and influential people that they are right for the job.

Federal Judges

Article III courts are those that make up the judicial branch of the federal government:

- U.S. District Courts
- U.S. Court of International Trade
- U.S. Court of Appeals Circuit Courts
- The Supreme Court of the United States

The federal judiciary also includes Article I judges, who preside over courts or tribunals (a panel of judges) of limited power and jurisdiction, often connected to government departments and agencies. These courts are different from those of the judicial branch. For example, judges who sit on the U.S. Court of Claims do require nomination by the president and Senate approval (like Article III judges do); however, they serve a fixed term of 15 years. Another example are judges for U.S. Bankruptcy Courts. Appellate judges of the U.S. Court of Appeals Circuit Court make these appointments. They provide jurisdiction over a particular bankruptcy court's territory. And some judges are hired. Article I Judges (administrative law judges) serve the hiring agency, such as the Social Security Administration's Office of Disability Adjudication and Review.

State Judges

The process for becoming a state judge is determined by each state constitution, and the qualifications vary. There are states in which the judge is appointed through a committee. Other states have elected judges. Some states require an appointment by the governor and approval by the Senate. The length of time in office varies from serving for life to serving for an elected term. In each case the process for determining a judgeship is set forth in the state's constitution.

Circuit Judges

In many western and southern states, because of the distance between cities and lower populations, there are not enough cases to warrant the establishment of a full-time judge. Judges are then asked to ride a circuit, which means a judge travels from one city to another on a scheduled calendar. These judges preside over a general jurisdiction, which means they may preside over any type of case, from traffic tickets to murder trials.

Municipal Court Judges

Municipal court judges are appointed by the local chief governing authority, such as a mayor, and approved by the local council. These are generally appointed for an annual term and require reappointment each year. The positions are very political and usually controlled by the local party.

SHERIFFS

The sheriff's position was discussed in chapter 3. Since ancient times the sheriff has had numerous assignments, including court security—the protection of judges, prosecutors, and others—and to transport offenders and suspected offenders between the jail and the courtroom.

CORONERS

The prosecutor's office oversees many functions critical to criminal justice. The coroner is one such position, whose average annual salary is $69,050.[18] The office of coroner is somewhat unique in its function since there is close cooperation between the coroner and the prosecutor as they prepare a case for trial. The coroner will advise the prosecutor what is evidence for presentation in a trial and what is not. In the media, the coroner has been portrayed as a medical doctor who performs autopsies to discover the cause of death (death that is unattended by a doctor, and to ascertain whether it is a homicide, suicide, or accident), and whether malfeasance has occurred. The coroner may or may not be a medical doctor, depending upon the specific state's requirements. Of course, if they do not possess a medical degree, then they will not be performing an autopsy. However, they will lead the investigation that prepares evidence for the prosecutor and then, if needed, testify in court.

FORENSIC SCIENTISTS

The forensic scientist is a newcomer to the criminal justice field with increased popularity and emphasis in the academic field, often with its own curriculum. The average salary of the forensic scientist is $65,000.[19] The courses are interesting and include exposing students to the more graphic side of crime scenes, as well as taking them through the process of crime scene analysis. Professor Joe Paglino (profiled in Appendix A), a retired detective for the Monmouth County, New Jersey, prosecutor's office, creates a crime scene somewhere on campus for his students to examine and evaluate as the final examination.

The forensic scientist is the latest member of the criminal justice profession and they are usually members of the prosecutor's office with advanced degrees in forensics, chemistry, and biology. They examine the evidence for accuracy and help to develop the prosecution's strategy for presenting their case in court.

PROBATION

Probation Versus Parole

Probation and parole officers are discussed in chapter 3 and other sections of the book (see index). However, they are worthy of mention here because of the special functions they perform for the courts. The terms *probation* and *parole* are often used interchangeably, although their functions are distinctly different. Parole is often under the jurisdiction of some larger state division, such as the Department of Corrections or perhaps a parole board. Probation is usually under the jurisdiction of a county court, and probation officers report to the judge. Parole officers are generally sworn law enforcement officers, whereas probation officers are not.

Probation Officers

The probation officer is the eyes, ears, and legs of the court. The functions of the probation officer are detailed in chapter 3. The work of a probation officer tends to be more diverse than that of a parole officer, and it is more geographically specific.

OTHER JUDICIARY STAFF

The work of the judiciary requires a diverse staff. We have already discussed those at the uppermost level (judges and attorneys) and considered that they generally require law degrees. Others, such as bailiffs, clerks, and reporters, are referred to as "officers of the court." Textbooks often downplay these positions or provide very little information about them. However, the job seeker should not ignore these positions. They pay a decent salary, have good benefits, and may be a stepping-stone to other positions in the judiciary or the criminal justice system.

Bailiffs

The bailiff, with a median salary of $46,100,[20] might go unnoticed in the courtroom except for when he announces that the judge is entering or leaving the courtroom—a very formal moment usually accented by the announcement, "All rise!" The bailiff's responsibilities are much greater and include keeping track of attorneys, witnesses, and prosecutors to maintain the court's working schedule. Other duties include informing the defendant's attorney of the outcome of a case.

Court Reporters

Court reporters, with a median salary of $58,657,[21] are also referred to as court stenographers. Court reporters may be hired as needed on a case-by-case basis or they may be salaried employees. They require special training as stenographers and for operating the machine upon which all court language is recorded. The court reporter must pass a state proficiency test. The court reporter must be very accurate, because their report becomes the official record of the court proceedings. In addition, during court proceedings it is quite common for the court reporter to read back to the judge what has transpired for the judge to make a ruling. There has been an effort to replace this position with more sophisticated recording equipment, but this suggestion has had its drawbacks: First, it makes recall more difficult and time-consuming. In addition, recording equipment will pick up all the noises of a courtroom, potentially making some of the more important parts of the recording unintelligible.

Court Clerks

The court clerk, with a median salary of $41,060[22] maintains the calendar for the court, and in court it may be referred to as "calling the calendar." The court clerk performs duties critical to the court's functions, including administering the oath, maintaining the files of the court, and keeping the evidence secure. This position may be a stepping-stone for someone preparing to become an attorney, or the position may be occupied by an attorney who is preparing for a position in the prosecutor's office. In some jurisdictions, the court clerk may prepare writs and other court documents as directed by the court.

SUMMARY

The court responds to criminal justice matters much like a case manager. Where does this case belong? Who should provide supervision? What resources are available? What resources are needed? The questions could go on and on. The court and its actors must be prepared to interact with police, probation, corrections, community corrections, and private non-profit agencies.

There are new functions for the courts that require specialized training for assigned judges and staff. This is the largest growth area with the most expansion in the judicial process. They include the special or problem-solving courts, such as drug court, domestic violence court, gun court, and reentry court. There are other special courts, which provide unique circumstances for judges who see the cases through from beginning to end, maintaining jurisdiction and oversight. Or, as in reentry court, the court may pick up the offenders as they are about to reenter the community and ensure a smooth transition in which the needs of the criminal justice client are met with appropriate resources.

More special courts have emerged around the country, following the documented success of drug court. This is not to suggest that these other courts will be as successful as drug court (there has been insufficient research to state that they are successful), but the model holds the potential for greater success. In these cases, the judge is no longer the generalist of the court, but becomes an authority in the special circumstances of victims and offenders as well as the more effective means of management to prevent future criminal recurrences, while maintaining the welfare of the victim, the offender, and society.

Program staff of the court, depending upon funding sources, may operate in independent units or may report to the probation department with work assigned to probation officers.

Working for the court, in any capacity, is distinctly different from employment in the other areas of the criminal justice system (law enforcement and corrections).

Chapter 5

The Federal Government

The federal government is comprised of a complex set of criminal justice agencies. Some agencies are relatively small, while others have been extensively developed. Each agency has its own set of requirements because of the legislation which established the agency. Some operate exclusively in the United States (such as the FBI), while others work exclusively beyond the continental boundaries of the United States (such as the CIA).

The U.S. Bureau of Labor informs us that the federal government is the largest employer in the nation with more than two million law enforcement and civilian employees, including about 95,000 who are authorized to carry firearms. These employees occupy more than four hundred different positions.

Employees of state and local branches of law enforcement may work their entire careers in one state or one community. However, federal officers know from the moment of the application that they are not constrained by location and may have sudden relocation not only to other states or areas under U.S. protection but also to foreign countries. Approximately half of the federal workforce is in the District of Columbia, New York, California, Texas, and Florida. These locales are the major sites of U.S. offices, border protection, import/export security, and other sensitive assignments related to U.S. security. The work of federal law enforcement is distinctly different from state and local police departments. Most local police work happens on the beat and while responding to motor vehicle violations. The federal law enforcement officer is more likely to respond to counterfeiting, white collar, corporate crime violence, drug smuggling, production and distribution, postal fraud, environmental threats, and protective services for the president and other high-ranking government officials, including when traveling abroad. A simple breakdown of officers is to describe them as either investigative or uniformed. Park police[1] and game wardens are among the uniformed service. The investigative force is extensive and includes the better-known agencies—the FBI, CIA, DEA, ICE, EPA, ATF, and the Secret Service. Some of the lesser-known would include the Postal Service and the Department of Agriculture. It is not uncommon for an overlap of services between the departments, cooperative ventures, and at times competition between the agencies because of events or investigations that enter into the responsibilities of more than one of the federal agencies. The list of agencies above helps to indicate the vast diversity of employment in the federal service.

THE FEDERAL GOVERNMENT EMPLOYMENT SEARCH

The federal government is somewhat unique when it comes to postings for positions and receives a greater number of job applicants than any state or local personnel office. The website for job openings is www.usajobs.gov, or the Federal Jobs Digest at www.jobfed.com. Note: Jobs are usually posted for one week only. This means that if you are interested in a specific job(s), you must visit the websites weekly for updates. The large volume of applicants has led the federal government to use private agencies to screen potential applicants for them. The application process must be meticulous. You should:

1. *Adhere to all dates*. If you are late submitting the application, it will probably be discarded. Be careful to send the application by the due date, as well as any supporting documents, or if given a time frame, then send the documents within the allowable time frame.
2. *Do not leave blank spaces on your application*. Blank spaces tell the reviewer that something is missing or that you may be hiding something. Blank spaces are a job killer. Blank spaces may result in the immediate rejection of your application.
3. *Double-check that your application is complete*. Go over the application line by line. Review the job posting. Highlight on the posting the application requirements. Check each requirement to ensure that you have successfully answered/provided for each requirement and each document.
4. *Review your KSAs*. Federal employment is very specific about matching the right person with the right position. *KSAs* refer to *Knowledge*, *Skills*, and *Abilities*. To put it another way, the KSAs should be represented on your application through the answers to the following questions:
   - What do you know?
   - What have you been trained to do? and
   - Can you apply this knowledge to real-life situations?

Knowledge, Skills, and Abilities (KSAs) are critical in your résumé. They are to be incorporated correctly or your résumé will very likely be rejected. These are the requirements needed to perform a job that is demonstrated through qualifying experience, education, or training.

Each vacancy announcement will list the KSAs required in terms of "specialized experience," or "selective factor" requirements. In determining whether you qualify for a certain position, reviewers will evaluate your education and experience against the KSAs for each position. Because each position is different, the requirements for each will be different.

When you apply for federal positions, it is important for you to show that you meet the "specialized experience" and "selective factor" requirements for the position in your application package.

You can do this by either including the information in your basic application or by addressing these requirements separately from your application. Go to the following website for KSA information: https://federalresumeguide.com/how-to-write-a-ksa-for-a-government-job/

If you choose to address your KSAs separately, you should keep your responses brief and to the point. You need to relate your responses to the requirements of the job for which you are applying, and you should give examples that clearly demonstrate how your knowledge, skills, and abilities meet the requirements of the specific position. If you choose to rely on your basic application rather than write separate responses to the KSAs, you should be sure your application covers all the KSAs so the reviewers don't have to read between the lines to connect your basic application to the KSAs. As the applicant, you are responsible for showing how your education and experience meet the requirements for the posted position.

If you are unsure of how to write a KSA, you have the option of going to the above-mentioned website. A second option is to visit www.writeKSA.com. This website will help you write your KSAs for a fee of about $30. Another website which provides sample KSAs https://federalresumeguide.com/how-to-write-a-ksa-for-a-government-job/[2]

1. *Make sure your résumé accurately answers the three most important questions*. These include: What do you know? What have you been trained to do? Can you apply it?
2. *Highlight your skills.* The reviewers of your application will be looking for those specialized skills, talents, and aptitudes that match you with the needs of the job.

5. *Do not assume that a résumé for one federal job is appropriate for all federal jobs*. Different jobs list specific KSAs. Make your résumé reflect the ways in which you possess the required KSAs. Prioritize them according to the position posted. In some cases, it may be best to create a section on your résumé that addresses the KSAs specific to the job posting.
6. *Do not assume that a résumé for one federal job is appropriate for all federal jobs*. Different jobs list specific KSAs. Make your résumé reflect the ways in which you possess the required KSAs. Prioritize them according to the position posted. In some cases, it may be best to create a section on your résumé that addresses the KSAs specific to the job posting.

CITIZENSHIP

You must be a U.S. citizen or become a naturalized citizen to qualify for federal employment. On very rare occasions, waivers are available to legal aliens for hard-to-fill positions when no qualified U.S. citizens are available; however, the applicant must also qualify according to U.S. labor and immigration rules.

EDUCATION REQUIREMENTS

The education requirement for careers in federal agencies varies from agency to agency. Some agencies, such as the FBI, are very specific if you consider the diversity of academic study that is acceptable: accounting, electrical engineering, information technology, or computer science, fluency in a foreign language, or a degree from an accredited law school. Consider these other requirements for the FBI: two or three years of professional work experience; one year of law enforcement experience may be substituted for an advanced degree; and the successful completion of the FBI training academy, with eighteen weeks of training located at the U.S. Marine Corps base in Quantico, Virginia.

AGE REQUIREMENTS

Many federal criminal justice positions have a maximum age at which employment must be initiated due to federal law enforcement pension requirements. However, in certain situations, a waiver may be granted that extends that requirement. Some federal agency age requirements include:

- The administrative office of the U.S. courts: maximum age 37; positions include probation officers, pretrial services officer, statisticians, and investigators.
- U.S. Marshal's service: minimum age 21 and maximum age 36.
- Federal air marshal: maximum age 40.
- Federal Bureau of Investigation agent: maximum age 34.
- Immigration and customs enforcement agent: minimum age 21 and maximum age 35.
- Immigration and Naturalization Service (border patrol) agent: minimum age 21 and maximum age 34.
- Bureau of Alcohol, Tobacco, and Firearms agent: minimum age 21 and maximum age 35.
- Drug Enforcement Administration agent: minimum age 21 and maximum age 36.
- U.S. parks police officer: minimum age 21 and maximum age 37; mandatory retirement at age 57.[3]
- U.S. fish and game warden:[4] minimum age 21 and maximum age 37.
- U.S. Secret Service agent:[5] minimum age 21 and maximum age 37.
- Treasury enforcement agent: maximum age is the date immediately preceding an individual's 37th birthday (see profile James F. Kenny, PhD, provided in appendix A).[6]

SALARIES

Federal salaries are commonly more generous than those found in state government. Salaries are affected by the type of job, length of service, and promotions. Salaries are based on performance and testing. For example, federal agent median salaries are $75,762 a year.[7]

BACKGROUND CHECKS

Applicants for federal employment will undergo rigorous background checks (called vetting) to eliminate anyone who may be detrimental to the work of the hiring agency. These are investigations into the personal conduct and character of the applicant. The background check will minimally include criminal history, references, previous employment history, credit checks, and checks of social networking sites. Qualified applicants must also complete an employment panel interview prior to final selection. Normally, interviews are held within the general area (about 250 miles round trip) from where the applicant resides. Applicants must pay travel expenses to and from the interview site and to their first employment location.

THE FEDERAL BUREAU OF PRISONS (BOP)

The Federal Bureau of Prisons (BOP) prides itself on its professionalism. Retired warden Robert Verdyn, who rose from the ranks of correctional officer to warden, has no tolerance for his officers being called "guards." They are to be called correctional officers because of their training and performance. He once remarked that being a "warden" was "the best job in the world." The BOP opened its first training academy for correctional officers in 1930 in New York, and it is among the earliest of prison systems to open an academy. (Bob Hood's profile is in appendix A.)

The BOP requires that an employee must be hired in the agency prior to their 37th birthday, but for certain job titles this may be waived to age 40:

> The Attorney General has determined that the initial appointment of employees into Federal Bureau of Prisons law enforcement positions must be prior to their 37th birthday, with the following exceptions: Physician Assistant, Medical Officer, Dental Officer, Registered Nurse, Nurse Practitioner, and Chaplains of some faith traditions. Psychologists may be waived up to the date immediately preceding their 40th birthday.[8]

The Federal Bureau of Prisons has a central office located in Washington, DC, and is operated through six regional offices throughout the United States. The BOP operates 185 prisons and camps, 14 privately managed facilities (which will be eliminated as their contracts expire), and 5 community corrections management facilities that house more than 215,000 federal prisoners.[9] A visit to their website will provide a broad perspective of the number of prisons and types of correctional services.

ORIENTATION TRAINING

All persons appointed to the Federal Bureau of Prisons must successfully complete in-service training as a condition of employment, including 200 hours of formal training within the first year of employment. This includes orientation to the physical plant, familiarization with policies and procedures, and techniques for supervising and communicating with inmates in their daily activities.

Several examples of positions in the BOP include the following:

- Chaplain
- Clinical psychologist
- Corrections officer
- Dentist
- Medical doctor
- Nurse practitioner
- Physician's assistant
- Registered nurse
- Social worker
- Administrative staff
- Warden

Orientation training includes:

- 80 hours of institutional familiarization at the facility.
- 120 hours of specialized training at the Federal Law Enforcement Training Center (FLETC), which serves as the BOP residential training center located at Glynco, Georgia,[10] normally within the first 60 days after appointment and as scheduled by the Employee Services Department. This training includes four components: firearms, self-defense, written academic test on policies and procedures, and the Physical Abilities Test (PAT).

The Physical Abilities Test consists of:

- Dummy drag: Drag a 75-pound dummy 3 minutes continuously for a minimum of 694 feet.
- Climb and grasp: Climb rungs of a ladder and retrieve an item; ideal requirement 7 seconds.
- Obstacle course: Ideal requirement 58 seconds.
- Run and cuff: Run one-fourth mile and apply handcuffs; ideal requirement 2 minutes, 35 seconds.
- Stair climb: Climb up and down 108 steps with a 20-pound weight belt; ideal requirement 45 seconds.[11]

All applicants must meet the physical requirements for the considered positions. The examination will be conducted without cost to the applicant, usually by a federal medical officer, and will include a urinalysis test for drug detection. Applicants should not wait to get to the academy to get themselves into shape. Successful applicants will be in good physical condition prior to reporting for training. The academy schedule is rigorous, and the applicant will not have time to diet and exercise outside the required program.

The Bureau of Prisons, in conjunction with the U.S. Public Health Service (PHS), offers well-qualified students an excellent employment opportunity through the Senior Commissioned Officer Student Training and Extern Program (COSTEP). Through Senior COSTEP, students in select health-related fields of study are commissioned as ensigns in PHS during the final year of academic study toward a qualifying degree or residency. Students receive full salary and benefits in exchange for an employment commitment at the sponsoring agency after graduation. For more information, call (202) 353-4110.

COSTEP is a work-study partnership between students, educational institutions, and various federal agencies. It offers students valuable work experience directly related to their field of study and provides formal periods of work and study while they are attending school. After completion of academic and work requirements, students may be eligible for permanent employment.

The Student Temporary Employment Program (STEP) provides temporary employment opportunities that can last for as long as the individual is a student. Employment does not need to be related to the student's academic field. These positions are located in the central office, in Washington, DC. For more information, call (202) 307-3177.

The Summer Temporary Employment Program creates training and work opportunities in a wide variety of positions for individuals who can work only during the summer months. The work ranges from office support, trades, and labor occupations to positions in professional fields. These begin about mid-May and end on September 30. Applications are typically accepted from December through April 15. For more information, call (202) 307-3177.

Over the past thirty years, the BOP has trained more than 400 doctoral-level psychologists. Each of the ten psychology pre-doctoral internship programs continues this commitment to training by providing eligible clinical and counseling graduate students with a well-rounded, high-quality experience. Each program strives to prepare interns for entry-level service as a practicing clinical or counseling psychologist. Individual training sites employ different training models to achieve this objective.

VOLUNTEER, INTERNSHIP, EXTERNSHIP, WORK-STUDY, AND SUMMER EMPLOYMENT PROGRAMS

To become a volunteer, you should contact the Federal Bureau of Prisons facility closest to you. Volunteers should apply six months in advance of their anticipated start date. This will allow for an appropriate background check to be completed. All inquiries should be referred to the attention of the Institution Volunteer Coordinator (IVC). A complete listing of IVCs may be found in the appendix of the *Community Volunteer Handbook* (see http://www.bop.gov/jobs/volunteer_handbook.pdf).

Each federal training site may provide interns with special training opportunities which will be specific to that site. Some examples include forensic assessment, substance abuse treatment, or behavioral medicine. Some training provides experiences with special treatment populations, including geriatric, female, HIV positive, or violent offenders.

Internship opportunities exist in many of the legal branches in the Office of General Counsel including labor law, commercial law, real estate and environmental law, litigation, discrimination complaints and ethics, legislative and correctional issues, the legal administrative branch, and the Freedom of Information Act (FOIA). Among the experiences provided are opportunities to handle projects that broaden legal experience and knowledge. Interns are taught to conduct legal research and to draft legal memoranda, opinions, and correspondence. Eligibility for employment includes completion of the first semester of law school. There are summer and full-year internships during which the student may volunteer.

The U.S. Department of Justice uses an online application process. Candidates may complete and submit an application electronically through the Office of Attorney Recruitment and Management's website at www.usdoj.gov/oarm.

SUMMARY

Federal employment opportunities are perhaps the greatest in the scope of any employment agency. Similar to other governmental employment, the process of finding a job that interests you, waiting for an opening, the application process (among the more rigorous of all applications), waiting for acceptance, going through training, and to finally be given an assignment is a long process. You will need patience and endurance to work through it from beginning to end. There are those who will become discouraged. We suggest that you look at the length of the process as an opportunity. Once you have decided to pursue this as a career path, there are many courses of preparatory action. In addition to what we have detailed, such as interview preparation, you can do more. The first step would be to review the specific agency of interest, learn its history and scope of operation, and familiarize yourself with some incidents (cases) associated with the agency. Make a list of what requirements you already match and which you may fall short of. Develop a plan that will allow you to address each shortcoming and set attainable goals. Review the KSAs and firm up any area that falls short or in which you are not strong. For that matter, review your abilities in each area and seek to improve them all. Personal growth must always be an ongoing process. Your strengths and abilities will determine the outcomes in your job search and your career advancement.

Chapter 6

Internships, Volunteering, Externships, and Part-Time Employment

Career preparation begins the first day in the first class of the undergraduate experience. This chapter addresses the academic experience as a preparation for a criminal justice career. In addition, there is a focus on the changes and challenges created by COVID-19. The value of first-year courses and professors to assist students with exploring student goals for the future has changed because of increased reliance on virtual modalities. The COVD-19 pandemic has intensified challenges far beyond the standard adjustments to college life. The new adjustments may be anticipated and more stressful because of virtual learning.

The student in these first few weeks of college may not believe it but this is also the time to take advantage of the new college environment, including the virtual environment, as an opportunity for growth. The current student and future professional would be wise to reflect upon the following quote by George Bernard Shaw, "We are made wise not by the recollection of our past, but by the responsibility for our future."[1] The adjustments to life away from home necessitate creating new relationships with classmates, professors, and other college staff, and discover from whom to seek help. This time is an opportunity to learn discipline and perseverance, to see the college experience as the occasion to understand that the classroom instructs students in new ways to acquire knowledge that will be incorporated into the career.

Many students enter college with some idea of what they expect after college, namely a job upon graduation. Unfortunately, even the best college experience—good grades, great professors, accolades such as achieving Dean's List, participating in the many clubs on campus, the field trips, and more do not immediately result in a successful job search despite having the degree in hand. COVID-19 is a new impediment to employment and the competition for jobs and especially career-oriented jobs is greater.

A career in criminal justice is more than a job. Appendix A provides profiles of successful career professionals to illustrate what can be achieved in a criminal justice career. Their success was not an accident. Success is a consequence of hard work, perseverance, and academic preparation. More importantly, the persons profiled serve as examples to be followed for a career path. Each professional who is profiled has had their success, at least in part, because of their academic preparation.

Academic excellence and experience will help prepare the student to obtain a job and then advance into a career. This chapter will provide guides to maximize the academic preparation for understanding career potential. The personal achievements, skill development, and real-life experience with which to obtain the job/career upon graduation can be accomplished during the four-year academic undertaking.

COVID-19—THE NEW WRINKLE OF THE ACADEMIC EXPERIENCE

The COVID-19 pandemic has changed academics and complicated the academic preparation for obtaining the first job of the career. Therefore, the student must approach the job/career preparation with greater diligence. Classes on campus have been shifted to online and, despite the best efforts of college planning, professors are less accessible. Criminal justice students traditionally do an on-site, hands-on internship for practical experience. Many agencies will no longer allow students to be on-site during the pandemic. There are alternative methods for contacting professors and for obtaining real experience through the internship.[2]

This chapter will present detailed information for gaining quality academic experience and adjusting to virtual internships to gain the maximum benefit from them. Think of COVID-19 as an opportunity—think outside the box, think critically, ask what else is possible, and then explore.

Note: The restrictions created by COVID 19 may be relaxing. However, we encourage prudence by university professors who supervise internships. First, there remains a possibility that a more virulent variation of COVID could appear and set everything back to zero. Second, just as COVID 19 was unexpected, we should remain aware of and preserve our experiences through the pandemic to be better prepared to face other unexpected events which can interfere with our efforts to best serve our students.

MAXIMIZING THE ACADEMIC EXPERIENCE

The academic curriculum is a defined path to the degree—a process of advancement from introductory courses such as The Criminal Justice System, a broad overview of the components of criminal justice: law enforcement, corrections, and the courts. This is followed by courses of greater concentration on specific aspects of criminal justice such as Introduction to Law Enforcement or Introduction to Corrections. The next level refines the student's understanding of theory and practice through such courses as criminology, victimology, or forensics as well as very specialized courses such as terrorism.

The bachelor's degree is the cornerstone for future success. Each semester will add to the student's development. The student should ask, "What else can I gain from each course?" followed by, "What else can I gain from the next semester?" The questions set the student up to get answers. The "else" in the first question refers to the student looking beyond the goals for a course as outlined in a syllabus. The questions seek to assist the student with personal enrichment based upon their interests.

The authors anticipate that understanding the undergraduate experience as a process will initiate a lifelong journey of always preparing to take the next step forward in a career. Sometimes the next step will be clear, at other times, the opportunity may not be seen at all, or perhaps will be presented at an unexpected time. Agencies operate from need and when someone has prepared themselves to take the next step, there is a greater likelihood that they may get the offer to advance and fulfill an agency need.

FRESHMAN YEAR—ADJUSTMENT

A career choice is not critical during freshman year. What is critical is to gather information—to learn about the breadth and depth of the criminal justice profession. There is a striking difference between media presentation and real life. Forensics on TV resolves crime quickly whereas in real life it is a tedious process conducted over time to ascertain the facts. The media exaggerates and limits the criminal justice profession. Criminal justice has opportunities that stretch across almost every conceivable academic subject area. The criminal justice profession is more than the apprehension and punishment of offenders, it is also understanding why things operate and what causes things to happen. All courses will have direct applications for a career. Many academic disciplines (sociology, psychology, and the sciences such as chemistry and computer science) share the landscape of criminal justice—a social fabric serving society and providing protection.

CAREER FOCUS

Freshman year begins the exploration for a future profession. Some will learn about what they have chosen for a career; others will be trying to affirm that they are making the right choice; and some will be exploring the many options in criminal justice for a profession. The maximization of the potential benefits from the college experience begins the first day of the class. The student will discover that the syllabus and the professor are key elements to help explore and from which to find inspiration—to guide the student toward a future profession.

THE PROFESSOR AND THE SYLLABUS

The professor guides a course with a syllabus which may or may not follow the organization of the textbook. The syllabus is vital to success in the class. The professor is vital to the student's future. Many professors of intro courses are adjuncts, who have been hired because of their career success and because they possess the credentials to teach the course. They bring experience, expertise, and passion into their courses. The adjunct will have limited office hours. When appropriate in class, ask about their careers or follow up after class. Among the questions are, how do I get a job in the profession? This is especially important if this is a field which interests you. How do I prepare for a job? Are some jobs better than other jobs?

Professors offer something different—a resource for career information. Asking questions in and out of class is begin a relationship. The professor can be a role model, mentor, problem solver, and a reference for internships and employment. Students often refer to the professors with whom they develop relationships as contacts. We discourage the use of the word contact and prefer the word relationship—begin to understand professionalism.

The student should assess why professors are passionate and discover their experiences. Two questions will help the student approach the professor for advice and later, for guidance: "Has the professor been successful in a career?" and, "Why?" The answers will include the job title(s), and the years on the job. An analysis of success may be more difficult. If the professor reveals accolades and awards, then there will be a sense of what achievements are possible.

Professors guide students through course material covering specific areas of criminal justice, the who, what, why, when, where, and how of it. Knowing your professors will help you to understand their perspective of the course content. They are the subject matter expert (SME).

Introductory courses are often large with as many as 150 students. While we like to think that someone will remember us, this is not the case. Students ask for a reference and I turn them down because while I may know the name and can look up the grade, there is little else that I know about the student. A relationship with a professor is more than sitting in class and getting a good grade. Additionally, while many students only read the syllabus at the beginning of a course, a weekly review is recommended to stay current on weekly topics and performance requirements. Review the syllabus for its content what is interesting for career information. The syllabus needs to be reviewed each week prior to class and read forward to the next week. This will allow the student to be prepared for class and ask question about next week's materials. Note: the question that is not asked, will never be answered.

Note: Use what is interesting (on the syllabus, in the textbook, from the lecture) to guide your papers. Explore the subject to gain additional information which can then be used to develop questions for the professor(s).

SOPHOMORE YEAR—CAREER DECISION

The course content becomes more specific with choices for specialties such as law enforcement, corrections, or perhaps law. The student who has considered their career path will most likely choose one of these courses to intensify their interest in a career path. We strongly suggest that the student take as many of these as possible to understand the relationship between the subsets of criminal justice. A career is a long time and personal interests do change. (Review the profile of Bo Orichowsky in appendix A.) He began his correctional career as a social worker and later changed to become a parole officer which he found more satisfying and in which he utilized his social worker training. Or consider Bob Hood (appendix A), who began as a teacher and became the warden of the most supermax prison in the world.

Sophomore year should begin serious discussions with the career counseling center and the internship director. Each will have strategies and resources to enhance the preparation for internships and job searches. The student will gain information about resumes, introductory and cover letters, interviewing, and conducting personal assessments (strengths, weaknesses, and skills for internship and careers).

The internship preparation plan begins during the sophomore year, the time to broaden awareness about opportunities in criminal justice and to advance personal knowledge of the types of available job opportunities within the subsets of criminal justice. See the discussion about internships in this chapter. Statistically, this is the time many students become frustrated with their chosen career path and drop out or change their major. This can be turned into a positive experience. The answer is that you have learned or experienced something which has altered your thinking. The internship is about making the best career decisions. First, you are completing about half of the degree requirements. Second, there is time to explore other career paths, perhaps within criminal justice or in another field. See your advisor or career services coordinator to help you move forward professionally. The answer may be as simple as taking an interest inventory or converting a minor course of study into a major. College is about exploring and preparing. Sophomore year is the time to move forward.

JUNIOR YEAR—TRANSITION YEAR

Students should begin to conduct themselves as professionals and view fellow students as colleagues. Criminal justice agencies require professionalism and expect that fellow employees are recognized as colleagues. This is the year of the internship, to experience work in the field and understanding the relationships between employees. The course will explain skills and abilities, while the on-site experience will provide the opportunities to apply the course content. The internship is the time to further assess career interests and affirm that the choice of future profession is correct or that the career objective should be altered.

SENIOR YEAR—PULLING OUT ALL THE STOPS FOR A CAREER

Senior year—fine-tune career preparations. A degree in hand is not necessary for all job applications. Many criminal justice job openings require a finalized degree by the time a job begins. Oftentimes, there are tests (for example Civil Service) to pass. An application puts you on a wait list for the next scheduled test. After taking the test, a score is assigned which establishes a rank and order from which applicants will be called. The applicant may not be on the first round of interviews which extends the wait. This is often a slow process. Taking tests is important because there is a learning curve to test taking; scores improve with each test.

ELIMINATING LOOSE ENDS FOR THE CAREER SEARCH

Senior year is the time to put the finishing touches on career tools such as a resume, cover letter, 25-year plan, my ten points, an employment portfolio, references, writing skills, and more. These are discussed in depth later in this chapter and in the appendixes.

SUMMARY—BEGIN BEFORE THE DEGREE IS IN HAND

Senior year will close with the degree awarded and if all goes well an appointment to an academy or the anticipation of a job which awaits you. The contents of this chapter, the information in other chapters, and the appendixes contain the tools for a successful career search.

INTRODUCTION TO INTERNSHIPS

Career preparation involves investigating the choice(s) for which you seem best suited. A process begins with introductory courses and follows up with professors and professionals who work or have worked in the field. The next steps are to explore some websites related to the chosen fields. Read them thoroughly and write down questions. Professors should be helpful answering these questions. These steps are best taken during the first two years of the college program as preparation for visits to agencies, police forces, court houses, private nonprofits, and other criminal justice sources. This is the time to observe and to seek answers for any questions not yet answered. These steps should help to firm up a career choice.

There are minimally four potential opportunities to experience the job and the work environment: internships, volunteering, externships, and part-time employment. The intent is to expose the career seeker to as many ways possible to explore and understand careers. The point is to enter the field of criminal justice satisfied with a career choice or, to put it another way, the person starting out on a career does not want to suddenly become aware that they have made a bad choice. The proposed process is to focus on the information to limit bad career choices. This process is to allow the job seeker to make an informed decision. Introspection (knowing yourself) is an important component of the preparation for careers. Among the concerns which the individual should address are what interest you about the career under consideration? What has motivated you to seek this career?

GOALS

An important activity for the first and second year preparation for employment is to list goals in three areas, professional (what level?), financial (how much?), and personal (what is included in your life to be?). Write them out (and if a 25-year plan is being formed, place them at the top of the plan) then they can be evaluated throughout the plan at the five-year intervals to ensure that goals work well together and do not conflict. A vital question to consider is why have the goals been chosen? Stating goals early will enable the individual to evaluate and reevaluate goals and their source. Goals that are well thought-out as career objectives will help the individual to a productive future. Successful goal achievement requires commitment. Goals should be specific, attainable, provide personal motivation, and measurable through the five-year increments of the 25-year plan. Goals attained are a source of personal pride. Goal achievement can be viewed as a process from smaller goals to larger goals—all do not have be attained immediately.

INTERNSHIPS

COVID-19 eliminated many opportunities for on-site internship experiences. However, there are virtual internships or volunteer work. Colleges generally require internships prior to graduation to help students explore career choices. Internships are generally assigned college credit whereas, volunteering is not. Internships or volunteer work in criminal justice frequently require a criminal justice background check. (Review background check specifications.)

Many students anticipate the internship; they want to go out and experience the field. Frequently, the internship is a positive experience that affirms for students that they have made the right choice for a career. In some cases, the internship provides exposure to other aspects of the career, which they can now explore as an alternate career choice. The internship ensures that those interested in a specific career have chosen wisely and enables the student to begin the next and official steps for entering the career field.

Frequent laments of students during the internship are the discovery of elements of the job (such as the volume of paperwork) not emphasized during the courses or of which they had been unaware. Unexpected events or environmental conditions can affect students' consideration of a position as their career choice. When this happens, the more extreme reaction is to change one's major to a different career path. However, another way of reacting is to reexamine the original career choice and find a more personally acceptable role for a criminal justice career.

The primary source of exposure to law enforcement is through the media, which portrays it as active, busy, challenging, and at times dangerous. In these capacities, heroic rescues are being made, offenders are being captured, and complex investigations are undertaken and solved. Inasmuch as most police work is patrol, it fails to resemble any of the descriptions just mentioned. When students wait too long to begin their internships (such as waiting until the year in which they graduate), their other degree requirements may already be completed. If they discover that the job of which they have dreamed is somehow not a good fit for them, or that they may not qualify (such as discovering that they cannot pass a background check), then they find themselves in a bad position. Emotionally, there is letdown and bewilderment about what to do with their hard-earned education and how to adapt their preparations to a different career choice. Too often, this disheartening situation also signals a change of curriculum/major. The consequences of such a change at a late date usually include needing to take additional courses, even adding on semesters along with the additional tuition expenses for a new major.

There are practical solutions to this dilemma. Participation in a combination of activities will help students make rational informed decisions before the final year of their degree work, preferably in the early stages of college preparation. Our electronic age makes a wealth of information available through the internet. Few students get through high school without becoming quite proficient at internet searches. Virtually all criminal justice agencies have their own websites. After an initial search of these websites, more specific searches can be conducted.

Volunteering is another doable experience. When done early, and we suggest beginning in the freshman year, volunteering may facilitate the timely discovery of new career options within a field of interest—or a non-fit for a career. When this becomes evident, a change of focus is less traumatic. Four activities (visiting, volunteering, reviewing websites, and interviewing) will help the student with the decision-making process by clarifying what seems to be the better path to follow.

We strongly suggest that college is one of the ways to prepare for a career. Similarly, you can prepare for your college internship by engaging in a few pursuits such as reviewing potential agencies available for your internship. Dorothy Taylor[3] has written a book that can help you with your internship preparation and guide you through the internship so that you get the most from it. It will help to ensure that you successfully coordinate your efforts with your college professor/advisor. Often there are internship requirements for your college degree that must be completed. Taylor's book can help you to understand the many tasks you must adhere to. For example, her second chapter will help define the goals of the internship, and chapter 8, the "Evaluation of the Field Placement Experience," will help to lay out what you must do to comply with your criminal justice department's requirements.

THE CRIMINAL JUSTICE VIRTUAL INTERNSHIP

Virtual internships have been a direct outgrowth of the challenges created by the COVID-19 pandemic. While the virtual internship was nonexistent prior to the pandemic, it seems likely to now persist. The virtual internship is not a substitute for the on-site internship experience. This opportunity will provide students with practical and authentic experience during which they will utilize laptops, tablets, smartphones, and other technology such as web conferencing. This experience, like the traditional internship, will help the student prepare for a real-world job/career. The virtual internship will have a broader reach of experiences which increase the scope of opportunities especially in other parts of the country or abroad. The student can have the opportunity to work from home or their dorm room to participate in an internship experience and to overcome difficulties which prevent or limit on-site participation.

The college internship coordinator can develop rigorous content which provides dynamic and innovative learning. The student is thus invested in the experience. Furthermore, there may be a transformation in how the student sees the profession about which they are considering for a career and how they see that career blended into the world around them. Among the skills which the student may acquire include agency etiquette, improved proficiency with technology, better writing skills for professional utilization, to critique the participating agency, and research experience. Finally, an evaluation of the experience may be regularly conducted during an internship class coordinated with the internship supervisor via a virtual collaboration.

THE PROS AND CONS OF THE VIRTUAL INTERNSHIP

The virtual internship has an upside and a downside. Each perspective will help the student to decide whether a traditional or virtual internship is best, that is, which will provide the most complete learning experience. The similarities include the application process, the submission of a resume and cover letter (and perhaps a writing sample). A major difference which will require some preparation is a phone or Zoom interview. Being prepared with My Ten Points will assist with the interview. At times, only a virtual internship will have the potential to meet personal needs. The internship is more than the achievement of three college credits.

First, the opportunity can affirm or help to decide career direction. It may happen what was thought as the choice of career is not appropriate. This is good. Now the student can consider other alternatives before being locked in with employment.

Second, the internship assists with job/career hunting development through gained experience, interviewing, preparation of résumés, and letters of introduction.

Third, a personal debate between a virtual or onsite internship is healthy. Experience, such as that obtained from an internship, is critical to making the right choice.

Fourth, the criminal justice field is constantly undergoing change.

The person best prepared for the job search will have the better adjustment once a position is obtained. No one anticipated 9/11 or the COVID-19 pandemic, or the current social upheaval and the personal and professional changes now under consideration. Take note that such events represent *opportunities* for the student to assess their preparedness to face apparent and not-so-apparent challenges and to adapt to change. A career is an experience of changes.

Fifth, a virtual internship can be a unique experience and, for others, it may be daunting. Some students will not know how to handle a virtual internship and will have trouble adjusting. The student should have an orientation, access to the internship coordinator, and an on-site mentor to help guide the experience.

THE UPSIDE

Awareness of the upsides of virtual internships, such as increased flexibility, are opportunities and may motivate the student to be more enthusiastic about the internship:

- Flexibility—The student creates a work schedule which better integrates into the demands of their time. Class and internship schedules are often hard to fit in a single semester. The virtual internship may free up time to better coordinate the registration for courses without conflict. Meetings with your on-site mentor will be done online, through a video chat, or over the phone. Your assignments will be digitized and can be accomplished on your time.
- Independence—The student is not micromanaged. The intern will be expected to always be on time. The virtual internship will minimize lateness and call-outs for personal problems including sickness. However, the virtual internship is not an excuse to avoid attending a scheduled

meeting or missing deadlines for assignments either from the site or for the course. Good time management skills are essential—a talking point for job interviews.

- Telecommute—Geographic boundaries do not restrict. This is very important if the agency the student is interested in is too far away for normal commuting—such as Washington or perhaps California. The student will probably have the basic tools for the experience—an internet connection and an email account.
- Communication—This experience will enhance effective communication skills. When a communication is sent there is a wait time for the response—the student will learn to craft responses carefully, effectively, and succinctly—a talking point for the job interview.
- Options—The student is not restricted to local internships—the entire world is possible. An internship not available locally may be a resume enhancement, provide a competitive edge, and a talking point for job interviews about the depth of personal experience.
- Relationships—Students often use the word "connections." Think in terms of professionalism, collegiality, and the potential references which are established during the internship. Professionally, they are relationships made for enhanced job/career achievement. A healthy discussion in an internship class.
- Personal Growth—The virtual internship may provide opportunity for self-assessment and specifically knowing when, how and to whom to reach out for help. Seeking help is not a negative trait, it is a strength. There is little which we can do best on our own.
- Technological Advantage—Technology has become increasingly more important in the work world. The virtual internship provides the opportunity to learn and work with new emerging technology and advance existing personal ability. These are résumé builders and discussion points during a job interview.
- Reduced Liability—You are not on-site which can mean less liability for the on-site provider and the university.
- Earn 3 college credits and a required course for your criminal justice major.

THE DOWNSIDE

Understanding the downsides of virtual internships are opportunities. Many of the downsides can be turned around during the virtual internship because of an awareness of them:

- Virtual Internships May Not Fit—They are not for everyone. Many criminal justice jobs require face-to-face contact. A self-assessment of the student's comfort zone in face-to-face encounters may reveal personal difficulties. Achieving comfort and expertise is more difficult in the virtual world, especially if the need is to develop skills in face-to-face situations. The virtual internship may be a bad fit, because of an inability to manage time, and not knowing when to seek assistance or guidance.
- Less Sensitivity—Distance does not cure all problems. The virtual intern may find that they are being treated more like an employee than someone learning. Personal interactions are limited in the virtual world and no one may notice that you are struggling. No one is present to observe and provide immediate feedback, thus diminishing the learning experience. Most students want to excel on their internship and through a virtual experience there is no one to notice that the student is putting too much pressure on themselves, thus reducing the effectiveness of the internship. Interns require guidance and the opportunity to ask questions, get clarification, support, and acknowledgment of their work. E-mails and texts cannot replace being on-site and having a conversation. The virtual intern needs to learn when to ask questions and to seek advice.
- Less Structure/Support—The virtual intern, while having a mentor, will not be as "in-the-loop" as they would be on-site. Lack of presence in the office means the loss of guidance at the time something occurs—support comes later should something be lost in the exchange between mentor and student.
- No Actual On-Site Experience—Less opportunity for on-the-job training. Opportunity is lost for experiencing an actual workday, observing, and participating as events unfold and new information arrives. The virtual intern cannot shadow an employee of the agency.
- A disconnect from the opportunity to understand the culture and environment which exists in an agency. A concept called "Environmental Press"[4] may be explored to understand the fit between the person and an environment. However, the student loses the application because they are not in an actual agency. Agencies rely on updates, information flow that keeps everyone in the loop, office chats, and other instances of spontaneity which occur on-site. The office workforce advances daily with the steady flow of information. The student misses the opportunity to observe office growth and advancement. In addition, all environments have and create stress which must be addressed personally and professionally.
- Requires the Student to be Self-motivated—The student needs to be attuned to events through improved analysis which allows the formation of better questions for in-depth responses.

- Lower Standards—There can be lower expectations for the virtual intern. On-site mistakes can be anticipated and expected because the on-site supervisor is present for immediate remediation. Mistakes may and can occur which will not be corrected because no one is aware of them. The student should be aware of this point as the virtual internship may be challenged during a job interview or an explanation asked for about the internship. My Ten Points is a good place to develop a response about the internship.

PROS AND CONS SUMMARY

The virtual internship experience is only as valuable as what is put into it and what is offered on-site. The on-site experience might be diminished but the student can take the initiative to expand through research, increased mentoring, and requested guidance to explore and expand on the situation. The internship may not be on-site but that should not deter the student from accepting the challenge and seeking additional growth potential with the virtual experiences. To put it bluntly, *the student can ask for more.*

The student should periodically perform personal assessment of their learning style. This can be discussed with the internship coordinator. The student is in control (something which may need to be learned and potentially as simple as asking, "What else is possible?") of the limitations or boundaries. Once the question(s) is asked then the internship opportunity may be expanded.

Co-workers will not be alongside of the student. However, the student can reach out for greater explanations. Similarly, the student does not have to wait for their mentor to appear online for another assignment—*Be proactive*. The student may ask, "What else is available or possible?" This question helps separate the average from the outstanding employee. This question keeps the student and the career conscious employee in a constant state of preparedness. This is an opportunity to develop self-discipline. If the student needs to take a five-minute break—learn self-discipline and be accountable to five minutes; develop a schedule—*Keep it.* Stay on point—be a self-appointed taskmaster. At the risk of sounding trite—the only stupid question is the one not asked!

THE VIRTUAL INTERN

Some student characteristics which help ensure a successful virtual internship (and can be applied to an on-site internship) include:

- Self-motivation helps the student gain or advance current skills which will prepare them for their career. This is more difficult to accomplish during a virtual experience. However, just as the virtual experience allows the student to expand their boundaries, the challenge of being off-site, for the student, becomes not just how to have the internship but perhaps what additional skill development is possible.
- Successful career preparation means that the student, prior to and during the internship, will be assessing their personal skill inventory and enhancing existing skills (review the KSAs for federal employment), mastering new skills, or recognizing that a skill is not possessed but is needed or is desired for career preparation. This should be part of a developmental plan for later attainment and may be included in the 25-year plan. The mentor and the internship coordinator can assist in this process of skill set development. (Note: Internship courses may encourage the participants to regard their fellow students as colleagues [a good practice] to rely on and build relationships just as would occur on the job. The sharing of interests and perhaps frustrations will also enhance the learning of the other student interns.) Once more, the relationship between mentor and student is critical. A weekly evaluation will help ensure the developmental flow of strengths and overcoming weaknesses. A mentor–student relationship may help to develop the student to recognize the value of self-motivation and, if lacking, to cultivate this characteristic.
- Prior experience can contribute to a successful virtual internship. For example, those with prior experience may understand the value of reporting on time, understanding the environment, their role as learner in that environment, being a team member, adapting to change, acknowledging shortcomings, resolving conflicts (with assistance from the mentor), and seeking appropriate assistance. Many students possess some prior experience in the field of criminal justice. This has been heightened by their interest in criminal justice as a career.
- A criminal justice virtual internship program can be personalized and provide opportunity to meet program objectives, complete with supplemental online activities such as microlearning simulations, and online for enrichment of the experience.

AN ORIENTATION TO THE VIRTUAL INTERNSHIP

An orientation should begin during the semester prior to the internship. The orientation will explain the process for the virtual internship; an assessment whether the virtual experience is appropriate for them; instruction for self-evaluation and the style of learning; and whether they possess self-motivation, discipline, and initiative. These are all good qualities for a successful virtual internship. At the conclusion of the orientation the student will be asked the most important question of all—"Do you feel that you will be successful with a virtual internship?" If the student is unsure, there may be a hybrid opportunity with some virtual and some on-site options and will depend upon opportunity, the evaluation of the internship coordinator, and whether a mentor can be found who accepts this challenge.

What the Prospective Intern Needs to Know

a. What will be the assigned tasks and responsibilities?
b. Will there be training and when and in what?
c. Are there a required number of hours per week?
d. Is the internship paid?
e. Will college credit be assigned and what are the requirements for credit?
f. Will the internship site provide a letter of recommendation?
g. Will the on-site supervisor provide a letter of recommendation?
h. Is there potential for full-time employment?

VIRTUAL INTERNSHIP TRAINING

The internship site discussion should include the project description—an overview of the agency, the role of the intern including assigned tasks, and the identification of a mentor for guidance and support. The virtual student interview will determine the compatibility of the student to the agency. An evaluation by the agency will occur at the conclusion of the internship.

Communication on the job, with the mentor, with the coordinator and with fellow student interns as colleagues is essential. Some of this may be part of the classroom regimen of the course while some will need to be undertaken prior to the start of the virtual internship. This is a time to refine professional use of language and to avoid street language.

Identification and development of a workspace for the internship. This would include the dorm, the home, the library, or potentially the coffee shop. What makes a specific space ideal (such as privacy from interruptions) as a learning environment and what can be accomplished in each space?

Scheduling—Students should have achieved this personal attribute prior to the internship. The adaptation to a worksite and the virtual site and how it is coordinated with other required activities becomes essential.

Work expectations need to be clearly understood prior to initiating the virtual internship. This will include the use of personal and worksite technology.

Relationships can be developed during the virtual internship. While expressions of personality may be more difficult, the virtual intern can learn to develop presence during phone, or virtual meetings such as video conferencing. The key will be for the student to be as prepared as possible and to make themselves be heard at appropriate times.

Goals and expectations—The student should specify their goals and objectives for the internship (what do they need to know or get out of the internship). While this is begun during the training, it can be enhanced and expanded upon with the internship coordinator and later with the mentor. This may be a more critical task for the virtual experience than the traditional internship. The host agencies and mentors may have provided at least some of these during the creation of the virtual experience. Some guidance for accomplishing this task may be gained from the position description developed by the host agency. Goals and expectations may include agency etiquette which is suggested or required at different levels of the agency, types of knowledge, skill sets, and tasks of the job.

The student should have a mentor from the providing site. In an ideal experience, the mentor will be matched to the student's interests to guide them through real-world experiences which align with criminal justice practices and the accompanying proficiencies.

The mentor is accountable for the intern's proficiency which assures a quality experience. The host agency and the mentor gain what is essentially free, dedicated assistance in positions which normally have few resources devoted to them. One outcome of the internship should be that the student will perform with excellence and be a potential employee for the agency at the completion of the internship.

THE INTERNSHIP COORDINATOR AND THE ON-SITE MENTOR RELATIONSHIP

An open line of communication between the internship coordinator and the mentor is essential to ensure effectiveness and efficiency. Communication with the mentor, in writing and/or orally about upcoming expectations and tasks, will help ensure smooth transitions of information between the host and the university. Information gained from the communication can be followed up on during the class sessions.

ONLINE SUPPORT AND FEEDBACK

The student should maintain a log and a journal of their experiences for at least weekly review. The student should have the availability of feedback from both the internship coordinator and the mentor. The feedback and its applicability are details for the journal.

EVALUATION OF THE VIRTUAL INTERNSHIP EXPERIENCE

A process of an ongoing evaluation is essential to the integrity of the virtual internship experience. There should be a formal evaluation at the conclusion of the internship.

Weekly verbal reports to the internship class and coordinator—This is critical to ensure student compliance with the terms of the virtual internship and should minimally consist of the previous weeks progress. This provides an opportunity for the intern to request assistance, adjust the plan, present log and journal notes from which to evaluate progress, and overcome problems. *Written feedback can be hazardous because too much must be interpreted.*

Personal Reflection—An analysis of the experience and an assessment of needs for future growth completed at the end of the internship experience.

Portfolio Journals—Reflections of interactions assessing the content and contribution of preparation for the work world including skill development.

Domains of Learning—The internship coordinator will examine all content provided by the student and in coordination with the agency mentor for the following:

1. Knowledge—An understanding of skills required on the job which enhance professional performance and enable the student intern to evaluate their future career aspirations.
2. Interpersonal—The ability to forge relationships to collaborate with the mentor and other staff at the agency. To have developed a network of colleagues.
3. Cognitive—To demonstrate critical and analytical thinking to organize and prioritize assignments on the job and in conjunction with other life activities.
4. Practical—To illustrate introspection, that is, analysis of personal goal achievement through alignment of satisfied goal achievement to enhance future career determinations.

5. Professional—To complete tasks in a timely manner presented and in accordance with the required etiquette of the agency.
6. Goals and Expectation—To meet the goals and expectation developed at the initiation of the internship.

SOME FINAL NOTES FOR THE VIRTUAL INTERNSHIP

The virtual internship program is a work in progress as both the college and the internship site learn to be more progressive and inclusive of each other's needs and the needs of the student. Part of the answer lies in creativity for what is missed from being on-site. Internship coordinators and mentors should consider general guidelines for virtual internships and specific guidelines to be followed on-site. The guidelines should specify available tools and resources for the mentor and mentee.

The college or the on-site internship provider can offer other experiences for the student including simulations, case studies, and on-line training. These experiences are opportunities for applications of what is learned or to hypothetically trouble shoot problems. As virtual internships expand, training materials can be developed to match the needs of on-site providers. Surveys, focus groups, and questionnaires help to discover the strengths and weaknesses of your online training strategy.

INTERNSHIP SUMMARY

Internships are a component of many college programs. The classroom cannot teach students all they need to know, nor can the classroom prepare the student for all careers eventualities. The internship can position students in settings to explore their interests with real-world experiences, to develop relationships, and build skills before heading out into their chosen field. Internship opportunities are hands-on learning that requires being both mentally and physically present. In recent years, many companies and students have begun to take advantage of the convenience offered by virtual internships. Just as with any opportunity, virtual internships have both positive and negative aspects. Prior to application the college and the student should consider whether the experience can meet the students' needs. Good lines of communication between all parties are essential for a successful internship experience.

A virtual internship can be rewarding. Like the on-site internship, a remote internship has benefits and drawbacks. Coursework, athletics, family, illness, physical hardship, and perhaps financial considerations may make internships difficult. If these instances or should other circumstances exist, a virtual internship may be an option. The pros and cons can be discussed with the internship coordinator. We wish all a successful virtual internship.

A RESOURCE FOR VIRTUAL INTERNSHIPS

Gottfredson and Mosher[5] outline the *Five Moments of Need Model* which can be applied to interns, learning for the first time in a professional work environment. They identify essentials skills with which to build, integrate, implement, and track performance support solutions aligned with goals, strategies, and practices. This model is especially important when things change or when things go wrong in the workplace. The point is that someone is learning, and the result of a failed moment does not have to have serious consequences. A problem, discovered timely, enables both the agency and the learner/intern to grow and benefit. Earlier we mentioned environmental press and in this case the intern develops work habits which are in sync with the work environment. The authors explain how to implement the *Five Moments of Need Model*:

1. Learning for the first time.
2. Learning more.
3. Applying what has been learned.
4. When things go wrong.
5. When things change.

VOLUNTEERING

Opportunities for volunteering will return after the pandemic. However, there are opportunities, some of which are in related fields, such as remote staffing of a crisis center or with private nonprofit criminal justice agencies, which are available. Volunteering entails the least risk and potentially the greatest gain for the student. The advantages of volunteering vastly outweigh the disadvantages. Some of the advantages include real work experience, real person interaction, references, knowledge, on-the-job training, an entry for the résumé, and availability to encounter changes and openings in the field as they occur. A volunteer does the work and observes others doing it as it happens or needs to be done. This is often different from the general job description. Volunteers are assigned specific tasks, but as other events or projects come up, the volunteer may be shifted to provide assistance and gain a broader view of the career potential.

Volunteering allows discovery of whether this work is appropriate. If the work is different from expectations, the volunteer does not have to stay. They can move on (but never leave the volunteer post unmanned; it is a responsibility) and try something else. Volunteering is time well invested. If nothing else, you have performed a service and gained experience as well as the realization that there are other aspects of criminal justice not previously considered, which may be more attractive for a career choice.

Volunteering is an unpaid experience. The smart volunteer treats the experience as a paid job. Dress appropriately, arrive on time, and do the assigned work. Greater responsibility can be requested, and questions may be asked about what is observed. If the position does not provide experiences of interest, ask for them. Most employers and employees understand the position of the volunteer as a learning experience and are willing to extend themselves and their staff to provide fulfilling opportunities.

EXTERNSHIPS

Externships have a variety of meanings and are sometimes referred to as apprenticeships or that they are like internships. Students, and especially freshman, are often unfamiliar with the term and are confused by it. They provide a short-term, practical, firsthand experience with a specific career or job through job "shadowing." Unfortunately, there are many occasions when this either is not possible or not allowed such as with law enforcement or correctional jobs. There are some possibilities when a police department will allow a ride along on patrol. The recommendation is to take advantage of such opportunities, when they are available, prior to an internship. While it may not be in chosen career area, it will provide exposure to depth of criminal justice potential for employment. A valuable way to access externships would be to utilize the college alumni network.

PART-TIME WORK

There are many reasons to engage in part-time work such an:

- Experience to determine criminal justice employment for a career.
- Experience for the résumé.
- Experience for interviews.
- Experience in other fields of criminal justice.
- Experience working in the field and interacting with employees.
- Experience with interagency cooperation.

Look at such web sites such as Indeed.com, Jobs2Career.com, or zipcruiter.com for employment which includes security, loss prevention, paralegal, investigator, facility monitor, and more. These websites may advertise jobs from out of state. Out-of-state postings may provide ideas for seeking similar positions in state. All jobs in the criminal justice field may not be posted as criminal justice jobs. Part-time positions generally do not require a bachelor's degree although some college, such as a two-year degree or the equivalent, maybe a requirement. Another reason for part-time employment is the salary which may be put toward college costs. Graduates often remark that it is tough to obtain that first job. The part-time job is getting a foot in the door which may lead to a full-time job. Anytime you are working, you will be exposed to more opportunities for full-time employment—all available jobs are not posted and are sought by word of mouth.

Never neglect the letter of recommendation. The letter may be a general letter to place in a portfolio or as a reference to be contacted when seeking full-time employment elsewhere. The reference from a part-time job should be discussed with a supervisor prior to terminating a part-time job.

There are disadvantages to part-time work such as distractions from course work. Stay focused on the goals for the part time job—it provides experience for a career and that it provides some salary to help cover expenses. Another risk to part-time work is that if you do it well then you may be offered full-time work. Criminal justice agencies appreciate hardworking employees. While the choice to change to full-time is a personal decision, this is also a time to stay goal oriented; that is, finish the degree and have a career.

SUMMARY

Part-time work does not have to be the desired career job. It is an opportunity to learn and expand personal awareness about jobs and careers in criminal justice. There is no place better than the work environment to improve skills development for a career. For a more in-depth guide to working part-time see the article, "6 Benefits of Working Part-Time Instead of Full Time."[6]

Chapter 7

Getting the Job, Entering the Field, and Career Advancement

This chapter provides the tools to prepare a search for *and to attain* employment and advancement in the criminal justice system. Hopefully, you have read about the different fields of criminal justice and are not too badly confused. Optimistically, you have begun to narrow the area(s) in which you might be interested. With any luck, you are not feeling overwhelmed with the diversity of positions, and you have begun to understand the difference between dramatized versions of jobs and the real work of the profession. There are strategies and tools which will make your employment search efficient and productive. Efficiency makes the process smoother, and in the end, getting the job is what matters. This may seem ambitious for one chapter. However, preparation for employment sets the stage for advancement in the criminal justice system. This is true whether a career is maintained with the starting agency, or the career is shifted as opportunity is presented into other criminal justice agencies, or outside the criminal justice field.

FINDING JOB OPENINGS

Finding job openings is vital to attaining employment. Part of the answer is to expand the areas to search for employment opportunities. In addition to the employment opportunities that are mentioned in this chapter, you should ask others who have jobs how they found their jobs, or where they looked. In either case, you may find places to look that previously were not explored.

In chapter 6, the value of visiting potential worksites, websites, professors, internships, and volunteer opportunities were discussed in some depth. This chapter will begin with more ideas for locating job openings, as well as discuss the importance of tools such as a cover letter, résumé, networking, identifying appropriate references, completing applications, preparing for, and sitting for an interview, entrance exams, academy training, some points on personal presentation, and conduct during the first days on the job. In this chapter and in chapter 9, there is discussion about what to do should you find that the job is *not* for you. The last point may come as a shock, but it happens. As you go through the process of the search, exposure, interviews, training, and reporting to the job, things occur that may warn you that this is not a job you want. If this happens, it is not the end of the world! It is simply a wake-up call and an opportunity to move on—to find more satisfying employment and life satisfaction elsewhere.

Jobs are posted on bulletin boards, websites, in human resources and personnel departments, in newspapers, through friends and colleagues, and via search agencies (or headhunters[1]). Some jobs are posted quietly, they are not advertised because the agency does not want to be overwhelmed with those considered to be non-candidates—they want someone special. You must be tenacious in your search. Some sources may be visited every day, such as Indeed.com, to find new postings. Other sources only come out periodically or are not posted at all. Some agencies or companies do not like to post for jobs and prefer a word-of-mouth search. Career fairs, networking, and taking advantage of every occasion to make yourself known, enhance the likelihood of an agency reaching out to you, a colleague, or by someone who is aware of your credentials and ability for you to fill the slot. The answer to this is to prepare, update, and continue personal development—*network, network, network.*

What follows is information about what to do when you find an appealing job opening.

READING THE JOB POSTING

Read the posting carefully and highlight the important points. *You must be able to respond to those important points in cover letters, highlights in a résumé, and during an interview. They probably can become some of My Ten Points.* Read the job specifications thoroughly, understand them, adhere to deadlines and specific requests. Understand exactly what the hiring agent is looking for and that you possess the qualifications for the job. Oftentimes, there are do's and don'ts listed in the postings. You must be able to fulfill the do's. However, when a posting tells you not to do something, *DON'T DO IT!* For example, the posting may state that you should *not* include transcripts or references because they will be requested later. Do not think that including them will help you when you are specifically instructed not to do so. Dates and deadlines are critical. You *must* adhere to them. If your application is late, it may not be accepted. If the posting says, "Until a choice is made," then you need to submit your materials as soon as possible. The postmarked date on the application (or the time submitted in the case of an electronic application) may count toward your score; that is, the earlier the submission the better. In some cases, the date on the application may even qualify you for a move up on the list because your application was received before another. A note of caution: Speed can become detrimental if you sacrifice quality. Make sure your supporting documents are well-prepared. See Document Portfolio in appendix G.

The search for employment will likely result in many applications being submitted simultaneously. Keep all job postings organized by creating a master folder titled Jobs and the year, ex., 2022. Maintain a section with information such as resume, references and contact information, sample cover letters, certifications, degrees, and transcripts, some or all, will potentially be used with each application. *Copies of all important documents should be in a "Document Portfolio."* The applicants' selection of specific information will be determined by the application requirements. Label a section in the folder as Completed Applications. The maintenance and update of this information will help with the efficient and accurate completion of new applications. This is information to be reviewed when an agency makes contact. Reevaluate the application for the information provided. This is especially important for interview preparation—there must be consistency between the application and the interviewer's questions. There will be times when there will be multiple applications to the same agency when different jobs are posted. The file will save time preparing applications for each posting. Once more, there must be consistency between the applications.

THE COVER LETTER

(See the sample letters provided in appendix B.)

Include a cover letter with your application that is professional in appearance and in content. At the top of the letter, include the title of the position for which you are applying and the position number if listed. A specific area may have posted for several positions—be sure that the application materials reach the appropriate reviewer. The cover letter is an opportunity to specifically state why you are applying and to briefly cover special skills, experiences, or events in your life that make you stand out—emphasize them because they enhance your presentation. These are generally themes that are not included on your résumé. The letter is your opportunity to state why you are the best candidate for the job, *not* to rehash your application or résumé. The points you emphasize may become interview talking points later. If you have never written a cover letter, see a counselor for guidance and a review of the letter.

Main Features of a Cover Letter

- Name
- Address
- Phone number
- E-mail address. (The e-mail address should be professional. If it is cutesy or includes terms meant to denote some aspect of your personality, such as "dark master" or another appellation, then set up a new e-mail name and address for yourself.)
- Date
- The name of the person to whom the application is being sent
- Their title
- Company name
- Company address
- Posted position title and position number
- Dear _________________, [salutation]
- Paragraph 1: Description of why you are writing. Explain why you are interested in the position.
- Paragraph 2: Description of your qualifications. Provide solid experiences and examples of strong qualities that make you a viable candidate.
- Paragraph 3: Addendums to your application package: résumé, references (upon request), the fact that transcripts (if required) will follow, and a request for an interview.
- Sincerely,
- Your name
- Sign your letter in black or blue ink. (Blue ink is often requested by some agencies because it indicates that this letter is not a copy of other letters that you have sent.)
- Enclosures
- The résumé
- References (if requested); otherwise say "upon request."

HOW IMPORTANT IS YOUR RÉSUMÉ?

A résumé will either get you the interview or result in rejection. Rejection may be the result of failing to meet the qualifications. How you develop your résumé to meet those qualifications will be determined by your status, which is whether you are right out of college, looking for advancement, hoping to change professions, you are in the middle of your career, or influenced by some other factor.

The résumé should qualify the applicant for the job and make the applicant stand out. Résumés that arrive in response to a job offer are often put in a pile and scanned later. A common practice by agencies is to hire an independent contractor to do a job search or résumé review. Some agencies and private contractors machine-read résumés for key words or phrases. Review the job posting for key words (such as: supervision, security, and experience using technology) and then list them. When technology is utilized by the agency, résumés will be selected using identified key words or phrases. A technique for attracting the attention of the machine reader is to create a header and then list the key words which apply to the applicant. The next step is to change the font color in the header from black to white. This enables the header to only be seen by a machine reader and not human reviewers of the résumé. The intention is to have the machine reader see the terms and select the résumé for employment consideration through the identification of key terms which apply to the posted agency position.

Therefore, the résumé must be accurate and present the information which will catch the eye of the reviewer for further assessment. The content is the opportunity to have your résumé receive more than a cursory glance. The résumé, by itself, will not earn you a job, but it may open the door for future consideration. The résumé must get you an interview where you can sell yourself.

On a very basic level, your résumé reassures the employer that you meet the basic requirements for the position and advise the employer what you bring to the table and convince them that you are an individual who possesses the professional standards and skills for the job. The appearance of your résumé can be the initial argument that you do possess the professional qualities and skills necessary for the position. Think of your résumé as an advertisement that must get the employer's attention. If not now, then later, as your resume grows to contains more information about you, then the resume will be tailored, or to say it differently modified, specifically for each job application. Never discard used applications keep them on hand for future reference.

Résumé Tips (see appendix D for additional help in putting together a solid résumé):

- Make it professional.
- Use good paper. Companies like Staples have Business Centers which will do this for you for a fee.
- Don't clutter the résumé with details in small fonts.
- Carefully consider any use of highlights, such as bolds and italics. Too many are distracting. Each emphasized item must make a point.
- Whenever possible emphasize on the résumé those personal abilities that correspond to the employer's stated needs (do not neglect KSAs). Place

experience first, education second. (If you have an excellent cumulative grade-point average, list it. If you graduated cum laude or summa or magna cum laude, list it.) Do not list it if it is under a 3.0.

- The exception to putting your experience first is if you are a recent graduate. In this case, list your education first because often the recruiter must verify that you meet the educational requirements.
- List education, experience, certifications, and other evidence of your talent (such as awards and accolades) in reverse chronological order (*most recent is listed first*).
- Cover the basic requirements of the position (education, experience, etc.), addressed in bullets 5 and 6.
- List memberships in and service to professional organizations.
- List any volunteer experience and community service work.
- Do not list references unless specifically required to do so.
- State the job you seek as an objective.
- Do not list your political affiliation.
- Be honest.

Once the résumé is completed, always carry copies with you. Note: *Copies*—more than one—because you never know who you will meet or how many copies of the résumé will be needed to jump-start your career.

JOB KILLERS

Hopefully, you are reading this sooner rather than later. We live in an electronic age that exposes all of us to examination by others. Employers now Google job applicants and research them on Facebook, YouTube, LinkedIn, and other social and professional websites for personal background information. Potential employers may ask for the passwords to your accounts. Give them the password but be aware of what they might find. The pictures posted (the applicant sprawled out on a couch with a liquor bottle in hand will not be seen as complimentary), the stories that are written (wild times at 3:00 a.m. on a weekday will not be seen as indicative of someone who is prepared to work), and the information provided (that new tattoo depicting gang symbols) on each of these sites says something about you. True story: One young man completed a DEA interview in which the interviewer asked whether he had ever experimented with drugs. The applicant emphatically replied, "No!" The interviewer then pulled out a picture of a social media posting of the applicant and his friend with what they described as the "world's biggest blunt"—which they had just rolled themselves. The interviewer asked for an explanation, and the applicant was turned down for the job. The applicant committed at least two major sins here: He lied, and he was seen with an undesirable substance on a social media post.

One careless slip may be enough for a potential employer to make a judgment which immediately removes the applicant from the pool of candidates. Once something is posted, it is out there forever. These are photos and statements that ultimately characterize who the applicant is as a person, and once posted, cannot be withdrawn.

An often ignored individual characteristic is the credit rating. This may be part of a background check because of a sensitive position. The potential employer may be qualifying the honesty of the applicant's responses and verifying personal responsibility for monetary affairs.

NETWORKING: THE MOST VALUABLE TOOL FOR YOUR CAREER

Networking Defined: The ability to meet people who may have knowledge, advice, or relationships that contribute to your career search, advance your career, or help to prepare you for life after your career.

Networking Tools: The résumé, references, personal presentation, speech, and dress.

The A, B, and C of Networking:

A. To help you select a career.
B. To help you advance your career.
C. To prepare you for what comes after your career.

Networks are lines of communication with important dependable colleagues and potentially lifelong friends. Colleagues developed through networking are invaluable sources of support, encouragement, advice, guidance, and information which improve the quality of professional lives. As we network, other networks become interconnected. Notice the impact that the professional networking site LinkedIn has already made on the lives of people. Notice how expansive LinkedIn and Facebook have become.

Former President Lyndon B. Johnson once attended a funeral of someone related to a senator with whom he only had a passing acquaintance. That senator later gave a vote to legislation that was important to President Johnson. This illustrates an important point about networking: Take advantage of opportunities available to friends and colleagues. You never know when you will need them or when they will be there for you.

Networking begins before the first job interview. By the time you are reading this, you will have already considered at least one career and probably several jobs. Now is time to get serious.

Whom do you know to speak with? You may have started down this path with a relative, perhaps a family friend, or through a presentation that caught your attention. Now is the time to learn more about your choice(s). Do some readings in course assignments. Read some more and start writing down questions you can ask of those you know and of others whom you may encounter. You want to be prepared for anyone you meet. Similarly, always review the list of "My Ten Points." You are waging a campaign for your career. You never know when you will meet a person who may be your entrée into your field of choice or perhaps even a career change that you have not considered. Career preparation and networking are daily activities.

Networking enhances the job search, advancement, changes of career path, preparation for life in retirement, and much more. Personal preparation is an ongoing effort. Whether you are just starting out, looking for advancement, preparing for a job that will open up, or perhaps seeking to make changes in your position, there are deliberate and calculated actions you can take. Think of this as a battle plan, a strategy that is designed to promote you, and to achieve what you want.

A STEP-BY-STEP NETWORKING STRATEGY FOR CAREER DEVELOPMENT

The following is a step-by-step strategy to help plan and negotiate a career from finding the first job to settling into a comfortable and satisfying retirement.

Design a personal strategy. This is preparation—the opportunity to chart a career. This is about what you want to accomplish, and the tools required to achieve the first position. Ask yourself, what is my ideal job? Assume you are successful, then ask, where do I want to be in five years? This should be followed by: In ten years? In twenty? When do I want to retire? What will it take for me to retire? This is the 25-Year Plan. At this stage, it may be a bit of a stretch to think about retirement. This strategy will set the stage for that time. All questions do not have to be answered. Some answers will begin the process and help to determine a future path. You cannot know where planning and experience will lead, or to put it another way, what doors may open. One door opening may mean an entire shift of future plans; those shifts may be the difference between success and failure or perhaps between just getting by and being satisfied in your professional life.

Caution: As you draft the plan, the future may seem intimidating. Role models and heroes may seem larger than life. Refer to appendix A for profiles of prominent people in the field of criminal justice. Select those most closely related to your personal aspirations. Read their profiles. Some started out in entry-level positions, and had they remained there, would have had careers served in anonymity. Those profiled were selected because they broke out—they had a plan and reached for new heights, even unexpected heights. This is not a matter of whether you can see yourself in their shoes, but whether you can implement your own plans. Think big, large, grand—what do you have to lose except success if you do not plan and instead leave your future to chance? You can and should place each idea into the plan. This is grist for the mill. This is material for evaluation now and in the future for what is good for you.

Put the plan into writing. If you have a home office or a workspace that permits a display, put the plan on the wall; keep it in your face. The plan is a combination of where you want to be, what you want to do, and what you hope to accomplish. This is an action plan and will undergo change with new experiences, accomplishments, and setbacks. Do not call setbacks "unfortunate"; look at them as opportunities or learning experiences. Did you ever notice that when times are bad, some people keep moving forward or manage to recover more quickly? They do not sit back and wait for an opportunity to come to them; they are preparing or are prepared for the next prospect, the next change, no matter how unexpected. Hint: Look up *paradigm shift*, an important and often misunderstood idea. Paradigm shifts are always the things to come, the unexpected. Preparation for the future is ongoing.

List all positions in which you are interested. Look at the list and determine which positions have qualifications you already meet. Remember, your career starts by getting your foot in the door. Prioritize the list. You can advance this step by recognizing that you are interested in positions for which you do not possess qualifications. Now, you can decide whether to get those qualifications. Or, if they are beyond your reach (and part of this decision-making process is to consider whether the pursuit of those credentials will be a future goal), determine whether they may be more attainable in the future.

Review your credentials for each position. Develop a document portfolio. (See appendix G.) Highlight the positions that meet your credentials. Which other positions are you interested in? Highlight them with a different color. There are at least three benefits to be gained by this step. The first is obvious. Those for which you already qualify will be your first applications into the job market. Second, you will know which other positions interest you and you can identify which qualifications you lack. Third, remember some people are always preparing for change. Pursue missing credentials for the other positions. Move forward; that which stops moving goes nowhere.

List anyone and everyone who has a relationship to each position and relist them if there is overlap. Utilize friends and others to provide references. From time to time update the list to include new references and their contact information. Anytime you meet someone new, ask for a card, then write on the card some notes about the circumstances of the meeting and especially if that person asked you to contact them for something. Do not dismiss such a statement. This person may have seen something in you that you have not considered. Volunteering is a valuable way to meet new people and to demonstrate personal skills. Volunteering can add to the diversity of your references. Here is a list of potential sources to start building a network. Remember, you may add to this list. As you encounter sources, they may say something that catches your attention. Your task is to enter the names of any contacts alongside each category:

- Family members
- Friends
- Former employers
- School guidance counselors
- Business owners
- Local politicians
- Neighbors
- Professors
- Former coworkers
- College career placement officers
- College alumni

Always be prepared to network. You never know when someone will just pop up, such as a fellow shopper in a supermarket or perhaps while you are relaxing on a beach. Chance opportunities do happen, and the value will be in your readiness and acceptance of the moment.

Prioritize who is closest to the positions of primary importance. Start with your A list, those closest to jobs for which you are already qualified. Contacting someone for the first time may seem awkward or be difficult for you. Perhaps someone you do know can be your first point of contact, and then become your entrée to those you have never met before.

Review your résumé, update, and make copies. Keep your résumé up-to-date. There are different types of résumés, and there is a skill to writing a winning résumé. This is one of the important tools that will help you get your foot in the door. If you have any doubts about your résumé or your ability to produce a good one, then it may be worthwhile to hire a professional service to review your résumé. ResumeEdge.com is one site that will do this for a fee.

Review your list of "*My Ten Points*." This was discussed in chapter 2 (also please see appendix C). Review these points periodically so that the responses come naturally and remain applicable to your most recent experiences. These are the points you want to make to potential employers, and they are safe responses to tricky questions. Remember, you do not want to be caught flat-footed during an interview with a question that confuses you or leaves you stammering for an answer.

Make an appointment to visit each of your contacts personally. (Be on time for scheduled meetings!) Make an appointment and be professional even if the person is a close friend or colleague—to be considered a professional, begin to act like one. Bring a résumé, the document portfolio, and a notebook. If the interviewer asks for a résumé during the interview that will be an opening to say, "I brought my résumé and other documents if you would care to review them." Your ability to produce a document upon request shows that you are prepared and proactive about your job search. There may also be questions about something you have not prepared for prior to the meeting. Perhaps the contact would like to see other supporting documentation. Make a note of what they request and specify when you will provide the documentation. This should occur within 48 hours or sooner after your meeting. Now, add those documents to the portfolio. Do not let someone move in front of you with their résumé and other information because you delayed getting the requested information to the interviewer—keep the process going—the ball is in your court.

Guidance for an initial meeting with a contact. First, be goal-directed and demonstrate that you know what you want. This could be one of your ten points; that is, you will make a specific statement about your goals. Keep your questions to the point. Your statement may begin with, "I am looking for a job in . . . " Your questions should include something like, "Is there someone you can refer me to?" Never forget to ask, "May I use your name as a reference?" Do not assume that it is acceptable to do this; your contact will appreciate the courtesy. You are establishing a relationship with that contact because they have already established their value in a field. Be sure to ask if they have any advice for you. People like to talk about themselves, and you are meeting them because they are experts. That question will allow them the opportunity to respond from their level of expertise.

You are learning about conducting a job search, beginning to anticipate what might happen during an interview, and discovering how you will respond to a job posting. You should assess the results for what will be said about you. That is, you do not want to ask someone for a reference unless you are sure of what they will say. For example, you do not want a letter to begin with, "[Your name] was in my Intro course and my experience with him was only for those fifteen weeks. I can tell you he received excellent grades, but the time period was too brief to provide other information." Such remarks will not help you get your foot in the door! You want someone to be able to say specific things, such as you were on time, work well with others, ask intelligent questions, and so forth. The reference must be able to provide specific examples of your work ethic and qualifications.

Those just starting on a career search, or are a seasoned veteran, make mistakes. After you make a contact, *be sure to follow up!* It is good manners and suggests to the contact that you are serious about your job search. In addition, people like to feel appreciated. *Follow up!* Draft a short thank-you note expressing appreciation for the help and advice. This may provide you with an edge—you are reminding them that you met, and a card is not imposing. Finally, even if the contact does not result in a job, send a thank-you note or make a personal call to let them know that they were helpful.

Maintain a network file. The computer, flash drive, other portable electronic device, or in the cloud is a good place to maintain and back up a networking file. The important points for the file include name, title, address, phone number, and agency. Make notes about how and where you met, colleagues you have in common, and discussions you have had.

You can never say everything about yourself in one conversation. In fact, one initial conversation may only allow for generalities. Most conversations do not allow you to present yourself with all your best attributes in an organized fashion. A résumé can do that for you. It is never too soon to prepare one, and after it has been prepared, continually update it with new accomplishments. (See sample résumés in appendix D.) Always carry a résumé and other documents from the document portfolio protected in an 8½ by 11-inch envelope.

You will begin to realize after a short while that your contacts have relationships with one another; your contacts have their own lists of contacts which helped them to excel in their careers. It is a small world, so act as you want to be treated and do not burn bridges. Your grace and respect for others will help you overcome many obstacles, and you will not have a bad reputation circulating among your contacts.

Networking is a two-way street. Network contacts also want to advance their careers. Through the network, you and they may share common goals. Seek opportunities that apply to someone in your network, go ahead and share. The information may be a job opening that does not interest you, or an article about something of someone else's interest. For example, someone in the network may be looking for a particular item, perhaps a book or a documentary that you happen to know. Send the information to them. Your generosity will be remembered. Keep in touch with those in your network. Send a brief e-mail to say hello—it can work wonders.

Don't burn bridges. A career is a long time. Along the way, you will encounter many people—both good and bad. They are liable to show up when least expected, perhaps as your newly appointed supervisor, or perhaps you have eclipsed them, and they are now your subordinate. In either case, you do not need either a hostile boss or a hostile subordinate. Try to leave every encounter, job, and advancement, on the best possible terms. (See the section titled "Career Changes and Moving Forward" in chapter 9 for detailed information.)

Maintain the network throughout your career. Your network is like the old TV game show on which you were able to call a lifeline. Your contacts are there to provide career guidance, help you prepare for new positions, help you explore new options, be of assistance during tough times, and more. They are invaluable.

Networking Safety, or What Not to Do. You will meet new people, in person and on the internet, as you build your network. Unfortunately, not everything about networking is positive. Things can happen outside the network that can hurt you. Similarly, there are things that you may do, outside an official capacity, that can hurt you. Our lives are transparent. Social networks by design and intention spread to others both good and bad information about you. Take caution when providing addresses, phone numbers, and personal information, such as Social Security numbers. Social networking has made it easy and attractive to reveal too many details about ourselves. Ask yourself, how much do you want someone to know about you? Is there information that you have revealed that is embarrassing? Has someone else posted something about you that (a) you would rather not have shared, or (b) you know is untrue? Pictures tell stories, and the viewer will make judgments. You cannot later say that something was unintended. If it is out there, you cannot bring it back. Sometimes it is about perceptions. You may think something is within acceptable limits, but others have their own perceptions. For example, perhaps an opportunity opens for someone, but as those in the hiring position discuss that person, someone remarks, "Oh, he's a drinker." The candidate was not known to have a drinking problem, but the person making the comment remembers that every time he has seen the applicant at a function, he has had a drink in his hand. Such a perception is almost impossible to recover from, just as things that go out into cyberspace can never be withdrawn. As our mothers used to say: If you do not have something good to say, then say nothing! This is sage advice.

A former director was out to dinner with friends and made some unfavorable comments about his agency. He did not realize that one of his superiors was nearby and overheard the comments—he lost his job the next day. Let us add to the advice just given: Think before you speak!

The Last Word about Networking—It Works!

You should work to keep your network in place throughout your career. The network is a tool that, when used to your benefit, will assist you in your job search and to explore career options. If you want a career, dress the part, speak like a professional, and be prepared with a résumé and supporting documents.

PREPARE, PREPARE, PREPARE

Stephen Covey's[2] *Seven Habits of Highly Successful People* is a powerful book to help you prepare for a career and be successful in that career. Each chapter provides good ideas. One of his foremost proposals is that as you develop and move forward, you must "*Sharpen the Saw*." For example, keep your contacts up-to-date with new developments in your life that are important to your career. There are several ways to improve and make yourself more attractive to an employer—and to future employers, such as, improve yourself as a writer. There is a notion that this skill is sharpened in college, that is not always the truth. We become better writers as we practice writing in different contexts. Those contexts include:

- Your résumé
- Letters (especially your skills in writing different types of letters)
- E-mails
- Reports
- Case notes
- Papers and articles

This is not a complete list of all types of required writing. It is a list of types of writing that you need to know about and in which you should hone your skills. The last item is one that students and others often find the most challenging, and for some it is intimidating. When we write and/or publish our work, we expose our ability for many others to see, be critical of, and challenge. You must take risks, but there are ways to minimize those risks.

Write and allow others to read and be critical of what you write prior to submitting it. Give it to someone whom you trust and let them be frank with you about what you have written. Many colleges have writing labs to provide assistance. There are general guides to writing, and some are more specific.

For example, and assuming that you are seeking a career in criminal justice, you may wish to pick up a copy of *The Criminal Justice Student Writer's Manual*,[3] a well-thought-out guide to many problems encountered by those who must write and there are specifics for different types of writing in the criminal justice profession. Note: Spelling and grammar check are aids but they are not absolute. They do not cover all problems such as *feet* and *feat*—they sound the same and are spelled differently and have different meanings.

There are many places you can seek publication for your work to get you started. These include letters and short articles to magazines and newspapers. The more challenging assignments will come as you hone your writing and research skills. These would include articles to peer-reviewed journals which provide status, and greater exposure to those in the field. In addition, they look great on your résumé. The point should be obvious: Do not neglect writing skills.

CAREER EXAMPLES

George seeks a career in community corrections. He has joined a professional association and attends monthly meetings. In the newsletter, there is a listing for a position at a halfway house. He goes on the internet to review the organization. He mentions the job to one of the members he has gotten to know, and that person knows a director in the organization whom he says he will call. The director is delighted to have a reference from someone he knows. George gets an interview and shows up well-prepared with his résumé and other documents. George gets the job.

Bill wants to be a corrections officer. He knows a family friend who is a corrections officer. The family friend explains that the work is tough, and the hiring process is arduous, but he should not be discouraged. The friend suggests that Bill follow the steps carefully and call him for advice as he needs it. The friend arranges for a visit to a correctional institution. Bill is enthusiastic and starts the process. He follows up with the friend periodically, who advises him what will be coming up in the process. Bill keeps his interest high. Bill is now making a career in corrections.

Margaret is unhappy with her current career choice and feels trapped because she has been with the same agency for ten years and is vested in their pension plan. She goes to Human Resources and speaks to a counselor, who reviews her résumé and experiences. Margaret learns that she can transfer from her present position to another one; however, she will have to qualify for the new position by taking a civil service test. Margaret has not taken tests for a long time. The counselor suggests that a prep book will allow her to see the kinds of questions on the civil service exam and to take practice tests. The counselor also advises her that the more often she takes the tests, the better she will score. Margaret finds several positions that interest her, reviews the specifications for those jobs, and watches for test opportunities. Margaret has now taken several tests and has scored well, ranks high on the lists, and receives calls for interviews.

Sam is having dinner with friends and mentions that he would like to become a police officer. One of his friends knows a police officer and arranges a meeting. The officer invites Sam to the station house and shows him around. He tells Sam that he will have to take the civil service test for law enforcement. In the meantime, he might qualify as a special officer, but he would have to go through training. As a special officer, Sam demonstrates his commitment to the process. After taking the civil service test and completing police academy training, Sam is enthusiastically welcomed to a position on the police force.

In each of these instances, there are some key points: (1) Be involved; (2) Take action; (3) Be prepared; (4) Present yourself well; and (5) Get the job! While these are fictitious examples, they are drawn from the authors' experience with students and others. These are examples of how to use the tool of networking.

PRACTICAL SUGGESTIONS

Many techniques, tools, and processes for networking have been discussed. However, there is more to learn. While there are a limited number of hours in a day, you must work to stay in touch with your network. There are times when you can do this casually, like over lunch or dinner, or perhaps during a game of tennis or a round of golf. An e-mail saying hello might be sufficient. Take the time to show an interest in the affairs of others; ask how they are.

Relationships should never be one-sided. There are times when one of your contacts may serve the needs of another of your contacts. A network is a chain of relationships with reciprocity. LinkedIn offers the opportunity to cite other members' skills. You do not have to wait for someone to cite you. Take a moment and cite them for their abilities. Business cards are a great tool for helping people remember who you are; give them freely but avoid handing them out indiscriminately or pushing someone to just "take one."

THE APPLICATION

As you progress in your job search, visit the LinkedIn website, https://www.linkedin.com/job/law-enforcementjobs/?trk=jserp_related_searches, for listings of criminal justice jobs. Applications have rules for completion, which must be followed precisely. If they require applications to be typed, then type! We further recommend that when you visit the LinkedIn website that you download several applications, some for jobs you might currently be interested in and some that are not as immediately attractive. There are three purposes for this suggestion. First, see the different types of applications and the various ways similar questions are asked. Second, each application is an opportunity to practice filling it out. Third, save your practice applications for when you fill out a real application. Your practice answers can save you time and, more likely than not, help you to prevent making errors when you complete a real application.

Some agencies allow you start an application process (such as submitting a résumé) on their website, to which you may return later. Note: Be aware of information about sending your application over the internet. This is particularly important if it specifies that the application process is complete once sent. *Be sure that you have included all appropriate and required information before submission.* Check the application twice before hitting "*Send.*" A suggestion: download the application and complete it away from the site. Once it is completed, go to the site, and fill it out in one sitting. Reread it thoroughly before submitting, correct misspellings, incorrect grammar, and anything else that does not read well.

PRIOR ENCOUNTERS WITH THE POLICE

Arrests, criminal charges, and convictions have consequences for criminal justice employment. They do not necessarily mean a dead end, but if handled inappropriately, they can result in immediate rejection from the employment process. There will be a box on the application which requires a *"check it"—if you have ever been arrested, charged with a crime, or convicted. Be aware* that this does not ask for a conviction alone, but whether you have ever been arrested and/or charged. Failure to check the box and answer all relevant questions about these matters is considered a *falsification of application.* Generally, there will be a space to elaborate on the circumstances of the checked box. And when you are selected for an interview, you will have the opportunity to explain the specifics of the encounter. You should be candid when you provide your explanation, neither downplaying nor embellishing. Do not make excuses, but if there are legitimate mitigating factors, then you may need to include them. As stated earlier, background checks are required by most if not all criminal justice positions—*Be honest.*

YOUR REFERENCES

Determine whether to submit references with your application. Some jobs do not wish to have the references included others do; some want letters of reference to accompany the application; and some application processes do not tell you that they want them or that they will request them later. Some application processes generate an automatic request for references as soon as you submit the application. Oftentimes, these applications also permit you to go back in and check the status of your application, and to see what letters, transcripts, or other documents have been received by the hiring authority.

Choose references carefully. Each reference provided should know you and be able to speak not only to your qualifications, but to your character, as well. (Review networking in this chapter for additional information about references.) While a reference does not need to be a lifelong best friend, they should be more than a recent or casual acquaintance. Think of what your reference can and is willing to say about you. Review the questions below to help in this assessment:

- Can they describe you in work circumstances?
- Can they describe you under stress?
- Can they attest to your knowledge and ability to deliver?
- Can they describe you developmentally?
- What do they know about your future aspirations?
- What can they say about your family or family background?
- Are they familiar with anecdotal incidents from your life?
- Can they speak to your successes?
- What do they know about the job to which you are applying and your suitability for the work?

These questions may help guide you in your selection of references.

You should be informed about the job for which you are applying, including the title of the position. You should also be aware of the type of work you will be asked to perform. For example, if the job requires you to drive and you have an expired or suspended driver's license, you are setting yourself up for a problem during the interview process. Interview questions may revolve around the expected work. Most job descriptions will include sample descriptions of the work expected, and there may be other types of required work at the same location. Contact the worksite and when possible, make a visit. Have a list of questions (*My Ten Points*) prepared ahead of time that address the types of work performed with that agency.

Quality preparation will be an asset when you request that someone write a reference for you. You may wish to provide them with some specific examples of work that is described in the posting and ask them to assess your ability to perform that type of task. Your reference can then address this specifically in the letter they will write for you.

THE EXAM

Many criminal justice positions require entrance or civil service examinations. You have a choice. You can go into the examination cold, or you can prepare for the examination. If your career is important, then we strongly urge preparation. There are a variety of ways you can do this.

- Read books, websites, and other material about the agency and the job.
- Enroll in a test prep course.
- Obtain books especially written for the type of job you will be tested on. (Prep manuals are listed in appendix H.)

THE INTERVIEW *(SEE APPENDIX C)*

Presentation is everything. The interview begins as the door opens. Presentation refers to your appearance, your walk, your talk, your greeting, and how you have prepared yourself for the interview. Do you know who will be doing the interview? Do you understand the expected work performed in the position? What do you know about the agency? Who is the supervisor? Who are the clients? What is the mission statement? What is the salary? How does someone advance in the position or the company? What are the benefits? These are some of the questions you should be able to answer *before* you appear for the interview. The answers you do not know should be prepared as questions to ask during the interview. At some point, the interviewer probably will ask you if you have any questions. Being prepared is impressive! Know your destination, plan the route, and plan to arrive early. Bring copies of all documents that you have sent ahead of time. In the event of multiple interviewers, someone may not have been presented with copies of your application, and it will demonstrate your preparedness if you can simply hand them out if that appears appropriate. Bring additional information, such as copies of certificates, licenses, or awards that are relevant to the position. (See Document Portfolio Checklist in appendix G.) Visit the hiring agency's website. Get answers to the questions listed at the beginning of this section. Make a note of any answers you cannot obtain from the website. These may become *your* questions during the interview. A special note about waiting for an interview: Don't sit there, do something. Bring a book, perhaps a book about the career work you intend to do or something else that is stimulating. This may be an excellent entrée into an interview. That is, the interviewer may see the book you are reading and ask what you think. Once more, this is a potential interviewing opportunity. Prepare a response about the book. In some cases, because of the security for the facility, you may not be permitted to bring anything in with you—Be prepared to leave everything, except what is specified, in your car. By the way, use the restroom *before* you go in for the interview—do it early rather than later—and do not keep the interviewer waiting. You do not know how long the interview will be, and you do not want to be uncomfortable or to have to ask to leave the interview to use the restroom. Again, you should be prepared.

Big Note: Turn off your cell phone! The interview is more important than your call. Answering the cell phone during an interview is rude.

THE TRAINING ACADEMY

(Review chapter 3, "Careers in Corrections," for detailed information about academy training.)

The training academy may take place in any of several environments. There may be an academy that serves a region or one that serves a state. Perhaps it will be at the county college, but if the agency is very large, then the academy may be sponsored by the hiring agency. The academy training cycle may last from a few weeks to a few months. The recruit will receive training that is likely but not exclusive to include classroom instruction, firearms on a range, self-defense, first aid, excessive force, emergency response, and material specific to a job or a state. The training academy is the beginning of your preparation for the job. Many recruits are aware that when it comes to the job, there is the textbook and then there is on-the-job training. Oftentimes, academy training will end with on-the-job training with a seasoned officer/employee.

PREPARING FOR THE TRAINING ACADEMY

The training academy tests your ability to learn and your physical endurance. Get in shape mentally and physically before attending the academy. Chapter 2, "Careers in Law Enforcement," has already discussed how participation in physical education classes and sports during college is preparation for the physical component of academy training. If you have been away from school for a while, you may wish to set up a training regimen for yourself, which should minimally include conditioning, endurance, and strength training. You should also prepare yourself academically. Get into the habit of reading and writing. Take some time each day, preferably at the same time, to read. After reading—write! You do not have to read the great books of philosophy (although they may be of use to you). Read novels, as well as some general texts or other books about your intended career. (See *Newjack*.) Then write about what you read.

Depending upon which agency you will be working for, you may be able to access their curriculum and expectations online. You can always contact the agency and ask to speak to the academy director or an aide for advice about the makeup of the academy training program.

FIRST DAYS ON THE JOB

You worked hard and have arrived! Now is the time to apply what you have learned. The classroom and the textbook present an ideal, and there will be vast differences between the ideal and the real, or the pragmatic. There will be many who will be willing to give advice and guidance, and there will be others who will help you reluctantly, if at all. As you report to work each day, there will be new assignments and with them come new challenges. Presuming that you have a supervisor who is a skilled and seasoned professional, you will be allowed to take your time and feel your way into the job. New employees come to the job with enthusiasm and in addition to training have had other experiences. The first days on the job are a time to learn, not to display what you know. Each job has its own environment and culture. Learn about each, and as you demonstrate ability there will be occasions to pitch in and be a team player. The caution (and at the risk of sounding harsh) try to avoid being a know-it-all. What you know is a strength. Build on what you know to improve, how, and when you may best contribute.

Unfortunately, criminal justice is a field which presents changes and challenges on a day-to-day basis, sometimes from minute to minute. Criminal justice events require immediate decisions and action to which you must bring into play all those things learned in so many settings from the classroom to the academy. Sometimes there is no textbook answer or established policy to guide you. You may need to decide on the spot and hope for the best. However, the better trained you are, the better you will respond to all circumstances.

No one can predict how events will play out, and they may not turn out like they are glamorized on TV. During your first days on the job, you may be assigned to a senior person in uniform, or perhaps a senior staffer. If not, then you will have to assess those around you and determine who is best qualified to answer your questions. What is important is that *you do not let questions and concerns go unanswered! Get answers!* Those answers may eventually protect your job—and even your life.

SUMMARY

Hopefully, this chapter has set you up to prepare for your career in the criminal justice profession. If you are meticulous in these preparations and follow through on them, the career and the future should be in good shape.

Chapter 8

Criminal Justice Ethics

There has perhaps been no time in criminal justice history when the legal and ethical practices of members of the criminal justice profession have so strongly been called into question. There is a difference between legal action and ethical action. The problem is that crossing the ethical line can (but not always) result in violations of the law. One of the best examples have been recent allegations of force and excessive force during the pandemic. Professor Jay Albanese has expressed a common sentiment about the essence of ethical conduct, "Being ethical is when no one else is looking." Law enforcement must exercise restraint procedures in the course of their duties and must make decisions about the degree of force necessary to ensure safety for the subject, the officer, and others, such as bystanders.

Broad media coverage reports about incidents, which officially may be within procedural boundaries, yet are presented to be excessive force. In all cases, because the United States is a nation of laws, apparent violators, regardless of position, are entitled to due process. Unfortunately, a deluge of media, pictures, recordings of events, and analysis by commentators lead the way to conviction in the media before a day in court. To take this one step further, the outcomes of justice (and sometimes injustice), the day in court, and the verdicts result in a failure to satisfy either the offenders, the offended, or the supporting parties. This is a conversation which exceeds the scope of this book. The student, future and present career persons, should keep themselves well-informed, well-educated, and well-trained to be prepared for the difficult circumstances of duty.

Normally, when things go wrong, it grabs the attention of the media for a short time. George Floyd, Breonna Taylor, Ahmaud Arbery, Eric Garner, Tamir Rice, and several others, as well as other incidents such as the accusations of assault of female prisoners at Edna Mahan correctional facility in New Jersey, are examples of severe incidents.[1] The responses to each incident have been explosive, built upon previous outbursts, both violent and peaceful, in the streets, nationally and abroad, and in social media which have once more raised concerns of racism, gender, equality, reparations, and more. The issues of Black Lives Matter, abolition of police and prisons, defunding police, women's rights, and the rights of the LGBTQIA have remained prominent in the news as perhaps never before. They have not disappeared in a short time and appear poised to remain conspicuous for some time to come.

Some of the responses have been to charge law enforcement officers with murder, other serious offenses, and procuring enormous liability judgments and settlements such as $27,000,000 in the George Floyd case. In addition, there have been numerous incidents of police, including ranking police being dismissed and resigning from their posts. More unfortunately, there have been suicides. In 2019, 228 police officers died by suicide, twice the number of 2018.[2]

Legislative and authoritative responses include a review of policy and procedure, training, and to introduce and pass legislation to institute reforms. These actions help to mitigate public outcry. On a more personal note, for the first time in almost 30 years of teaching criminal justice, students have challenged whether criminal justice remains a viable field for a career. In effect, the students were asking if they assumed roles in criminal justice would they be able to do their jobs or be placing themselves at criminal and civil risk.

The attempt to answer such apprehensions is difficult. Part of the response as mentioned above is to encourage students to be objective, continue to be aware of events as they unfold, and to update their education especially regarding the official outcomes. It is important for students to acknowledge their awareness of such serious events, how they will affect their performance, and how the events may impact careers. The challenge for the internship coordinator or career counselor is to ask students to be introspective and to examine whether they are likely to be involved in unethical behavior. Secondly, the student can be encouraged to examine their ethical grounding and that examination of their ethical grounding is a function of career maintenance. The following questions will help the student to achieve and maintain their ethical grounding.

1. What can they do now and progressively throughout a career to ensure that they maintain an ethical posture?
2. Do they have examples of members of the criminal justice community who, despite the challenges to the status quo, perform their jobs to the best of their ability, and serve as examples for successful careers?
3. Who do they have to speak with who is "on the job," or perhaps has administrative and supervisory functions and can help them understand the impact of the recent events on the ability to perform their job?

Criminal justice students have the opportunity (not available to the general public) in their college and university courses to examine, with their professors, past and present instances of both illegal and unethical conduct to understand its impact and importance for careers. The student can follow up, that is, track incidents, as opposed to making decisions based on incidents as they occur and the immediate reactions to them. Careers are about the long run, the 20 to 30 years in a profession.

Criminal justice is a profession which is always subject to review and revision. Among the many actions are legislative (the passage of new laws) and judicial (consent decrees) which affect operations. The following incidents are recommended for review to understand both short and long-term outcomes from incidents: *Miranda v. Arizona*;[3] Serpico;[4] George Floyd;[5] Rodney King;[6] Scottsboro Boys;[7] Amadou Diallo;[8] and Trayvon Martin.[9] In addition, it is also important to follow the current incidents to their conclusion and consequences for operations, such as training and enforcement. The ethical mandate is that the law must be interpreted fairly without encumbrance from media representations, religion, personal values, previous experiences, and personal agendas. *The Importance of Ethics to the Criminal Justice Practitioner*[10] addresses the application of ethics to such practitioners as defense and prosecuting attorneys, law enforcement officers, the judiciary, and others.

Students with doubts about pursuing careers in currently challenged areas of criminal justice should seek assistance and must resolve doubts about career paths. These events do contribute to and may cause additional stress and doubt about the ability to perform assigned duties during serious incidents. These are frequently addressed in articles in journals, trade magazines, and academy training to sharpen performance when encountering serious and especially life-and-death circumstances. Increased awareness of ethical considerations is specifically applicable to a personal career path. There are many agencies such as ACA, APPA, and IACP which offer ethical guidance. Each of their codes of ethics can be found in appendix P.

The quote listed at the beginning of this chapter is the subtitle to a book by Jay Albanese.[11] In this simple statement, he manages to sum up what confounds those who examine the actions of members of the criminal justice profession who violate ethical standards. A vast amount of the responsibility of each component of the criminal justice system occurs out of sight from the public (and can be a great source of temptation). For example, prisons operate behind tall walls protected by armed guards who allow neither admittance nor exit from the prison. Police do not invite civilians to accompany them on investigations, to crime scenes, arrests, or other circumstances. Non-police personnel are excluded from most law enforcement circumstances. Access to the evidence files of prosecutors is not allowed except as they are offered up as evidence (disclosure) to the defense as required by law. Criminal justice operations exclude the outsider from observations of its practices. Many courtroom activities take place outside the courtroom and are never recorded by the court stenographer. Those conversations occur in chambers, in private offices, and in other places. In those settings, determinations are made about the applicability of constitutional law, the plea bargain, the admissibility of witnesses, and even what the witness will or will not testify about. For example, Derek Chauvin took "The Fifth" and would not take the witness stand during his murder trial of George Floyd.[12]

Awareness of unethical conduct often occurs when someone recorded it, unknown documents are discovered, a witness comes forward, a "sting" is conducted by an investigating unit, a message is posted on Facebook or on a video on YouTube, or something else happens that thrusts the act into the forefront of public knowledge. When this occurs, an advocate, an investigator, or perhaps even the media grasps hold of the problem and does not let it go. Then, like a dog with a bone, interested parties scrutinize and analyze the incident until more and more people are aware of it and the increased attention leads to some form of resolution. The consequences are that names such as Rodney King or Mark Fuhrman become, at least for a short while, household names or around which some special commission or governmental investigation occurs. In other cases, such as that of Serpico or the New Jersey State Police (for racial profiling[13]), entire agencies become suspect of wrongdoing and more serious action is taken. The Knapp Commission[14] is an example in the first instance, or the agency like the New Jersey State Police, is placed under Federal Consent Decree[15] in the second instance. The agencies and the professions are connected by the tarnished reputations, and public confidence is eroded. The incidents from the past year, such as Breonna Taylor,[16] George Floyd, the January 6 disturbance at the nation's capital, Rayshard Brooks,[17] Jonathan Price,[18] and others have become household names. Reactions to these serious events are just beginning to impact on the criminal justice field. In the aftermath, there have been general and specific responses to some, and more will likely follow.

Ethical issues affect everyone, and no area of the criminal justice profession is immune from them. They are broad in their types of occurrences and impact on individuals and their public perceptions of professionalism. They erode the general confidence of society and may compromise the ability of each criminal justice area to perform its touted functions. While colleges and universities offer ethics in most career programs, the uniqueness of ethical conduct in the criminal justice profession goes beyond good and bad or moral and immoral—it is directed by the state and U.S. Constitutions, codes of conduct, and rigid construction of policy and procedures. Criminal justice professionals have considerable power, which at one extreme includes decisions of life and death (such as police shootings and executions) and at another extreme includes discretion, turning a blind eye, or acknowledging that someone had to be held accountable for a crime, even if it was the wrong person—an innocent person.

There are several purposes for including an ethics chapter in this book. They include helping the future professional to:

- be an ethical person who understands ethics for their profession and will protect their careers as they contribute to the field.
- develop critical and analytical skills—to go beyond the status quo.
- understand the pressures that will be placed upon them.
- understand the types of ethical dilemmas that occur in practice and that conflict with training, policy, and justice.
- become more open to the exercise of moral and ethical judgment at the toughest times, such as when no one is looking.

The actions of professionals and the public are influenced by various sources of information, such as social events, media, personal interactions, colleagues, and training. The many events of 2020 and 2021 remind us just how precarious is the balance between ethical and unethical conduct. There is a job to be done, and sometimes even the best of people fail to maintain ethical standards. The famous Stanford prison experiment was conducted by Dr. Philip Zimbardo.[19] He used graduate students to assume the role of guards and others to be the prisoners. His students ultimately became aggressive, abusive guards, and the student prisoners accepted the posture of the convict and became subservient to the prison conditions and then responded as prisoners creating a hostile adversarial relationship. His findings suggest that the role determines the actions of the player.

Abu Ghraib, a military prison for prisoners of war, became a painful real-life example of the Zimbardo experiment, with more serious consequences for the guards. The prisoners endured a variety of abuses, such as being forced to be naked and then have physical contact with one another. One of the more damning pieces of evidence was the widely publicized photo of PFC Lynndie England standing with her rifle on her hip, a cigarette hanging out of her mouth, and one foot placed on a prostrate naked prisoner. Perhaps, as we often hear, she was only following orders. Perhaps her actions felt like a patriotic thing to do at the time. In all likelihood, however, she received encouragement from the wrong sources, her superiors—and her conduct resulted in a prison sentence. These abusive acts violated standards for the treatment of prisoners of war, as well as violated the prisoners' cultural and religious traditions, mandates, and practices.

After the egregious events of Abu Ghraib, Zimbardo wrote again about the abuses that occur when power is not regulated, calling it "The Lucifer Effect."[20] We could postulate that at least some of those who engaged in the abusive behavior believed that they were doing their duty, or at the very least were being loyal to their country and what it stands for. Nevertheless, what they did was wrong. In this case, they were soldiers in military uniform who represented the United States.

Stanley Milgram conducted a Shock Experiment which focused on obedience to authority and personal conscience. The experiment showed that participants were willing to shock unknown individuals with sufficient voltage to kill a human 65 percent of the time when instructed by an authoritarian figure.[21]

Every individual is responsible for maintaining a balance between their personal beliefs and their actions. We often refer to this as "being objective." The criminal justice professional is surrounded daily by events and persons that represent the worst that can occur. Maintaining objectivity is difficult in the face of so much input that encompasses illegal and immoral behavior.

The simple explanation for being ethical on and off the job is to know the difference between right and wrong and to make the correct decision (sometimes in the face of considerable pressure). Professional posturing suggests that criminal justice professionals are trying to do what is correct, such as attempting to safeguard society. However, the personal dilemma comes when the answers are not so clear cut. One way to view this is to ask the questions, "does the end justify the means?" and, "does my decision transcend the single event?"

Perhaps we can all agree that achieving safety because of taking action is the satisfactory attainment of the goal. However, our society is governed by a constitution as the foundation for democracy, and the result must be judged by the process that achieved a particular conclusion. This discussion is not about the legality or the illegality of what someone does. Specifically, if someone steals, that is a crime and unethical. However, if someone decides that the only way to safeguard society is to deny someone else a basic right, then that too is unethical and possibly illegal, even if the motivation is correct. Unfortunately, there are many examples both in fact and in fiction where the denial of rights has resulted in an unlawful conviction, detention, and even execution. The process must be considered as it affects outcomes. Persons in responsible positions must adhere to the law and the policies and procedures which dictate their actions.

THE SLIPPERY SLOPE OF CRIMINAL JUSTICE

A slippery slope develops when the first unethical indiscretion occurs, is not responded to, and then advances as the actions progress to more egregious forms of misconduct which may then be illegal. This is especially destructive when the actions result in a personally desirable outcome and justifies the process in the mind of the agent, thus encouraging future acts of unethical conduct as the means of ensuring that the job is successfully completed.

Ethical violations cover a wide range of unacceptable and illegal behavior. Inappropriate conduct can occur both on and off the job and will include circumstances caused by greed, opportunity, an improper sense of duty, the unwritten code of unprincipled conduct, the existence of personnel gone rogue, supported by subcultures, bad and inadequate training, as well as substandard oversight. Unfortunately, there have been too many and frequent examples throughout the history of criminal justice.

Managerial responses have often failed to acknowledge or have ignored misconduct or have been fraught by powerful unions hampering efforts to attempt remediation. In addition, there have been administrations who appear not to care, will not address it, will not sanction those who violate promulgated policy of professional conduct, or who harbor abusers because it is part of an unethical set of standards. Unfortunately, there are also administrators who view themselves as powerless. "The line between good and evil is permeable and almost anyone can be induced to cross it when pressured by situational forces."[22]

There is a perception that offenders of the criminal law are deserving of whatever they get, suffer unethical retaliation, and thus are unwanted figures in society. Those unfamiliar with the justice system have incorrect assumptions about the purpose of criminal justice. It is understandable that there are times when ideation becomes uncompromising resulting in aggressive and abrasive conduct, supported by authoritarian relationships within criminal justice.

However, the question remains whether the criminal justice professional is always required on the job to acknowledge and respond to unethical conduct, and if such responses might be counterproductive to the expectations of the criminal justice profession to accomplish justice. Finally, we may suggest that unethical traits are developed in training academies, reinforced on the job, and contribute to and encourage lasting misconduct.

The significance of unethical conduct and its impact on societal relationships has become more painfully obvious. On the one hand, and for those that are interested, there is a volume of data, both academic and media generated, to support that contention.

The continuous history of misconduct, unethical behavior, corruption, and criminal acts are almost surely a by-product of the somewhat concealed hidden nature of criminal justice. The environment is isolated by a virtually impenetrable wall of armed law enforcement, the "blue wall," the unions, the insignificance of the criminal offender, a lackadaisical attitude by the public, a dearth of suitable and qualified guardians, or advocates for those who cannot advocate on their own behalf, and perhaps confusion about what the job is supposed to entail.

Unethical conduct "is both thorny to research and problematic to document although its existence is well known and has been widely publicized, in book form, film documentary and, most recently, in a seemingly non-stop torrent of reports in various media forms."[23]

TYPOLOGIES OF MISCONDUCT

Those who work in the criminal justice profession possess positions of considerable power, some much more than others. Often unethical conduct is a matter of circumstance. Some examples include setting quotas for tickets, racial profiling, stealing during an investigation, sexual harassment and other sexual misconduct, substance abuse (both on and off the job), sleeping while on duty, creating a hostile work environment, favoritism, accepting gifts or discounts because of one's uniform or position, and many more. Some of these acts are illegal, and the consequences in such cases are severe.

A reflection on the research of misconduct includes the lack of an accepted or inclusive typology of misconduct. There have been several typologies developed or proposed as ways to examine, quantify, or otherwise measure it. Keep in mind typologies have shortcomings. This discussion will rely upon the following as an explanation with which to assess misconduct. What follows has been edited and it is recommended that each be reviewed for its implications and consequences on the job and during a career.

"*Malfeasance*," *misfeasance*, and *nonfeasance* are terms with legal implications.

Malfeasance is a wrongful or criminal act perpetrated by a public official or other person of authority. *M*alfeasance is done intentionally, disregarding the fact that the action is morally or legally wrong and will cause someone harm.

Misfeasance is a lawful act, but performed in an unlawful, illegal, or injurious manner. Generally, misfeasance is different from malfeasance in that the actor does not have the intent to harm, but the harm comes through the actor's irresponsibility or negligence.

Nonfeasance is the failure to do something that one is legally responsible to do; an intentional failure to live up to one's legal or moral duty in a given situation, a refusal to fulfill one's obligation."[24]

THE CONSEQUENCES OF UNETHICAL CONDUCT

The consequences of unethical conduct are many. Individual consequences range from reprimands to criminal charges. In some cases, the conduct may be far-reaching and may result in dismissals, demotions, transfers, and changes to policy and procedure. In other cases, the misconduct breaches constitutional guarantees. In such cases, the severity is greater and can include a Federal Consent Decree.[25]

Overall, acts of unethical conduct erode confidence in governmental operations. Public service is one reason for the existence of the components of the criminal justice system. Law enforcement, the judiciary, correctional officers, and civilian employees appear less as providers of public service when illegal acts and unethical conduct become known. Criminal justice professionals may have forgotten who their client is and for whom they perform their services. This is especially true when they operate outside the limits of ethical conduct and the law or when their behavior is guided by selfish motivations.

A FEW PRINCIPLES TO GUIDE CORRECT AND ETHICAL DECISION-MAKING

Equality in the eyes of the law is a fundamental principle. An individual's position in the criminal justice profession is not to be used to single out persons or groups.

- Law must be the determinate of our behavior. Criminal justice personnel are the instruments of the law, and they must operate within the boundaries of the law and the written policies that specify their limits of behavior.
- As agents of the law, criminal justice professionals may not take advantage of either situations or people.

All too often, criminal justice professionals find themselves on a slippery slope of correct action because of very simple events. They may question, *what harm is it if I accept a doughnut, a free meal, a bottle of Scotch, or an envelope of cash?* The doughnut may seem to be a small offering, but what are the implications of an envelope of cash? If the professional accepts such gifts, is he or she then obligated to provide special favors? What will be expected? Is he or she now obligated to operate or to allow others to operate outside the boundaries of the law? In many respects, the criminal justice professional must be held to a higher standard. They are public servants who are expected to adhere to ethical dictates, not only on the job but also in their private lives.

Members of sworn law enforcement service are never "off the job." They maintain their authority even when off-duty. They still possess their badge and their weapon. Likewise, civilian members of the criminal justice profession represent their agencies at all times. The criminal justice professional needs to be mindful that when they say something detrimental about their agency or their fellow employees while "off the job," someone else may hear the comments or see them acting inappropriately.

WHY DO VIOLATIONS OF ETHICAL CONDUCT OCCUR?

There are many reasons to account for violations of ethical conduct. Each area of the criminal justice profession engages in training and oversight to ensure ethical conduct among its employees. The police and correctional officers are overseen by internal affairs units, and the courts are armed with administrative units to review the work of judges, prosecutors, and defense attorneys.

A primary reason for unethical conduct is inadequate training. Training academies usually have curriculums approved by agencies (such as the New Jersey Police Training Commission) or a board which certifies the course content. In some cases, however, the content may be taught inappropriately, or important points may be deemphasized. In other cases, the on-the-job training may undo the academy training. (See *Newjack*.) In some cases, an individual(s) may just "go rogue," that is, for whatever reason, knowingly and willfully decide to violate policy and standard operating procedures.

No one likes everything that they must do while on the job. However, laws, rules, policies and procedures must govern our behavior and dictate appropriate standards (of conduct) with others. Power is never an acceptable reason to exceed these standards.

RESOLVING THE ETHICAL CONTROVERSY

The criminal justice career will have many intersections from the point of hiring, to attending the academy, to continuing education, to training and retraining exercises, and to memorandums that serve as reminders of what is expected, that is, what is appropriate conduct. Administrators control these occasions to help maintain ethical conduct. At the same time, administrators, supervisors, and managers must also be role models for the expected behavior. Constant vigilance, review, and oversight are essential to maintaining ethical conduct. Many criminal justice associations seek to promote ethical conduct and good practices. Many are listed here, and others in appendix L.

CORRECTIONS

The American Correctional Association (ACA) developed its code of ethics in 1975. Since that time, it has promoted ethical conduct in the corrections field and has established various training programs to develop certified professionals. The ACA has also established a certification process for correctional facilities. The process to become certified is quite involved. Correctional institutions will spend months preparing for the inspection process that leads to certification by the ACA. Accreditation is voluntary. (See the ACA Code of Ethics in appendix P.)

Many private nonprofit agencies seek to promote professionalism and excellence in the field. They include:

- The International Community Corrections Association (ICCA): www.iccalive.org
- The International Corrections and Prison Association (ICPA): www.icpa.ca
- The Correctional Education Association (CEA): www.ceanational.org

PAROLE

Information about the American Probation and Parole Association (APPA) and its code of ethics may be found at www.appa-net.org.

POLICING

Primary law enforcement membership associations include:

- The National Sheriff's Association (NSA): www.sheriffs.org
- The National Organization of Black Law Enforcement Executives (NOBLE): www.noblenational.org
- The International Association of Chiefs of Police (IACP): www.theiacp.org
- The Police Executive Research Forum (PERF): www.policeforum.org

The Commission on Accreditation for Law Enforcement Agencies, Inc. (CALEA, http://www.calea.org), was formed in 1979. Some functions carried out by CALEA include maintaining a body of standards that has been devised by members of law enforcement to address topics such as, racial profiling. Accreditation by CALEA is voluntary. The CALEA Standards can be found in appendix P.

THE COURT AND THE PURSUIT OF JUSTICE

The court is an arena of highly charged personal, political, constitutional, and emotional decision-making. The extraordinary talent of Alan Dershowitz, emeritus (a Yale University Professor of Law) is well chronicled. His understanding of the ethical complexities of adhering to the law in the pursuit of justice is quite clear in what he describes as:

RULES OF THE JUSTICE GAME

- Rule I: Almost all defendants are, in fact, guilty.
- Rule II: All criminal defense lawyers, prosecutors, and judges understand and believe Rule I.
- Rule III: It is easier to convict guilty defendants by violating the constitution than by complying with it, and in some cases, it is impossible to convict guilty defendants without violating the constitution.
- Rule IV: Almost all police lie about whether they violated the constitution in order to convict guilty defendants.
- Rule V: All prosecutors, judges, and defense attorneys are aware of Rule IV.

- Rule VI: Many prosecutors implicitly encourage police to lie about whether they violated the constitution in order to convict guilt defendants.
- Rule VII: All judges are aware of Rule VI.
- Rule VIII: Most trial judges pretend to believe police officers they know are lying.
- Rule IX: All appellate judges are aware of Rule VIII, yet many pretend to believe the trial judges who pretend to believe the lying police officers.
- Rule X: Most judges disbelieve defendants about whether their constitutional rights have been violated, even if they are telling the truth.
- Rule XI: Most judges and prosecutors would not knowingly convict a defendant whom they believe to be innocent of the crime charged for a closely related crime.
- Rule XII: Rule XI does not apply to members of organized crime, drug dealers, career criminals, or potential informers.
- Rule XIII: Nobody really wants Justice.[26]

The bold, tongue-in-cheek statements of Dershowitz help to indicate the difficulty for practitioners (judges, prosecutors, defense attorneys, law enforcement officers, and correctional personnel) to be instruments of justice, especially if these are truly the beliefs held by criminal justice practitioners. The American Bar Association (ABA) developed the Model Code of Judicial Conduct[27] as a guide for judges. This code is intended to help steer judges in the right direction given the unique circumstances of their position. Judges must exhibit impartiality in their determinations of constitutional fairness. Pollock[28] points out the five canons of the code:

1. Impropriety and the appearance of impropriety
2. Impartiality and diligence
3. Personal affairs
4. Extrajudicial activities
5. Political activity

SUMMARY

The professionalism of employees is important to the image of criminal justice. The image that others hold of the profession is determined by the conduct of the many actors in the criminal justice profession. The ethical person will earn the respect of colleagues and the respect of citizens.

The candidate for employment has examined the options, pursued the job, and earned the opportunity to be an employee in the field of criminal justice. As employees, choices will be made about personal conduct and the way to respond to others. This is not a matter of political affiliation. This is a matter of right conduct that rises to a level above that necessary for the ordinary citizen. The criminal justice professional is a public servant.

Read the available codes of ethics that govern the job—and apply them. The failure to understand ethical precepts will result in poor decisions which violate those codes. Persons who violate codes of ethics risk suffering consequences for poor/illegal choices. Unethical conduct can ruin a career. Review some of the strange and inappropriate behaviors which have recently caused severe consequences for criminal justice personnel. Type "criminal justice misconduct" into the Google search bar to find examples of unethical and illegal misconduct. The many examples will help explain inappropriate conduct described as misfeasance, malfeasance and nonfeasance. All three types are unacceptable for the career professional.

Chapter 9

Career Transitions in Criminal Justice

This chapter has been constructed in four parts:

Part A—Career advancement briefly addresses some things to keep in mind from the first day on the job through retirement.

Part B—Career Changes offers recommendations and suggestions when opportunities become present. Career changes are those occurrences when something unanticipated happens. The successful change is the ability to gracefully negotiate the event. Successful change is often the result of growth and ongoing development after the career has begun.

Part C—Career Crisis is concerned with the threat or the realization that a bad career choice was made. This could occur on first days on the job or later in a career because of personal and agency change or social crisis. Personal change may include being unable to advance or unexpected events which disrupt a career path (e.g., the pandemic and the social crises which accompanied it). The reader may consider the challenges to the way law enforcement performs its duties.

Part D—Life After the Career—or Retirement. A career will come to an end. This is not a dramatic statement but a reality. Just as there has been an emphasis on preparation for a career, this section emphasizes preparation for retirement. The personal discovery is to determine satisfaction and personal fulfillment in retirement. Preparation for retirement must begin at the start of the career.

PART A—CAREER ADVANCEMENT (SEE PROFILES: LOUDEN, BRIGHTMAN, KENNY, ROYSTER, GUADAGNO, AND FERRANTE)

This topic is much too involved for this book. Nevertheless, it seems appropriate to provide a few suggestions. (See chapters 2 and 3.) Advancement is about more than getting to the next position; it is about doing what is important for you to achieve your next step. Keep in mind the *big picture*, your 25-Year Plan for five years, 10 years, 20 years down the road, and retirement. Take care of your whole person, including your physical, educational, and financial health. Staying in shape physically will help keep a career from being derailed by illness. Join a gym or at the very least stay active. Your fitness will contribute to a more satisfying and healthy retirement.

Education can be an ongoing journey to help with a current career, to change careers, and to set yourself up for a new and perhaps entirely different career when you retire.

Financial health is current, ongoing, and essential for the future. Getting the job is not a signal to rush out and start spending wildly or running up credit cards. Any failure to maintain good financial status can have an effect along the continuum of life. The creation of a financial hole (debt) will affect future plans. At the very least, as the career begins, attend a seminar or a course in personal financial management. There are rumors that Social Security and other pensions that have been relied upon in the past may not be around, and individuals will have to assume more responsibility for their financial futures. Unfortunately, for many, even if pension and Social Security remain, they may not be the same or sufficient to ensure a secure and fruitful retirement. There are many ways to build a nest egg to supplement incomes, but to do so requires your planning and action as soon as possible.

PART B—CAREER CHANGES

A career is an active experience. That is, where you begin is not necessarily where you finish. What is important is the personal preparation needed to advance, transfer, or even change fields. Some people do grow out of their careers or find that they have accomplished all that it will allow them to do. Unfortunately, this may happen long before the person's eligibility to retire. For some, life gets in the way (physical and mental illness, criminal events, hardships, a bad boss, and more), and a career ends at an awkward time.

Staying in a career that lacks satisfaction or that no longer provides a sense of personal worth is not healthy. A suggestion from management or human resources, at such times, is to seek other employment when the job lacks satisfaction or causes stress. The best choice may be to change jobs or careers. How easily that is accomplished will depend on what was done prior to starting a career and after the career has begun. Hopefully, and before the career takes off, take the opportunity to build a solid foundation. Some career shifts are made from the civilian side into law enforcement (see Bo Orichowski's profile in appendix A), while others move from law enforcement to a civilian career (see Len Ward's profile in appendix A). Some simply leave the criminal justice profession altogether.

There are a variety of questions that may be asked:

- What do you want to do?
- What are you capable of doing?
- What are you qualified to do?
- How can you obtain the credentials and experience to make the move?
- Is funding available (such as scholarships or grants) to assist you?

The answers to the questions are likely to include such responses as a better salary is desired, the job has been outlived, or that administration and supervision are obstructive, the passion for the work is gone, and new challenges are needed. Two final reasons for job change are stress or perhaps a personal life change has occurred, and a better balance is sought. Any one of these responses can be compelling for personal change. The consequence of changing a career because of these concerns may include improved happiness or satisfaction because stress has been reduced and there can be better fulfillment of life objectives.

CAREER CHANGES AND MOVING FORWARD

There are at least two perspectives to this scenario. The first is when the supervisor recognizes a problem. Employers generally help the new hire fit in and learn the job. Unfortunately, despite the best efforts, there are circumstances in which the employee does not work out. One of the more difficult tasks for a supervisor is to tell an employee that they need to move on. The job might have been hurting them, they were hurting someone else, or potentially could harm someone else.

The second case is the discovery that the career choice is wrong. Many things, on the job, provide signals that something is wrong—stress, unhappiness, being argumentative, not seeing eye to eye with coworkers, not accomplishing tasks, and more. A little honest soul-searching will provide some reasons. The job is not what it was anticipated to be. Perhaps once this decision is reached, you will wonder how to manage *without* a paycheck. The paycheck, however, while important, is not the primary reason to hang on to a job; your happiness and well-being are the most important. If you hang around too long, then you or someone else may be harmed. When job situations deteriorate, you risk damaging your reputation, as well as any hope of getting a good reference for future employment. This can damage future job opportunities.

THE AWKWARD DEPARTURE

There may come a time, for any number of reasons, when a departure may be awkward or unpleasant, such as when the agency is shorthanded or supervisors in your agency do not respond kindly to those seeking new jobs or are being considered for new positions. First, do not advise supervisors, or even fellow employees, about your plans. Second, advise potential employers that you are experiencing a hostile work environment. While this may hamper your effort to get a new position, honesty with a potential employer is better than a reference check on your work record which produces a negative response. Caution, never badmouth, or express a string of negative statements about the current position. Remain positive about your work performance and what you have accomplished on the job. Refer the employer to your references who will defend your personal and work record. Third, follow all other suggestions, such as giving appropriate notice and writing an appropriate letter of resignation when you are ready to move on.

LEAVE EVERY POSITION GRACEFULLY

This is advice for any change of career—A professional acts like one. You will meet those you leave behind, as colleagues who also have moved on, as subordinates, or your supervisors.

There are many ways to make a graceful exit. Express kind words to fellow employees, such as, "It's been great working with you. Please stay in touch. Here is my contact information." The same advice applies to supervisors: "You have been a terrific boss and I learned a great deal. I have really appreciated the opportunity to explore my potential and it has prepared me for new opportunities. Please call me if any questions come up about the projects I was working on." Of course, the most considerate thing you can do as you depart from a job is to finish any open assignments, or at least leave them in good condition for someone to pick up. *Never* leave a position without giving adequate notice. The norm is two weeks' notice.

Generally, a letter of resignation is suggested. Take the time to write it well and include some of the remarks listed above. Always leave on the best terms possible. Remember your boss can give you a reference, know of someone hiring, or have other positions for you to explore. Your supervisor will probably appreciate your candor that the job is not working out. Too often, an unhappy employee develops into a problem employee, and this circumstance may be paving the way for the employer to terminate the employee. This is a mark that no one wants on their record.

THE LETTER OF RESIGNATION

When a decision to leave is reached, do not immediately submit a letter of resignation, and stop reporting to work! Some options to take include scheduling a visit with your supervisor or an employee assistance program, go speak with a personnel counselor. This book has discussed that in the work world, it is important to place the right employee into the right position.

The decision to leave a position (or move to a promotion) is important. You have probably heard the expression, "Don't burn your bridges," or "The people you passed on the way up, you will see on the way down." The point is that life presents us with a variety of opportunities—and the occasional curveball. There are two important points of order: First, leave every position gracefully. And second, treat people as you would wish to be treated.

PERSONAL EVALUATION

Changing careers is often easier said than done. Nevertheless, an organized plan of action will be a step toward improving an unhealthy situation. (Review the section on Self-Assessment.) First, examine the 25-Year Plan and determine if personal goals have changed. Second, understand why the goals have changed. For example, have there been changes in your life which have redirected your objectives. Adjust the 25-Year Plan to reflect changes in interests and any improvements in skill development. Taking an interest inventory (RAISEC Inventory,[1] Strong Interest Inventory [SII] Test),[2] and there are others, will help align goals and values.

The circumstances described above may indicate that a career change is critical. The first step is not to take one. Do not jump from the frying pan into the fire. A constructive and beneficial change may require a lengthy period of preparation. Examine the following recommended criteria:

- First, read this plan before doing anything.

- Second, it is easier to move from one job to another than to seek a job from unemployment. Employment pays the bills. Once the decision to change has been made, you should feel some relief. Recognize that what has been causing the unrest can be put behind you.
- Third, change is a personal decision for your professional well-being—"Tell no one," especially your boss and co-workers. Prematurely revealing your intentions could result in retaliation and sabotage. However, we do urge caution, if your boss is supportive then that person may provide invaluable assistance.

Consider these steps toward a transition.

Step One: Take the 25-Year Plan and use it to assess your stability, that is, your strengths and weakness for change especially in the categories of: Professionalism, Financial Stability, Personal Condition, and Goals.

Step Two: Consider which fields might be a better career choice. Your review of the Plan should establish what you are interested in and your areas of expertise. If there is uncertainty there are free assessments available such as the Myers-Briggs Type Indicator (MBTI),[3] which will provide you with ideas about several potential career choices.

Step Three: Just as internship preparation was described, research potential career choices.

a. Review agencies and occupations. Go to the websites, read thoroughly, and write down questions. Remember to also review the benefits. Retrieve applications and fill them out carefully. Follow the instructions meticulously. Save completed applications for reference with prospective jobs. Always go over the filled in application *twice* before submitting. Many applications are now completed online and once submitted, the information cannot be altered. The information on applications must be accurate.
b. Review current job opening in desired professions through LinkedIn, Monster, and other job search engines. What are the required qualifications? What skills are desired? Review KSAs. Do you have the skills, or do you need a new degree or certifications? Do not be daunted by the idea of a new degree. Learning can be fun and if there is a goal(s) then there is motivation—the desire to move forward.
c. Go visit the places for a potential career change. Take the questions from the website review and get answers. The visits may raise new questions. Talk to people who are doing the work and assess their level of satisfaction. Ask why they are satisfied? Get specific details both positive and negative.

d. Seek what is available for you to experience these potential career paths. See chapter 6, "Internships, Volunteering, Externships, and Part-Time Jobs." The idea of a part-time job may not be appealing. However, if you have credentials and experience this will open a door for this type of career exploration.
e. Evaluate your Financial Status. A complete review helps to assess debts and assets. For example, a spreadsheet of your outgoing living expenses each month, such as mortgage/rent, utilities, household and personal expenses, groceries, loans, and credit card debt will be in black and white to evaluate a financial status. Get a notebook to record where money is spent and how much. Establish how long you can afford to be out of work. In other words, what are your assets? The rule is you should have cash for six months of expenses. Finally, calculate the cost of retraining, a new degree or certification.
   i. Warnings:
      1. You may have to make some sacrifices to move on.
      2. This is not the time to run up credit card and/or accumulate additional debt.
      3. A new job may not provide a salary increase. You may start a new career with a lower starting salary.
f. Prepare for applications:

   Update the resume—emphasize skills and experiences closely related to the job.

Update the cover letter. Think of something that makes you stand out. Think of it this way—you are selling yourself. Use keywords whenever possible, which are related to prospective jobs, and which illustrate the kind of person you are. Provide one example during which you best exhibit a skill. Keep the letter to one page. If the job posting uses specific language use it in your cover letter. When seeking a job change address it in the cover letter. How do your existing skills relate to the new field?

g. Prepare for interviews:

   Update My Ten Points—have examples for keywords used in your cover letter.

Review successes and failures (see toughest interview questions appendix C)

Practice mock interviews such as responses to questions given by an interviewer.

h. Review your references and relationships:

References should be related to the job posting.

Relationships, not contacts, are persons who know you, will vouch for you, and advise you when they hear of an opening suited to you.

SUMMARY TO PART B

Life changes are accompanied by difficulties. How smoothly you can deal with those changes is in your hands and will be the result of your preparation: personally, professionally, and financially. A career is too long a time to be unhappy. The Japanese have the expression "kanji," which loosely translates into threat or crisis and opportunity. The Japanese represent an excellent role model for their ability to rebuild and establish a stable economy. Remaining in an unhealthy or unsatisfying job is to remain in crisis, transition is healthy. Planning is essential to ensure that transitions are not a movement from one unhealthy circumstance to another. Rather, a good plan, well-executed, is likely to produce satisfying results. So much more could be written on this topic which is outside the scope of this book. We also suggest that moving forward is essential and after considering the suggestions above, go speak with trusted colleagues or professionals who can advise and assist with a productively formulated career change.

PART C—CAREER CRISIS

There may come a time to leave a career in criminal justice whether, for a better opportunity, retirement, conflict, or perhaps the career choice was wrong. The popularity of criminal justice does not mean that this field is the "right career" for everyone. The field of criminal justice is fraught with stress, change, corruption, ethical challenges, conflicting goals, controversies which seem to undermine or conflict with goals, racism, bias, discrimination, gender inequality, and more. In many cases, the issues, and especially those which are unresolved, result in personnel conflict causing a departure from a chosen career path.

The remarks made in this chapter and in this section are not an attempt to persuade someone to remain or to encourage someone to leave the criminal justice profession. The intention is to create a healthy awareness about what causes career changes, how to assess your current state, and how to properly plan for the future. Part of the decision-making is to determine whether what you are doing is a dissatisfying career or that you are in an unhealthy job. Consider this, should you begin to arise in the morning and dislike the idea of going to work, it is probably time to look for a new job—perhaps in the same field or leave the occupation for another. An optimistic note is that the individual who persistently improves themselves frequently discovers new opportunities in other segments of the profession or for other prospects outside the profession. (See Mark Ferrante Profile.) The authors stress that the criminal justice profession is broad and encompasses most subject matters of academia. Law enforcement and civilian opportunities are plentiful. See this website for the various jobs available in criminal justice: https://www.monster.com/career-advice/article/best-jobs-criminal-justice-0317.

Criminal justice is chosen as a career because something about the profession was exciting and interesting. If that excitement fades, then exploring other opportunities may be a first step toward deciding what to do next, for example, a transition from law enforcement to civilian or community corrections.

The recent social unrest during the pandemic has caused many to leave the criminal justice profession. The social unrest has resulted in calls to disband and defund police and prisons. In the past year and a half, legislation has been passed which previously might have seemed improbable, or perhaps should have come sooner. Chokeholds have been banned, body cameras mandated, and "no-knock" warrants eliminated. The protection of civil servants from civil suits with "qualified immunity" created at the federal level has been eroded by states passing legislation for "civil action for deprivation of rights" and the removal of law enforcement certification for excessive force when found in incidents. Many civil servants view this as threatening their careers when, by definition, the career work places them in personal jeopardy. The new laws bear the names of the victims who have suffered excessive force or bad judgement. There is more than what is mentioned at this time and the likelihood is that new legislation will continue and present new challenges for those who have careers and for those wishing for a career in criminal justice.

Sometimes, we are blinded by our passion for our career choices and can never envision ourselves in another career. However, no one is happy in their career 100 percent of the time. Transitions are often difficult, but not impossible and many of the same tools (résumés, interviewing, references, etc.) used to seek initial employment are recommended at this time. A discussion of those tools may be found in detail in the preceding chapters and in the appendixes.

The good news is that you are better prepared now than when you were first seeking to enter a career path. This is one more reason to have a solid updated 25-Year Plan. If the Plan is in place and has been used as a guide for ongoing professional development, then many pieces of personal preparation have already been initiated.

CONFLICTS IN CRIMINAL JUSTICE

The criminal justice profession has a well-documented history of persons and agencies that find themselves embroiled in conflicts and controversies. Understanding why conflicts occur may help with your level of satisfaction and awareness of the reasons for the conflict, on and off the job. Each component of the criminal justice system has specific tasks that seek to accomplish specific goals. A few examples will help to illustrate the depth of those conflicts and controversies.

Willie Horton was released from a Massachusetts prison on a community release program. He absconded and committed a violent offense. The governor was accused of being soft on crime. In reality, the governor had nothing to do with prison programming but because of the magnitude of the event, he was forced to withdraw from the presidential primaries. There is more to this story, and the curious can explore the complexities through several websites. The Willie Horton story is an interesting criminal justice and criminological conundrum that demonstrates the incongruous mix of politics, media, and expectations for the correctional/criminal justice system.

The get-tough legislation that began in the mid-1970s caused prison populations to skyrocket. States were not prepared for these increases and suffered financial hardship. Due to cutbacks and massive overcrowding, which in many prisons exceeded 50 percent, reductions were made in budgeted programming. The complexity of the problem results in steady failure rates after prison. Violence and other events have been publicized in recent years.

The goals of the criminal justice system (rehabilitation, deterrence, retribution, and public safety) are not always clear or understood by those inside and outside of the criminal justice profession. The goals are not straightforward (nor correctly understood) when aspects of law enforcement and corrections attempt to fulfill their tasks.[4] Other goals include restoration and restitution. For example, there is some expectation that once the offender has served a sentence, the debt is paid. Restoration for the offender is difficult to achieve because of the myriad civil penalties, referred to as "collateral consequences." Collateral consequences often involve lifetime exclusions. On every front, restitution is a commonsense criminal justice objective. Unfortunately, the ex-convict will usually have difficulty finding employment that permits even a poor standard of living, and they are unable to make good on restitution. Understanding the goals may add clarity to the manner in which the professional will manage a career.

Criminal justice is often referred to as a system. Unfortunately, it is more a collection of parts with little coordination between them. An oversimplification is that the police arrest, the courts adjudicate, and corrections is the place of punishment. Police officers wonder why judges grant probation after they have worked so hard to catch the wrongdoer. The courts are often frustrated by a lack of available sentencing options. Correctional facilities, due to a mass incarceration policy, suffer extreme overcrowding and a poor budget allowance with which to provide programs matched to the specific needs of offenders. Students who wish to enter the field of criminal justice would do themselves justice (no pun intended!) to be familiar with all aspects of the criminal justice field, its limitations, its abilities, and the restrictions with which to interact. Chapter 8 serves as an introduction to the ethical dilemmas encountered in criminal justice careers.

PART D—LIFE AFTER THE CAREER—OR RETIREMENT

The Post-Career Transition

Your criminal justice career has not begun, so why consider retirement? The response is simple. Many fail to consider retirement because it seems too far away. Of course, by the time retirement is considered, too often at a mid-career point or later, much valuable time has elapsed, and planning now must be rushed and may not produce the best results.

The career employee, at the beginning of their career, can begin to address retirement issues by asking four questions. The answers to these questions will not produce the final answers, but they will initiate retirement planning. That is, as life events unfold, personal needs and priorities change. All life experiences cannot be anticipated and there will be unexpected encounters that may change future goals and objectives. Those experiences very well may alter your plans and cause you to shift course in your goal setting. Ask the following questions:

1. How should I retire?
2. When should I retire?
3. What do I need to retire?
4. What will I do in retirement?

THE FAILURE TO PLAN

I sat in my first retirement seminar when I reached the 25th year of my career. I believed I had started early enough to be financially prepared for retirement. I took notes throughout the morning session and nodded my head knowingly as point after point suggested that I had done okay. However, I had a great deal to investigate before I signed the papers for my retirement.

The afternoon session began with a new speaker. A financial advisor opened with a startling remark: "For many of you in this room, I hope that you will run out of money in the first six months of your retirement." He paused, and I sat in disbelief. Others looked on in shock. How could he tell these hardworking folks who, after twenty or more years of effort, and had their retirement in front of them that they needed to return to work? I could see the panic in the eyes of several people in the room.

He clarified his remark by saying that even with their pensions and probably with Social Security, there would be insufficient income to maintain current lifestyles and financial obligations. He emphasized that many of them would not be able to live as they had dreamed of living during retirement. He went on to suggest that the sooner they returned to the workforce, the better to obtain employment to provide the required income to provide for their needs if things got tougher. This was sound advice. He also mentioned that the cost of living would increase, and that cost-of-living adjustments, or COLAs, would not keep pace with inflation.

RETIREMENT AND THE 25-YEAR PLAN

The authors stress that the 25-Year Plan should include retirement. Retirement goals should minimally be updated at regular intervals or annually. Criminal justice and law enforcement careers come to an end for many at a relatively young age with a generous pension and benefits which provide the freedom to select from a wide range of post-career activities. This is not true of all careers. We strongly suggest a quick but not a careless decision about returning to some type of employment as soon as possible after retirement. That is because the longer you are out of the workforce, the more difficult it may be to return. If you are fortunate and have prepared well for employment after retirement, you should have provided yourself with the means to live very productively in your retirement years and for fruitful activity during retirement. But if you have not, you can expect to have to work until much later in life at jobs which are not satisfactory.

For some, retirement provides the opportunity to do what they have always wanted to do but could not because of the career path. The question is, have you set yourself up to move on? Retirement can open the door for a second career or the opportunity to pursue an avocational interest. Those options hold the potential to be rewarding: professionally, personally, and financially. Please read some of the profiles in the appendix for suggestions.

RETIREMENT READINESS

The following checklist may be used just prior to retirement to determine personal readiness. However, using it early may be handy to ensure personal and financial well-being as you progress through your career. The responses to any point on the checklist may start out simple and become more complex as your career advances, such as being prepared for any transition during the career. Some items, such as your personal success, may require the assistance of a financial planner or an attorney. There are resources to help with choosing qualified and reliable financial planners and attorneys with the right specializations. Social Security also has a retirement checklist.[5] You may wish to create your own checklist divided into several categories for (short and long-term) goal creation. Those categories should include Financial, Lifestyle, Personal, and Location. You can fill in and fine-tune as you advance through your career. The subcategories, listed below, will help plan personal readiness. You may have to make new decisions to provide for your answers to the questions.

- Inventory personal financial assets
- Understand Social Security
- Understand pension
- Establish an emergency fund
- Minimize, manage, and eliminate debt
- Family (spouse, children, grandchildren)
- At what age would like to retire
- Set goals for retirement
- Where will you live
- Determine insurance needs (life, long-term care, housing, automobile)
- Estate planning (house, wills, trust)
- Sources of income or for emergency needs
- Retirement activities (sports, travel, hobbies)
- Health (exercise)

SUMMARY

The authors hope that this book has provided the tools with which to formulate a successful fulfilled career. We have provided our contact information in "About the Authors" should you feel the need to follow up and seek assistance.

Chapter 10

Privatized Criminal Justice (Careers in the Private Sector)

EMPLOYMENT OPPORTUNITIES

Private CJ careers receive little attention in traditional college CJ programs compared to the attention given to jobs in the public sector. This is unfortunate. There is great employment diversity in the private sector which translates to opportunities for jobs and careers. For example, there are approximately 36,200 employed as private detectives and investigators[1] and, in 2019, there were 1,126,370 in private security,[2] which includes armed and unarmed guards as well as mercenaries. The work is comparable to that in the public sector and some jobs, such as private detective, will be familiar because of the entertainment media. Privatized corrections, police, security, and risk management will each be discussed. The employment depth in these three areas prohibits listing all possible jobs.

The private sector of CJ is a resource for second careers after retirement from the public sector or it may supplement a primary job. Public sector employees are valued because they are already trained, are licensed to carry a firearm, and are experienced. Second careers in the private sector are attractive for retirees because of the salary which will supplement a pension and benefits from public employment. There is the possibility to earn a second pension in the private sector.

A seldom addressed opportunity in the private sector is the use of public professionals, prior to and after retirement, as consultants and trainers. These positions often have salaries above $100,000 or they are contracted employees. Prior experience, credentials, and career success are often critical to obtaining a private position. The work includes reviewing and developing policy and procedure, reviewing existing training, developing training, reviewing security, and overseeing change to existing security protocols, investigating problems, and making adjustments. A background in IT, and especially if the person is credentialed, is an asset for private security firms.

A couple of notes about these positions. First, there is shortage of persons to fill these positions. Second, some have starting salaries in the $30,000 range. However, the person with the educational background and managerial experience is likely to quickly advance and after training and gaining some experience becomes more attractive for private supervisory and managerial positions. Third, available positions cover the breadth and depth of CJ from worker to program manager, therapist, researcher, guard, supervisor, nurse, and many more.

There are some cases in which private companies have replaced public services as well as jobs that are not present in the public sector. Bounty hunters, which recently became a media sensation with the reality television show, *Dog—The Bounty Hunter*, are absent in the public sector, and are employed when someone skips bail and must be found.

Historically, many private-sector jobs are a carryover from much earlier times. Great Britain provides the model or origin for many private CJ occupations. The Thief Taker became the model of modern private police and bounty hunters who perform law enforcement functions while lacking official law enforcement status. Similarly, the watchman has its origins in medieval Europe and England and has become the night watchman who performs security for businesses, manufacturing plants, and buildings with objects of high value such as jewelry, stores, museums, information, or anything else requiring protection. Privatized positions come very close to official law enforcement as operators (such as bounty hunters, watchmen. and prison guards) often have a license to carry a firearm and use a weapon for protective purposes.

EDUCATIONAL BACKGROUND

This book emphasizes the importance of academic excellence for CJ employment and does not need to be repeated. Many private jobs require a minimum of a high school diploma, a degree, and in some cases a graduate degree, or specialized training for licensing. The requirements vary from state to state. However, a degree(s) in CJ will improve the likelihood of career-oriented employment and rapid advancement, especially with corporations and large private CJ agencies.

The content of the courses is valuable. Courses, such as psychology, political science, social work, economics, and finance, or research and statistics, which round out a degree, provide information and understanding about the

CJ process, ethics, law, corrections, and law enforcement. This diversity of information has relevance to a career decision in the private sector. An important note is that military experience is valued, and when combined with an academic degree, the job applicant will experience a broader selection of career opportunities. Traditional colleges and universities have degree programs which tend to be more conventional. Degree programs for private CJ careers are more diverse for colleges with online programs. The point is, after consideration of career goals and understanding personal characteristics for career success (see chapter 7), the student will be better able to determine the degree path best suited for a private CJ career. Explore the curriculums of colleges and universities for degrees, certifications, or program specialties linked to careers in private CJ. For example:

Southern New Hampshire University offers the following:

- AS Criminal Justice
- BS Criminal Justice
- BS Criminal Justice with a concentration in Criminology Crime Analysis
- BS Criminal Justice with a concentration in Security Management
- BS Criminal Justice: Corrections
- BS Criminal Justice: Police Administration and Operations
- BS Cyber Security
- BS Information Technologies: Cybersecurity
- MS Criminal Justice
- MS Criminal Justice: Public Safety Administration

INTRODUCTION TO PRIVATE DETECTIVES, CORRECTIONS, POLICE, AND RISK MANAGEMENT

This section will primarily focus on positions which, with a degree or other credentials, have career potential. Among the positions seeking persons with academic credentials include management, security, cyber-security, research, consulting, loss prevention, risk management, surveillance, and fraud investigation which require basic and/or advanced education and specialized training. In some cases, and especially those of less complex organizations, the training may be on the job. While such training is often job-specific, it may be the jumping-off point to greater career opportunities.

PRIVATE INVESTIGATORS OR DETECTIVES

The private detective/investigator is as old as the profession of law enforcement. Among the earliest inspirations for the profession was Eugene François Vidocq, who possessed very interesting credentials—first a colorful life as an on-again/off-again criminal (frequently imprisoned), a spy, a police informant, and finally a detective or criminalist. He is considered the father of modern criminology. He was also the founder of the *Surete Nationale*, now the National Police of France, as well as what is considered to be the first private detective agency. Vidocq became the model for detectives and especially those called *noir* stories starting a trend that continues today. While Vidocq had Paris for his location, Dashiel Hammett placed his fictional character in San Francisco and the seedy waterfront, and the television series *Magnum, P.I.* was set in Hawaii.

The real private investigator is less dramatic and less colorful, although engaged in a similar activity to the hard-boiled *noir* detective of story and film. *The Occupational Outlook Handbook*[3] reported that in 2019 there were 36,200 private detectives with a median salary of $53,320 per year. The expected growth of private detectives is about 8 percent per year. The modern private detective in most cases is required to have a license, time will be spent in an office researching financial and legal matters, or in the field pursuing personal matters, interviewing, or performing surveillance.

PRIVATE CORRECTIONS

Private corrections, or for-profit corrections, involves the contracting of services to private entities to perform tasks which, in most cases, are performed by government agencies. Privatization is controversial with strong arguments such as that they are cost-effective and operate more efficiently. A principal argument against them is that the practice is unethical, that punishment is a government function. Nevertheless, privatized corrections is a growth industry which, since the mid-1980s, has expanded the services it provides, specifically prisons (now managing approximately 10 percent of the national prison population), halfway houses, and reentry services. There are diverse employment opportunities available. Contracted services may be used for purposes of confinement (including architecture, building, and management), for community corrections, consultations, research, reform, therapeutic, medical, food services, and more. Some corporations, such as CoreCivic have been publicly traded since 1986. CoreCivic operates in 20 states. Employees have generous benefit packages including health, dental vision, life and disability insurance, retirement, and more. Visit Corecivic.com for a complete list of locations, benefits, and salaries (e.g., Correctional officer starts at $18.50 hr.). At the time of this writing, there were 447 job openings.

PRIVATE POLICE

There are distinctions, although there may be overlap, between private police and private security. Private police are regulated by the state in which they serve, are licensed, sworn law enforcement officers (sworn to uphold state laws) generally with limited jurisdiction and powers (in some cases, they may possess full police powers). There are also special police. The term special police may apply to police who report to a government agency or a nongovernment agency. The information, in this case, will refer to those hired by a nongovernment agency such as a private railroad. These officers are also sworn law enforcement, with duties such as the protection of property, employees, and patrons. There are opportunities for someone who is retired, plans to retire, or may offer off-duty employment.

PRIVATE SECURITY

Private security is an industry which provides many services including protecting institutions, colleges, communities, property, buildings and their contents, infrastructure, people, intellectual property, and much more which cannot be as effectively performed by public police. To be clear, when private security is employed, it places individuals, often with a supporting structure, on the spot for immediate attention to what requires protection. While definitions vary about what constitutes private security, other services include concierge and gate security. Private security is a solution to ensuring that companies and sensitive information are protected through pre-employment screening and investigations. Employees of private security may be uniformed or in plainclothes depending upon whether the work is part-time or full-time, the types of designated tasks, and the nature of the work such as patrol or undercover security. The median salary for a private security guard is $27,155.[4] Depending upon credentials and experience, private security contractors may earn more than $100,000. For example, a degree in public administration and experience in the public sector may qualify for upper level-positions. Some positions represent better opportunities for benefits than others. Generally, those positions which represent part of a corporate structure are more likely to have better benefits.

RISK MANAGEMENT

Risk management has been singled out because it involves private CJ positions and career opportunity. There are many titles associated with risk management including: Loss Control Manager or Representative, Risk Management Professional, Operations Risk Analyst, and Asset Protection Planner or Investigator. Risk Management involves many roles neglected in the literature and in course work. The Risk Manager seeks to understand and identify areas of possible negative outcomes (loss) within a business entity, a preventive measure intended to avert a management crisis. This can include security measures, loss prevention, mediation, and in some cases taking legal action. It includes synchronizing operational policy with regulatory requirements. Loss prevention is part of the responsibilities of a successful program of risk management. Many times, the risk management function includes mediation and/or trial participation. As an additional responsibility, it means maintaining best practices in the industry while conducting an ongoing operational risk assessment of the business units. The average salary for operations risk professionals is around $61,000–64,000. The possible actions for risk management include:

- Avoid the risk of total loss
- Reduce the probability of the risk occurring
- Reduce the impact of risk
- Transfer the risk
- Accept the risk[5]

JOB RESPONSIBILITY, EDUCATION, AND CREDENTIALING

Risk Management Professionals responsibilities include and are not limited to establishing and monitoring key risk indicators, implementing corrective action plans to mitigate risks with technical functions that include transactions analysis, internal reports preparation, and reviewing financial information for potential fraud. It is not uncommon to create policies, procedures, and control assessments in response to identified risks along with providing training and technical support to management and employees regarding risk management strategies and programs.[6]

There is information about careers, career paths, career development, training, resources, and exam information for certification available at https://www.acfe.com/career-center-main.aspx.

CERTIFICATIONS

Professional certifications for Risk Management Professionals include the Certified Fraud Examiner (CFE), Certified Risk Analyst (CRA), Certification in Risk Management Assurance (CRMA), Financial Risk Manager (FRM), and Professional Risk Manager (PRM).[7]

The job or career which is sought will, in part, be determined by educational credentials and certifications. Some titles of training and self-training provided by the Association of Certified Fraud Examiners include:

- Overcoming bias in investigations and fraud
- Protecting against emerging cyber risks
- Auditing for internal fraud
- Investigation on the internet
- Virtual CFE exam review course

A PROFILE OF A RISK MANAGEMENT PROFESSIONAL

Richard Halverson is a prime example of a career path in risk management. He is currently the Organized Retail Crime (ORC) Investigations Manager at Kroger, Greater Houston Area. He has a BA in Business Administration, degree from Michigan State University. His experience includes Assistant Special Agent in Charge, Homeland Security Investigations (HSI), Unit Chief; Global Outreach and Training, National IPR (Intellectual Property Rights) Coordination Center, HSI (Homeland Security Information), and visiting professor—College of International Security Affairs, and National Defense University. Halverson is in his second career after Homeland Security. At Kroger he is the lead for ORC investigations, operations, and training within the Houston division. He collaborates with division-wide asset protection teams to mitigate theft, criminal activity, and shrinkage at assigned stores and distribution centers. His experience at the federal government level enables him to facilitate relationships with federal, state, local law enforcement, prosecutors, and industry representatives to dismantle and disrupt criminal groups and their illicit activities.

LOWE'S ASSET PROTECTION AGENT8

The primary function of the Asset Protection Agent (APA) is to meet asset protection objectives, prevent inventory shrinkage, and deter criminal activity. This includes coaching/training of associates and store leadership to identify and deter external theft. The APA will coordinate efforts with the Senior Association of Certified Fraud Examiners (ACFE) and Advisory Panel on Substance Misuse (APOSM) to identify key merchandise and stores that are being externally impacted. Based on external and Organized Crime activity the APA will leverage data/resources to create a plan addressing exposure with training and external focuses to reduce theft activity. The APA is responsible for investigating and resolving issues related to criminal activity in accordance with local, state, and federal laws, and company policy. The APA (primarily focused on asset protection, operations, and safety policies/procedures) will monitor merchandise, customer, and associate activity as needed, reporting infractions to store and AP leadership. The APA will also support investigations of all company policies/procedures violations. An individual in this position may on occasion need to effectively respond to potentially violent and/or physical altercations and will therefore make quick, effective decisions and maintain an appropriate level of composure. The Asset Protection Agent is responsible for completing other duties as assigned.

Appendix A

Directory of Profiles in Criminal Justice

1. Len Black, Correctional Manager, State Use Industries
2. Heath "Hank" J. Brightman, EdD, Professor and Director, Applied Research and Analysis, War Gaming Department, U.S. Naval War College
3. Mary-Ann Conte, BA, MSW, DOC Corrections Social Worker
4. Ania Dobrzanska, MS, CCM, State Policy Advisor, Bureau of Justice Assistance (BJA)
5. Mark Ferrante, Consultant, American Institutes for Research
6. Kimberly McFadden Guadagno, JD, Sheriff, Lt. Governor, Corporate CEO, Connell Foley LLP Partner, Executive Director, Mercy Center
7. Robert Hood, MEd, Warden, ADX Florence (Supermax); Correctional/Criminal Justice Consultant
8. James F. Kenny, PhD, Federal Treasury Agent and Supervisor (Violence and Terrorism Prevention), Professor, Fairleigh Dickinson University
9. Roger Lichtman, Correctional Architect
10. Robert Louden, NYPD Lieutenant; Hostage Negotiator; Director of Criminal Justice, Georgian Court University
11. Bohdan Orichowsky, Juvenile Parole Officer
12. Joseph Paglino, Detective, Monmouth County Prosecutors Office; Professor
13. Raymond Rainville, PhD, Department of Criminal Justice, St. Peters University; New Jersey Probation Services
14. Ralph Rojas, Officer, Port Authority Police Department; Assistant Professor of Justice Studies
15. Brian L. Royster, EdD, New Jersey State Police Officer; Professor, St. Peters University
16. Darcella A. Patterson Sessomes, PhD, DSW, LCSW Assistant Commission NJ DOC
17. William Ussery, Police Officer, Professor, Clinical Psychologist, Clinical Psychologist

18. Len Ward, Parole Officer, Professor

The profiles in CJ are more important than ever for those seeking careers. Recent tragic events have cast doubt for many about whether a successful career in service is possible. Future CJ professionals are provided with positive role models who have had exemplary careers untarnished by ethical misconduct. They are a small sample of model professionals. These are personal stories of inspiration and for guidance of pathways through careers. A lesson which may be taken from the profiles is that a career may start along one path, but events, planning, education, and training can and will provide career trajectories which could not be foreseen. Transitions are part of the adventure, the unknown, the sense of achievement, and satisfaction that comes from a career. Each person discloses information about their careers in their own way. We asked for this so that the reader would have an opportunity to see each professional in their careers, with twists and turns, through each person's perspective on their experience.

Examine the career profiles for each individual's demonstration of the use of networking, career advancement, professionalism, education, collegiality, organizational change, association in professional organizations, accolades, and planning for and productively living in retirement. Each profile explores how these focal points contribute to satisfaction and fulfillment. May you find your inspiration from their successes.

LEN BLACK, CORRECTIONAL MANAGER, STATE USE INDUSTRIES

I came into the world of CJ by accident. I had never given it a thought. I met a gentleman who ran an organization in the Department of Corrections, and he suggested I get some business background and contact him afterward about joining his organization.

It happens that I did leave the field of social work and got some experience in the newspaper business. After about a year, I contacted the gentleman to see if there was still an opportunity available. There was, and he brought me in as an assistant buyer. The organization was the Bureau of State Use Industries within the NJ Department of Corrections. This organization operates the manufacturing shops in the state's correctional institutions.

Over the next few years, I worked my way up in the organization to become a buyer and eventually the assistant chief, chief, and director. During that time, I earned a certified public manager credential and obtained my master's in public administration from Rutgers University.

During my career, we opened new industries, moved into the services arena, and provided inmates with unique work opportunities. The most important thing I learned, and it's still applicable today, is that you need to play well in the sandbox. Nothing in any organization gets done without the help and support of others. If you alienate people, you won't go far (in my opinion).

It also helped that we changed our organizational structure to support the implementation of Enterprise Resource Planning software. With the assistance of a consultant, we changed our organizational structure and developed individual business units and a strategic plan with measurable results. You might ask, what does all this have to do with CJ? Well, it's all about life and managing within an organization. If you don't set measurable goals, you'll never achieve them. How can that help your stakeholders or customers? Whether it is in CJ or in rocket science, the core requirements for success remain the same.

During my career, I became active in many related professional organizations. First and foremost was the American Correctional Association (ACA) and the New Jersey Chapter of the American Correctional Association. Directly related to my job was another professional organization affiliated with the ACA, the National Correctional Industries Association (NCIA). I eventually became the President of the NCIA and would later serve as board chairman and the recipient of their highest honor, the Rodli Award. I also was a member of the Association of Government Accountants and the Trenton/Princeton/Monmouth Chapter of the American Production and Inventory Control Society (APICS). As you probably have determined, I feel very strongly that membership and participation in professional organizations can be and is very beneficial.

The decision to retire from my career with the State of New Jersey was not difficult. What I didn't do well was to plan what I was going to do when I reached Florida. Fortunately, due to many of the friendships and associations I'd made over the last thirty years or so, I had many opportunities. I decided to start my own consulting firm and provide consulting services to both government and businesses.

An opportunity arose that I could not refuse, and that was the chance to work with my wife, who is an instructional designer. So, I am reinventing myself and I'm applying things I've learned over my career to my new job as a senior consultant for Learn2Perform. I will be involved in strategic workforce planning and workforce analytics. I recently obtained my certification of strategic workforce planning through the Human Capital Institute.

I wanted to touch on some other areas. First, get all the supervisory experience and education that you can. As a matter of fact, get all the education you can, period—especially if it's free. Even if it's not free, get it! Second, join professional organizations. Take the time to make friends within these organizations and use them as a resource. Their experience can be very valuable to you.

HEATH "HANK" J. BRIGHTMAN, EDD, PROFESSOR AND DIRECTOR, APPLIED RESEARCH AND ANALYSIS, WAR GAMING DEPARTMENT, U.S. NAVAL WAR COLLEGE

As I look back over my twenty-five years of experience in the CJ arena, no one quotation more aptly describes where I have been and where I am traveling in my professional career that the following. "The first river you paddle runs through the rest of your life. It bubbles up in pools and eddies to remind you who you are."[1] This "bubbling up" began with my earliest opportunities as a law enforcement ranger and as a chief park ranger with the National Park Service, where I worked on a variety of environmental issues, predominately focused on illegal hazardous waste disposal activities and natural resource management improprieties.

Later, as the criminal research specialist for the Newark field office of the U.S. Secret Service and as the Department Chair and an Associate Professor of Criminal Justice at Saint Peter's University, my understanding of white-collar criminal investigation—particularly environmental fraud and money laundering, deepened into the darker, murkier pools and depths of exploring public corruption. Ultimately, this awareness of corruption control strategies and cultural challenges to ethical decision-making has become the cornerstone of my post-9/11 research for the U.S. Navy, the organization for whom I have worked in both a military and civilian capacity for the past twenty years.

If the CJ arena represents the overall environment, and white-collar criminal investigation, fraud, and corruption control depicts the river, tributaries, and inlets of my career thus far, education is definitely the paddle that has afforded me the opportunity to successfully navigate these waters.

Although now more than two decades into my career, I still find myself seeking out new opportunities for learning within the social sciences. I hold a doctorate, three master's degrees, and a bachelor's degree in fields as diverse as natural resource management, education, criminal justice administration, mental health counseling, and organizational leadership.

Even when equipped with the proper paddle, it would be nearly impossible to negotiate the turbulent waters of white-collar criminal investigation and corruption control without a boat crew equally adept at identifying these obstacles. Garnering the ability to read these challenging navigational charts is greatly aided by professional organizations such as the Association of Certified Fraud Examiners and the International Association of Law Enforcement Intelligence Analysts.

The river of CJ research and practice runs wide and deep and is best traversed by those who hone their coxswain's skills though discipline, repetition, and teamwork.

Lifelong learning, intellectual curiosity, and a commitment to serving others are critical to keeping the boat afloat, even in times of the most formidable turbidity.

MARY-ANN CONTE, BA, MSW, LCADC, ASSISTANT SOCIAL WORK SUPERVISOR

I often wonder how I ended up as a social worker with incarcerated individuals. My journey has led me to the most stressful yet rewarding job. When I graduated with my bachelor's degree, I was working as a cocktail waitress in Atlantic City, unsure of the direction I wanted my life to go.

I traveled around the world to Thailand, Spain, Belgium, Italy, Morocco, and the nations of Africa learning about other cultures, religions, beliefs, and history. I returned to college to pursue my master's degree with a different attitude. I wanted to change the world and if I could change one child's life, it would be worthwhile. I was a rare breed in my classrooms. Many students only worked part-time, but I had bills to pay and worked full-time. There were no other options.

During my graduate coursework, I had to intern at two different locations. My first internship placement was at a hospice. The hospice held an annual grief camp and I counseled children for a weekend at a local campground. I did grief counseling for families and clients during their greatest time of need. My clients began to die. I had become so close to the families and shared so many laughs that when I attended the funerals, not only was it depressing, but no longer would I see the family again. I felt that I had lost a friend, and I did not think I could handle a job with so much death and despair.

My second year of internship involved placement in a middle school. I was being supervised by a child study team, and I thought that working in a school system would be enjoyable. I facilitated a life skills group with special needs children who need a lot of attention. I looked forward to spending time with them every day. I realized I wanted to work with more challenging clients. I noticed the Juvenile Justice Commission was hiring social workers. I sent my résumé and interviewed for a job working with incarcerated youth at a residential community home in Trenton, New Jersey. I was hired soon realizing that this was the job I'd been searching for. I wanted to work with females. A position opened for a social worker at the female residential community program.

I had heard that working with the female population could be quite challenging. I was a little nervous, but I realized that females need a lot more attention and have gender-specific issues. I worked with the female population for ten years, and it was the most rewarding time of my life. Females have child custody concerns, molestation, sexual abuse, gang initiations, and problems that I had never imagined.

I am educated by them. Today's society is different from when I was a juvenile. Building trust is the most important piece of advice I can give to future correctional social workers. One must *always* tell the truth, even though those listening may not want to hear it—never "sugarcoat" anything. The females I counseled have committed crimes as serious as vehicular manslaughter and minor crimes of a violation of probation. Symptoms of PTSD have increased, as well as molestation. This is the struggle that social workers face. The females from the inner cities have witnessed crimes that no one should ever see in their lifetime—neighbors shot, domestic violence, drug dealers—all part of their daily lives. Most of them have become numb to violence—they are desensitized. You hope and pray that you can give them enough knowledge and coping skills to succeed in life and not become another statistic.

Some give birth and the families take care of the child while the juvenile completes her sentence. Young mothers miss out on the "first steps" and "first words." Building a bond with a child is important during the first year but cannot happen if the mother is incarcerated. My job ensured that the family visited regularly and to have community agencies assist with transportation.

I returned to college and became a Licensed Clinical Alcohol and Drug Counselor. I transferred to the Department of Corrections as an Assistant Social Work Supervisor to supervise social workers. The highlight of my job is facilitating groups in the institutions with the adult male population. I enjoy meeting new people and the men come from different backgrounds and have different life experiences. The men volunteer to be a member of the group, so they want to educate themselves and change their behaviors.

The most interesting thing about working with juveniles and adults is that the majority of incarcerated individuals have remorse for their crimes. The offender understands they made a wrong decision and needed to pay the consequence. Social work is difficult and challenging, but if you can change one life then you are successful—you change the individual, the family, and the community; you stop the cycle of incarceration.

ANIA DOBRZANSKA, MS, CCM, STATE POLICY ADVISOR, BUREAU OF JUSTICE ASSISTANCE, U.S. DEPARTMENT OF JUSTICE, WASHINGTON, DC

If you talk to a man in a language he understands, that goes to his head. If you talk to him in his language, that goes to his heart. I have always been interested in how people think, feel, and what life experiences drive them to a life of crime, as well as how they cope with incarceration, and life after. In my career, I followed my heart. Sometimes I bit off more than I could chew but I was driven to take on as much as I could to learn and grow. Today I love what I do. You can teach people skills, but not passion. You must let passion drive you. I believe that the key to my success has been my courage to find excellent mentors who believed in me, pushed me, guided me, and helped me grow. I never had a plan for my education or career, and just pursued what I love each step of the way. I will admit that I was lucky to never look for work in my career, because positions that were right for me were offered. I believe that my dedication to excel in school, taking on two majors with a minor, full-time job as a mental health counselor, and internship at the New Jersey Juvenile Justice Commission with Dr. Sheridan have paved my path to success.

My experience has been enriched by service in state, private, nonprofit, federal, and academic pursuits. Research has always been my driving force. I worked closely with corrections administrators, direct program staff, program managers, policy makers, professors, federal partners; and mental health professionals to assist individuals with complex needs; offenders; and those managed by criminal justice who are challenging and require a level of sensitivity (i.e., PREA). I learned about controversial criminal justice policy.

When I initially came to RU I started off as a food science major. Shortly after I realized I knew too much about food and did not want to analyze everything I ate. I took an elective course—Prisons and Prisoners—I felt like an anthropologist examining everything about prisons pixel by pixel. Professor Welch advised us one day to first go after what we love, and then go after money. That is exactly what I did, and I changed my major to Administration of Justice and Psychology. I decided I wanted to be a warden, however, this plan changed during my graduate studies. This was not my calling.

Dr. Sheridan delivered a guest lecture, and I immediately knew I had to work with him. He was the catalyst to my career with DOJ, for which I will be forever grateful. I gave him a call and convinced him to take me under his wing as an intern, and this was the best decision I have made for my career. He believed in me, mentored me, and pushed me. I vividly remember when he said that one day he wanted to sit down and pick up my published paper and read it because he wanted to and not because he had to. As a result, I produced a solid list of publications.

My publication portfolio includes several articles in *Corrections Today* on issues of professionalism in corrections and leadership. I am a co-author of a chapter on the history of prisons in *Prisons: Today and Tomorrow* (Pollock, 1997), a widely used text; and co-author of an article on the adjustment of life-sentence prisoners published in *Corrections Compendium*. I am also a published writer of fiction and a playwright. My short story, "Dances with Dragons: Memories of the Hole," appears in *The Crying Wall*, a book I co-edited. I served as a co-editor and a contributor of fourth edition of *Life Without Parole: Living in Prison Today*, released in March 2008.

Dr. Sheridan provided guidance on selecting my path for graduate studies, helping me align my passion with the right school. American University was the right match for me, and I couldn't be more grateful.

While at ACA, my supervisor recruited me to teach an online course at UMUC on *Juvenile Delinquency*. He was a former Commissioner of Corrections in Maryland and supported my plan to become a warden. This teaching position was a great experience because it made me realize that I do not want to pursue a career in teaching. When I was offered to stay and teach another course, I politely declined to pursue my career outside of academia.

At AU, Professor Robert Johnson took me under his wing, and we began a study of inmates coping with incarceration. I continued to publish, and he next recruited to me work with him on capital cases. Upon graduation I was accepted into the PhD program. However, I decided to take the year off to continue to work and decide if the doctorate was the right path. I loved research but I knew I was not interested in teaching.

While at AU, I also accepted a part-time position with the American Constitution Society for Law and Policy. I conducted research on legal and policy dimensions of communities in which ACS national lawyer chapters were planned. I analyzed information collected with the president of the organization as well as the legal community on the legal issues for research. I realized I did not want to pursue a career in criminal law.

After graduating with my MA, I accepted a position with the Moss Group, Inc. who had entered into a cooperative agreement with the National Institute of Corrections to implement the Prison Rape Elimination Act (PREA). In addition to the research, I assisted in design and administration of national training programs, prepared program management guidelines, and wrote a manual to provide regulations to the team of consultants on the management of the complex programs undertaken by The Moss Group, Inc.

While at The Moss Group, I was persuaded to apply for a position with DOJ. My employer, who also mentored me, pushed me to apply for the position. I was hired in 2007 to work for the Bureau of Justice Assistance to conduct research, perform program reviews, scan the field for emerging issues, advise on legislative initiatives, and much more.

My workload is intense, and my success is evident from high review rankings, timely production of high-quality work, and positive relationships with the field and co-workers. My key to success continues to be my passion for what I do. I believe it is imperative to pursue what you love in order to be successful.

Editor's Commentary

Ania Dobrzanska provides a prime example of the twists and turns from undergraduate to graduate student, while taking advantage of opportunities as they are presented, performing self-assessment, and making informed career choices. Career paths are seldom a straight line and aspirations will change. Who would have thought that a beginning in the study of food science would evolve into a career of diverse experiences which includes conducting research and obtaining a position within the Bureau of Justice Assistance. She is recognized for her contributions to criminal justice with 13 peer-reviewed publications, chapters, and other contributions to several academic books, an editor for a convict's autobiography, co-author of works of drama, co-editor and contributor to three works of fiction and two works of poetry. She has won awards such as the Commander-in-Chief's Coin of Excellence and Plaque of Appreciation, Military Order of World Wars, 2005 and the Tacenda Literary Award, Best Short Story for 2006. Ania Dobrzanska is a role model of career identification fostered by internships, progression under the guidance of mentors, and success built on hard work. Her accomplishments and achievements can be described as journey culminating in personal fulfillment.

MARK FERRANTE, CONSULTANT, AMERICAN INSTITUTES FOR RESEARCH

Although I did not study CJ or plan to go into this line of work, I was hired as a budget analyst for Mercer County, Trenton, New Jersey, shortly after graduating from Rider College with a degree in business. Soon after joining local government, I was asked to manage federal funding for the county's Human Services Advisory Council. It was not until at least five years later that I embarked on a career in the juvenile and CJ fields when I was given the opportunity to become the Assistant Youth Services Commission (YSC) Coordinator in Mercer County. A few years later, I became the YSC Coordinator and went on to serve as the Co-Chair of the statewide organization of County Youth Services Administrators in the late 1990s.

In 2000, I left local government to join the state's recently created Juvenile Justice Commission as the Assistant Director for Program Development and Prevention Services. In that capacity, I also served as the State's Juvenile Justice Specialist, managing over $4 million in federal formula and discretionary funding. This role entirely changed my perspective as it allowed me to meet leaders from across the country who were working to reform the juvenile justice system and to bring many of those initiatives back to New Jersey.

One such model was the Annie E. Casey's Juvenile Detention Alternatives Initiative (JDAI). In 2004, JDAI was launched in New Jersey in five pilot sites. New Jersey would later go on to become the first model state, bringing to scale the reforms created at the local level. Working alongside the gubernatorially appointed Juvenile Justice Delinquency Prevention (JJDP) Committee, I helped bring additional best practices to New Jersey's juvenile justice system. I also had the privilege of serving as the National Juvenile Justice Specialist from 2005–2007.

In 2007, I left state government and moved to DC to join a national nonprofit serving State Advisory Groups (SAGs) for juvenile justice. My role was to direct national and regional training efforts and to develop leadership within the SAGs.

After nearly four years of hosting conferences and trainings with some of the smartest and most dedicated professionals in any field, I left DC to move to New York City to join the NYC Department of Probation as the Commissioner's Senior Policy Advisor. Here I was able to spearhead both juvenile and adult probation reforms centered on evidence-based practices and principles and lead an inter-agency task force on bringing youth sentenced to out-of-home placements closer to their families and communities.

A few years later (following a change in administration in city government) I had the opportunity to join another national nonprofit, the Council of State Governments Justice Center, where I had the pleasure of providing technical assistance to states working to improve reentry policies and practices and to support county and state-level probation reform work. It was during this time that I was able to serve as co-facilitator, panelist, or keynote speaker at several national conferences, something I deeply enjoy.

A few plot twists later, I began the shift to consulting work, first leading a project to update performance measurement tools for federal grantees.

I currently serve as a Technical Assistance Consultant under two cooperative agreements within the Department of Justice's Office of Justice Programs: The National Reentry Resource Center/Corrections and Community Engagement Technical Assistance Center (NRRC/CCETAC) and the Center for Coordinated Assistance to States (CCAS).

KIMBERLY M. GUADAGNO, JD, SHERIFF, LT. GOVERNOR NEW JERSEY, CORPORATE CEO, CONNELL FOLEY LLP PARTNER, EXECUTIVE DIRECTOR, MERCY CENTER

Kimberly M. Guadagno is an exemplary role model for those interested in the legal profession. Guadagno earned her law degree at American University, Washington College of Law, and graduated cum laude. She has had a distinguished career in both public and private service highlighted by her groundbreaking roles as the first female sheriff in Monmouth County, first Lt. Governor, and first female Secretary of State for New Jersey. She has been the President and Chief Executive Officer of FulFill, the Foodbank for Monmouth and Ocean County. She is a partner in the law firm of Connell Foley LLP, specializing in economic development, white collar investigations, and litigation, and the Executive Director, Mercy Center.

Guadagno began a career in public service as a federal prosecutor with the Organized Crime and Racketeering Strike Force in Brooklyn, New York. She later became an Assistant United States Attorney for the Eastern District of New York and the District of New Jersey, where she was twice awarded the U.S. Department of Justice's highest honor for her prosecutions. She served 10 years with the United States District Attorney's Office and rose to the position of Assistant U.S. Attorney and Deputy Chief of the Corruption Unit.

Following her years of federal service, she became a senior member of the State of New Jersey Attorney General's Office where she oversaw statewide criminal investigations. In 2001, Guadagno left the public sector to work in private practice and taught Legal Research and Writing at Rutgers School of Law in Newark for six years. In 2005, she was elected Commissioner in her hometown of Monmouth Beach, New Jersey, and two years later, Guadagno became the first woman sheriff in Monmouth County where she led the 650-member, $65 million law enforcement agency until inaugurated New Jersey's first Lieutenant Governor. Guadagno has returned to her law practice as a partner with the law firm of Connell Foley LLP.

As President and Chief Executive Officer of FulFill, the Foodbank for Monmouth and Ocean County for two years, Guadagno lead the organization during the most challenging years of the pandemic. The demand for food was greater and Fulfill served 3.5 million more meals than the year before the pandemic. It awarded more than $2 million to food pantries and feeding agencies impacted by COVID-19. The restaurant program served half a million meals while participating restaurants were supported during this difficult time. A partnership served more than 20,000 meals through a collaboration with local hospitals. The food bank was facing a $1.5 million budget gap when

Guadagno began as CEO. Under Guadagno's tenure, the organization closed the $1.5 million budget gap, installed solar panels, assumed management of The People's Pantry at the B.E.A.T. Center in Toms River, and had sponsors donate services and materials to expand Fulfill's service driveway and lot for delivery vehicles. That came while Fulfill saw upward of a 50 percent spike in need, and food costs increased 200 percent because of COVID-19. Under Guadagno, contributions jumped from $22.6 million in 2019 to $32.6 million in 2020, according to Fulfill's most recent tax filing.

ROBERT HOOD, MED, WARDEN, ADX; CORRECTIONAL/CRIMINAL JUSTICE CONSULTANT

Bob Hood is a nationally recognized correctional professional with over 36 years in local, state, and federal CJ experience. He retired from the Federal Bureau of Prisons (BOP) as the warden of the nation's most secure institution—the U.S. Administrative "Supermax" Penitentiary in Colorado. He was responsible for the most violent, disruptive, and escape-prone inmates in federal custody.

Mr. Hood's career started as a correctional educator (teacher) after completing an internship within the New Jersey prison system. He found work with student offenders rewarding on many levels. Since almost 97 percent of his students would eventually be released to the community, it was satisfying to assist with their individual reentry needs.

His career advancement required additional academic and work experiences. He received a MEd in special education with a concentration in CJ studies. At work, he volunteered for many activities and signed up for training whenever available.

Advancement within the field of corrections required mobility. After working for the New Jersey prison system, he relocated to teach within the Texas prison school district. Eventually he moved again to join the Federal Bureau of Prisons (BOP)—again as a correctional educator. As relocations occurred, he taught CJ studies at local colleges and universities.

During Mr. Hood's tenure with the BOP, he was the warden of three major correctional institutions, the chief of Internal Affairs, and the assistant director of the Federal Law Enforcement Training Center (FLETC).

Security magazine identified Mr. Hood as one of the "Top 25 Most Influential People in the Security Industry," and CBS aired a *60 Minutes* special on his ability to effectively manage the most secured prison in America.

Now retired from the BOP, Mr. Hood continues to consult on correctional matters. He serves on advisory boards to several companies and CJ colleges.

Mr. Hood is an active member of the American Correctional Association, the North American Association of Wardens and Superintendents, and the International Association of Corrections and Prisons. He sees great value in membership to professional organizations and consistently attends their annual conferences.

As Mr. Hood reflects on his career, the most important aspect he recalls is working with other people. Once he prepared for a career in corrections, work became more than a job—it was a rewarding lifestyle.

JAMES F. KENNY, PHD; FEDERAL TREASURY AGENT; PROFESSOR, FAIRLEIGH DICKINSON UNIVERSITY (FDU)

After graduating from college (with history and political science majors) in 1978, I decided to continue my graduate education (with an MA in social studies and political science and a PhD in CJ) part-time at night while working full-time during the day.

I began my professional career in insurance management and as a Congressional aide. In early 1981 I accepted a position as a U.S. treasury officer, and later assumed several management positions (as a supervisory U.S. treasury officer, a training group manager, the chief of review, the chief of advisory, the district director's representative, and the district quality officer).

While my official posts of duty were located in New Jersey, the Agency sent me to complete short-term assignments in Washington, DC, Texas, Massachusetts, Rhode Island, New York, Pennsylvania, and Connecticut.

My career at the treasury department prepared me for a successful career in academia. My law enforcement experience provided real-life illustrations for teaching CJ courses. Being trained as a federal instructor and encouraged to develop programs in workplace violence and threat assessment provided skill sets for future classroom and professional training.

In addition to working full-time with the government, I began to teach college courses (Criminal Justice, Criminology, White-Collar Crime, Western Civilization) part-time, and conduct professional seminars/webinars on school/workplace violence, threat assessment/reduction, and bullying in schools (high/middle/elementary), other federal agencies, the NJ Department of Education, and private companies and associations. One of my most challenging assignments was working with the Virginia Tech faculty, students, administrators, and community after their shooting tragedy.

Since 1999 I taught CJ courses at FDU. I attained the rank of full professor and received the Distinguished Faculty and Outstanding Teacher Awards. I serve as both the graduate and internship coordinator for the CJ Department.

I started and chaired the threat assessment team at FDU for 10-years. I am the author of *Hiding in Plain Sight: Deceptive Tactics and the Criminal Victimization Process*.

ROGER LICHTMAN, CORRECTIONAL ARCHITECT

As a young architect, I knew I wanted to work on large projects with a social impact. In other words, I did not want to design homes or shopping centers for wealthy people, but rather I wanted to provide the tools to improve a social infrastructure. This basically left two avenues for my pursuit: health care and CJ. Early in my career, I was presented with the opportunity to develop justice projects exclusively, and I have since been working with clients to envision their dreams in jails, courthouses, juvenile facilities, and prisons. I have never looked back. I have over thirty years' experience with CJ architecture, and I have experienced all aspects of CJ design. This includes architectural programming, needs assessment, studies, site selection analysis, master planning, security design, construction administration and documentation for new construction and for renovation and rehabilitation projects.

I have had the opportunity to work all over the United States on a variety of justice projects. Additionally, our firm was hired by the commonwealth of the Northern Mariana Islands to develop a comprehensive CJ master plan that included a jail, a juvenile facility, and an immigration facility, and renovation to the holding facilities on the more remote islands. The project lasted over six years.

Today's CJ student would be advised to keep an open mind to new opportunities. One of the more successful avenues to accomplish this is through membership in professional organizations. In that manner one can work with colleagues for the betterment of the field. It also presents an opportunity to present a sounding board for new ideas.

ROBERT LOUDEN, NYPD LIEUTENANT; HOSTAGE NEGOTIATOR; DIRECTOR OF CRIMINAL JUSTICE, GEORGIAN COURT UNIVERSITY

On June 20, 1966, an almost-college graduate—with one course left in a bachelor's degree in business, which was completed the following summer—entered the NYPD Police Academy as a rookie cop, a probationary patrolman. He did not know or care that nationwide only approximately 3 percent of policemen and-women had completed college. On July 1, 1966, he and his approximately 1,000 classmates hit the streets. Entry-level NYC-mandated training would occur irregularly until February 1967. Their mission was to assist the department and the city to counter urban unrest, and the riots that were plentiful throughout the country that summer. Eight, ten, and twelve-hour tours of duty in the inner city were not uncommon. Sometime after completion of my BBA from Baruch College/City University of New York (CUNY) in 1967, I was contacted by the Police Academy and encouraged to apply to law school or graduate school. I declined the law school suggestion, but I began the applicant process for graduate school.

A few years earlier in 1964, CUNY had created a new college, John Jay College of Criminal Justice, which I entered in the fall of 1969 in pursuit of an MA in Criminal Justice. Thanks in large part to the U.S. government, based on recommendations contained in the 1967 *Challenge of Crime in a Free Society*, cops such as I were able to attend college or graduate school with our tuition paid by the Law Enforcement Education Program (LEEP) of the Law Enforcement Assistance Administration (LEAA). I earned my degree in 1977. In the interim, I was detailed to a headquarters staff position (house mouse), largely because I had a college degree; I was promoted to sergeant (1971) and moved back to patrol duty, this time in Greenwich Village; and subsequently transferred to the Detective Bureau and charged with monitoring confidential investigation funds, including informant payments, because I had earned a business degree.

I remained in the NYPD Detective Bureau through two more promotions, to lieutenant (1980), and then to commander of the detective squad (1983), for another 10 years, eventually retiring in 1987.

Although I may not be able to directly link my relative success in policing and later in academia, I still value and endorse college education for police officers for a variety of reasons, including the ability to acquire new knowledge, skills, and abilities that can be applied not only on the job, but also in the other real worlds that one inhabits. I also found that following the classroom-related routines of reading, writing, and engaging in critical thinking helped me to prepare for and pass the civil service promotion examinations. Good police departments and good colleges are, as they should be, value-based institutions. The potential synergy between the two provides for a better society.

In some ways, I look at the collegiate experience as having made a trip through Oz! Through it, we can enhance what is already in our heads, unlock parts of our personalities, and strengthen our resolve to do the best we can.

BOHDAN ORICHOWSKY, JUVENILE PAROLE OFFICER

Bohdan Orichowsky is an excellent example of someone who has worked in various capacities in and around the CJ field. Bo served four years in the United States Marine Corps and holds a BA in psychology and an MA in counseling. He has worked in the CJ profession for more than 23 years.

Bo began employment in the adult mental health field, moved to after-school programs and developed an after-school program for emotionally disturbed children in Camden County, New Jersey.

His career began as a social worker in the adult prison system, first working in the general population and shortly thereafter in the administrative segregation unit (the lockdown unit). After about two years, massive layoffs occurred, and he transferred to the juvenile division, assigned to what is referred to as a "special needs" program. The program is an off-grounds residential program for incarcerated juveniles deemed to have psychological issues, thus requiring more specialized treatment than is offered in the juvenile jail.

He worked as a social worker in juvenile residential services for eight years and served as a parole officer for 15 years—a capacity in which he believes he better served troubled youth.

After several years, he became disenchanted with his career choice and decided to try another career. After a few unrewarding jobs, he returned to the field of social work, and through a friend, was referred to a position with the State of New Jersey.

One of his responsibilities was case planning—setting up after-care services for the juveniles prior to their release back home, specifically mental health and counseling services, and when applicable, assisting in enrolling them back in school, as a majority of those returning to school were classified as "special education students."

Later in his career as a social worker, the state created the Juvenile Justice Commission, which in part included juvenile parole. He took an interest in parole and found that juvenile parole was more involved in dealing with the young men than adult parole. For example, when juveniles are released, they are seen on a weekly basis for at least two to three months or longer before being considered for less contact. He found that case planning as a social worker was being utilized in parole, and that parole officers were more involved in making sure that the juveniles were participating in mandated counseling services. He believed that there was more good working with the young men in the community rather than in the program. The young men all had great ideals that they claimed they wanted to achieve upon release. Bo knew all too well that without a strong presence to guide and encourage them on the outside, their enthusiasm would quickly lose out to the lure of the streets that had gotten them into trouble in the first place.

Bo was accepted for the Juvenile Parole Officer Program and successfully completed the training program and a probationary period as a parole officer. He was assigned to work in various counties, and usually worked alone in some of the major cities in New Jersey.

Bo came to Parole without any high expectations of having his parolees be successful. Experience had taught him that not all juveniles were determined to do well in life. However, there were those who did strive to do better. Some were able to turn their lives around. A few examples included one who became a truck driver, another who became a certified underwater welder, and others who went into vo-tech schools, the business field, and even college.

Bo's attitude toward parolees is that he would work toward ensuring that conditions of parole were met and to help all under his supervision. For those who wanted the help and sought improvement for the quality of their lives, he did all that was possible to assist them in working toward their goals.

JOSEPH PAGLINO, DETECTIVE, MONMOUTH COUNTY PROSECUTORS OFFICE; PROFESSOR

Joseph R. Paglino was born and raised in Brooklyn, New York. After obtaining his Bachelor of Science degree in CJ from Saint John's University, New York and obtained the position of confidential investigator for the Office of the Chief Medical Examiner in New York City. As part of this assignment, Joseph was tasked with the investigation of homicide crime scenes in all five boroughs of New York.

Joseph subsequently advanced in the field of law enforcement securing the position of detective for the Brooklyn District Attorney's Office in Brooklyn, New York. While there, he was assigned to the Major Offense/Career Criminal Unit, the Transit Crime Bureau, the Auto Crime Unit, the Supreme Court Bureau, and the Night Fugitive Strike Force.

Upon relocating to New Jersey, Joseph achieved the position of detective with the Monmouth County Prosecutors Office in Freehold, New Jersey. Joseph served in the White Collar Crime Unit, the Child Abuse/Sex Crimes Unit, and the Bureau of Technical and Forensic Services. In that capacity, he personally investigated a multitude of homicide, suicide, suspicious death scenes, kidnappings, robberies, burglaries, participated in undercover "sting" operations involving stolen property, and internet crimes against children. He earned the President's Award for outstanding police service in 1992 and 2001.

His professional affiliations include the International Association for Identification, the Fingerprint Society (United Kingdom), and the American Translator's Association.

An instructor, Joseph has taught courses in fingerprints, photography, crime scene investigation, and Spanish at police academies, colleges, and universities. He is an adjunct professor of psychology and CJ at local universities. Scholastically, Joseph is the recipient of a master's degree in forensic psychology and is currently pursuing a PhD in CJ.

Additionally, Joseph is a published author, collaborating with his partner, Mauro Corvasce, in the works *Modus Operandi*, a writer's guide to how criminals work, and *Murder One*, a writer's guide to homicide, both published by Writer's Digest Books.

Joseph has appeared in numerous media outlets, such as television and in print. Additionally, he has worked as an advisor to the Discovery Channel in the production of a mystery CD-ROM.

RAYMOND RAINVILLE, DEPARTMENT OF CRIMINAL JUSTICE, SAINT PETERS UNIVERSITY; NEW JERSEY PROBATION SERVICES

Moving to New Jersey as a 13-year-old, I entered an exciting cosmopolitan environment. After finishing high school, I moved on to college with the desire to be a high school history teacher. When I graduated from Monmouth University in 1966, I discovered, much to my dismay, that there was no real need for history teachers. I did what many young people in Monmouth County do: I hopped on a bus to New York and found a job in the commercial credit industry. In early 1968, I was summoned to jury duty. One day during the lunch hour, I accompanied a college friend (who was unhappy in his employment) to the county personnel department. The county personnel director asked if I wanted to fill out an application. I asked what jobs he had open, and he asked whether I had a degree and in what area. After I told him my degree was in history, he asked if I wanted to be a probation officer. I said "no," that I didn't want to chase kids around. He said that I would be a counselor to kids with problems. After the interview, I finally agreed and entered my life's journey of probation services.

During my seven years with the Monmouth County Probation Department, I did everything: adult and juvenile, supervision and investigation and family services. I soon became the department's training officer and the representative to several county social agencies. As the department grew bigger and began to diversify, I specialized in handing juvenile cases, which had been my original goal. Later I was given the opportunity to organize the Volunteers in Probation program.

With my training background, I was offered a position with the Administrative Office of the Courts, Probation Division, as the assistant chief of probation training. My boss was temporarily reassigned to be the head of a probation department and I became the acting chief of probation training, soon-to-be chief of probation training. During my time in training, I reorganized the program and built a truly comprehensive training unit. Since I was working with professionals in the field, I decided to further my education and was accepted to the doctoral program at Fordham University. During this period, I served as chief probation officer of Union County, NJ, a large urban-suburban probation department. During my tenure at Union, the department won three national awards for new and progressive programs (the first job bank for offenders in New Jersey, specialized caseloads for alcoholics and substance abusers, and the Union County Volunteers in Probation program).

I returned to the Administrative Office of the Courts with the goal of using my new field experience to revive the training program. I was approached to take over as the director of the state's Child Support Enforcement Program. I first declined, because I wanted to work on the training program; I reluctantly agreed to cover the position for six months. Six months began a span of twenty years in child support enforcement. After receiving my doctorate in sociology/CJ, I began to teach at the university level, which led to my next career in teaching CJ.

After retiring in 2001, I decided to put my education and experience to work. I taught at the College of New Jersey and Brookdale Community College, and I joined the faculty at Saint Peter's University. In 2008 I became the chair of the CJ Department.

RALPH ROJAS, OFFICER, PORT AUTHORITY POLICE DEPARTMENT; ASSISTANT PROFESSOR OF JUSTICE STUDIES

Ralph Rojas Jr. is the Assistant Professor of Justice Studies at Southern New Hampshire University. Professor Rojas holds an MPA (Master's in Public Administration in Administration of Justice) and an MS (in criminology) from Long Island University, New York and an AB (sociology) degree from Fordham University, New York. He is presently writing his dissertation on police drug abuse at the University of Baltimore, Maryland.

Professor Rojas has over thirty years of CJ experience—including teaching, administrative, managerial, and consulting roles in higher education and posts in law enforcement, corrections, prosecution, and criminal courts.

He has held several educational positions in teaching, course development, program modification, and program development in the fields of police, corrections, and forensic science at colleges and universities in New Jersey, New Mexico, and Colorado.

Professor Rojas retired after a distinguished 20-year career with the Port Authority of New York and the New Jersey Police Department. Earlier, he worked for the New York State Department of Correctional Services and the Brooklyn District Attorney's Office in New York City.

Professor Rojas is a member of the Academy of Criminal Justice Sciences (ACJS), certified CJ program reviewer; the American Society of Criminology (ASC); the New Jersey Association of Chiefs of Police (NJACOP); the New Jersey Association of Criminal Justice Educators (NJACJE), where he was a past president; the New Jersey Association of Forensic Scientists (NJAFS); the founder and past president of the Colorado Association of Criminal Justice Educators (CACJE); the founder and president of the New Hampshire Association of Criminal Justice Educators, the Northeastern Association of Criminal Justice Sciences (NEACJS), where he has held numerous executive board positions, including as the delegate for New Jersey and presently the second vice president; and the Southwest Association of Criminal Justice (SWACJ), where he was the October 2008 Denver Annual Conference site coordinator.

BRIAN L. ROYSTER, EDD, NEW JERSEY STATE POLICE OFFICER; PROFESSOR

In the beginning of 1985, I was uncertain about my future. During this time frame, I had already joined the U.S. Army Reserves, but I didn't want to be a full-time soldier. I had no idea what I wanted to do in life. By happenstance, a friend walked in and I noticed that he had lost a significant amount of weight. He was a former Newark, New Jersey special police officer. I inquired about his sudden svelte appearance. He told me he was in the New Jersey State Police Academy. At the time, I was not aware of this agency. He said a test was being given and suggested that I take it. My expectation of passing the test was not high, because I had never taken my education very seriously. I subsequently passed with a score of 61 out of 100. I later learned that I was accepted under an affirmative action policy, which made me feel like a "special case." Back then I didn't realize the importance of this policy, but I vowed never to feel like that again.

I entered the NJSP Academy in the fall of 1985 and graduated 26 weeks later, in January 1986. The academy was rewarding because it gave me the mental and physical discipline that I needed at that time in my life.

My first assignment was working at Hope Station in Warren County, New Jersey. It was an eye-opener for me because I had never been in that part of the state. As my career progressed, I ultimately became a detective after serving seven and a half years in the state police uniform. My duties changed; a detective must take numerous investigative courses before conducting investigations. The detective functions require an analytical mind-set because you're always trying to figure out a criminal's next step.

Over the course of my career, I had the pleasure of being assigned to some of the most prestigious units. A few that stand out include Central Security, EEO/AA, Electronic Surveillance, Solid Hazardous Waste, Organized Crime North, and Counterterrorism, but the one that was most rewarding was being a part of the FBI Joint Terrorism Task Force (JTTF).

The JTTF is comprised of officials from federal, state, county, and local agencies. The task force's function is to investigate cases involving potential acts of terrorism. Non-FBI members on the JTTF are sworn in as U.S. Deputy Marshals and are afforded powers to travel within the 48 contiguous states and outside of the U.S. to effectuate arrests. Everyone on the JTTF is required to have a top-secret national security clearance and CIA security clearance. My inclusion on the JTTF allowed me to assist in the tragic 9/11 investigation. This assignment was by far the most satisfying of my career because I saw firsthand how agencies could put aside any internal conflicts and work collectively to solve the most heinous crime the U.S. has ever witnessed. It was while on the JTTF that I received my first non-commissioned promotion to detective sergeant.

In retrospect, my entrance into the NJSP set the stage for upward mobility. I realized, early in my career, that education would set me apart from my contemporaries. Beginning in 1987, I attended community college to further my education. I couldn't sit back and watch others advance and not be a part of the process. My insecurity from believing that I was a "special case" in being accepted into the NJSP was the impetus for me to seek out my advanced degrees.

During my 25-year career, I have attained two associate degrees from Essex County College, a bachelor's degree from Montclair State University, a master's degree from Seton Hall University, a master's degree from New Jersey City University, a post-master's degree and a doctoral degree from Seton Hall University. It took approximately 22 years of going to school on a part-time basis while working full-time in the NJSP, but it was worth it. In addition, I attended the FBI National Academy, considered the most prestigious training for law enforcement. I firmly believe that education is important because it shows dedication, which should be a requirement for all future leaders.

My goal, after retiring from law enforcement, was to teach prospective police officers about the good and bad aspects of law enforcement and allow them to be more informed. When I subsequently retired in 2012, I obtained a full-time faculty position at Saint Peter's University. This position has afforded me the opportunity to join outside CJ educators' associations and network with my colleagues.

Professor Royster is the author of *Conflicted Journey of a New Jersey State Trooper* and the co-author of *Historical Dictionary of Criminal Justice.*

DARCELLA A. PATTERSON SESSOMS, PHD, DSW, LCSW

The letters following Dr. Sessoms's name say a lot about the person and indicate a personal drive to achieve. However, they do not inform us of her journey from a humble beginning on the periphery of a CJ career to one of steady advancement to a position of distinction as the Assistant Commissioner of Corrections for the state of New Jersey. Dr. Sessoms has successfully managed a career with community service as a volunteer, a worker for youth, and a citizen dedicated to contributing to social causes.

Darcella Anita Patterson Sessoms is a well-known leader in correctional social work education, policy, and professional practice. September 2004, she assumed the position of Assistant Director for the Office of Transitional Services with the New Jersey Department of Corrections. May 2007, she was promoted to the position of director. After having served almost ten years in state government, April 2014, she was promoted to the rank of Assistant Commissioner.

Assistant Commissioner Sessoms manages the Division of Program and Community Services, which is responsible for the following prison system services: social work, education, religious services, victim services, volunteer services, residential community reentry programs, the intensive supervision program (ISP), and county services.

Her career in social work spans over twenty years. During the past two decades, Darcella has worked in various arenas of social work policy and practice, which include but are not limited to domestic violence, HIV/AIDS, addiction, homelessness, juveniles, and incarceration. She is a licensed clinical social worker (LCSW) with the states of New Jersey and Pennsylvania.

Dr. Sessoms is certified as a student in field instruction supervisor, and she is responsible for the oversight of the field placement experience for many social work students in the tristate area who are interested in a career in forensic social work with a specific concentration on reentry and corrections. Dr. Sessoms also serves as a part-time lecturer for Rutgers University, the

Department of Social Work, where she teaches coursework on Diversity and Oppression. Additionally, she serves as a part-time lecturer for the University of Pennsylvania, where she teaches American Racism and Social Change and has served as a teaching assistant for the course Criminal Justice Issues: Implications for Social Work.

Dr. Sessoms received both a Bachelor of Arts in sociology and a master's degree in social work from Rutgers University, New Brunswick campus. She received her doctorate from the University of Pennsylvania, School of Social Policy and Practice. Dr. Sessoms credits her success to her faith, her loving family, and the strong mentors in her life.

WILLIAM USSERY, POLICE OFFICER; PROFESSOR; CLINICAL PSYCHOLOGIST

I joined the force in 1969 during the Newark riots. A good friend asked, "Why would you join a police department? You are smarter than that." My response was a phrase from Ben Franklin: "It seems that everyone is talking about the weather, but no one is doing anything about it." I was raised in an autocratic household, flunked out of military school, and spent four years with the USMC. These experiences confirmed that I could follow orders in a military environment, and I truly believed that I needed to contribute this background to a police career.

Finding a job was fairly easy; everyone was hiring. One department could not get my fingerprints because of my labor as a mason's helper. (They told me to use Jergen's lotion for a few weeks!) Another department had an entrance application that was so long and involved that my ADHD personality could not finish it. I was exempt from the NJSP at that time because I wore glasses. A mentor from the state police told me that I could get a job anywhere else, but *not* in my hometown. Well, the application was only two pages long and I didn't listen.

Highlights are difficult to recall. I was promoted to lieutenant after a relatively short time in Patrol and jumped over all sergeants. I credit this to almost completing my Associate's Degree in Police Science.

A specialty of mine was investigating fatal motor vehicle collisions. I attended most if not all of the post-autopsies performed in our community. In fact, one highlight was a DWI conviction that had been corrupted by several breathalyzer readings and a blood test at the ER. Due to my contacts in the pathology unit at the hospital, a doctor described a chart that indicated that the readings (venular, as well as arterial) had fallen within an acceptable variance. This case was a MV collision that involved several fatalities.

My decision to take an early retirement was available due to military time served, and I saw opportunities to use my talents in other venues. I believed that being 52 years of age was more marketable than being 55.

William J. Ussery, MA, LPC, has been a counselor since 1984. He received a MA in psychology from Fairleigh Dickinson University and a license in 1999. He has been employed by the COP2COP program at UMDNJ/UBHC since September 2000 as a Mental Health Clinician II with duties that include answering a helpline for law enforcement officers with mental health and substance abuse needs. These calls require assessments, referrals, peer counseling, and often a response to his specialty, critical incident stress debriefing.

Mr. Ussery has been trained in all levels of Critical Incident Stress Management (CISM) and he has been involved in crisis response since forming the Apollo team in 1984. Mr. Ussery was also certified to train peer counselors for CISM and QPR, a suicide prevention strategy. He has over 25 years' experience as a clinician, specializing in anxiety, trauma, and stress disorders. He was appointed an Associate Professor at the College of Saint Elizabeth, where he taught crisis intervention courses. Currently, he teaches crisis intervention to master's level students at Fairleigh Dickinson University.

LEN WARD, PAROLE OFFICER; PROFESSOR

Lenny Ward served as the Director of the Divisions of Parole and Community Programs for the New Jersey State Parole Board (NJSPB). As director, he oversees almost four hundred law enforcement officers and command staff within the Division of Parole, and he manages over $37 million in contracted services that provide direct support to the over 15,000 parolees under supervision in New Jersey.

Lenny entered state service in 1990 and has served in multiple capacities within the Department of Law and Public Safety, the Department of Transportation, and the Department of Corrections.

Lenny graduated from Jersey City State College in 1973 with a BA, attended Brooklyn Law School, and received a master's degree in Public Administration from Fairleigh Dickinson University in 1997. He is certified as an instructor by the New Jersey Police Training Commission, is certified by the U.S. Department of Justice in community-oriented policing and is an adjunct professor at Fairleigh Dickinson University.

Appendix B

Interest, Inquiry, and Cover Letters

Good communication is a key to success. Written communication provides the reviewer with the idea that you are a competent applicant and serious about the position. Many young people are accustomed to communicating by e-mail. This can be a fatal mistake when applying for a position. Many people see e-mail as a temporary message; often e-mail is not copied or filed. Once read, most individuals tend to ignore e-mails. A good written letter is usually read, filed, and attached to the appropriate file. Letters, or written correspondence, as attachments, are a good practice.

Note: The letter must make your point. However, you must also keep your letter short enough to ensure that your recipient will read it. The letter should be no more than two pages long. Here are some steps to follow:

First, type your letter. This demonstrates a professionalism.

Second, at the beginning, state the type of position being sought and the department or section of the agency. This will help ensure that your letter goes to the right person and that it will be assessed according to agency need. Research who should be the recipient of the letter and address it to him or her with the correct title. State in the first paragraph that there are attachments such as a résumé. (See Appendix D for sample résumés.)

Third, briefly, but succinctly, describe your contributions and emphasize the strong assets you bring to the position.

Fourth, state your interest in the agency and why they should be interested in you. Make a statement such as, "I have the experience relative to the needed tasks of the agency," or something softer when you don't have the experience, such as, "I am confident that I possess the competence to adapt to your workforce." Another approach would be, "I believe that I am an excellent match for this position because of my preparation and experience." You may reiterate the job requirements listed in the job posting, followed by your specific qualifications and examples of matching work that you have already performed and are executing. Address your talents (assets) with positive examples of applications in the past. This is the time to mention internships, volunteer work, professional associations, and other relevant experiences. You should also mention if you had any opportunity to be innovative during these previous experiences. This is also the place to mention any academic assignments that you completed that have relevance to the job you are seeking.

Note: Your remarks should be specifically addressed to the agency of interest. That is, find out about the agency (examine their website) and its work to target its mission and vision with your experience.

Fifth, in your final paragraph, request an interview to accomplish one of the following:

A. Explore a current job opening.
B. Explore your options if there is no current opening. This is the exploratory approach for you to get to know them and for them to get to know you.

The point is to get your foot in the door, to let them to see your face, and place your résumé in their hands. You want them to remember you.

Sixth, include all pertinent information that will enable them to get in touch with you—your full name, address, phone (and cell) number, and e-mail address.

Note: Carefully review all correspondence and documents for accuracy. Correct misspellings, poor grammar, and incorrect punctuation. *Do not rely on spell and grammar check.* Write your signature clearly—it should not be a quick autograph.

Note: This is the time when you should be giving out your phone number. Consider the introductory greeting on your phone. How would it sound to a professional calling in a response to an inquiry from you? Make sure your phone greeting (the first impression) is simple and polite.

End the letter strong. Leave the reader with something memorable about you. Look at the "My Ten Points" that you developed and see if there is one strong statement that can sum up why they should hire you. Think of yourself as a product to be sold—sell yourself with a strong message about yourself; after all, no one else is selling you. Utilize what makes you stand out.

If you take the time to go online, you will find many helpful examples of letter styles (in addition to the format we include in this appendix) that will emphasize the type of writing to be done, the language you should use, and the format or construction of the letter that would be the most helpful.

Here are two sample letters to consider for reference and style:

Letter 1: Letter of Interest Sample

Peter Smith

107 Sixth Street, Apt. 2B Middletown, NJ 07001
Phone: 555-761–6111

e-mail: psmith123@gmail.com

May 21, 2022
Chief Ron Smith:
Middle Village Police Department
123 Main Street

Middle Village, NJ 07777

Dear Chief Smith:
I am interested in law enforcement as a career, and I would like to inquire about any open positions at the Middle Village Police Department. Middle Village's training program for Police Special Officer II has been recommended to me by my CJ advisor as a place to start. I would be interested in learning more about your department's program and about any available opportunities. I have a bachelor's degree from Saint Peter's University in Criminal Justice. My concentration in that degree program included police administration and procedure, as well as courses in police culture, community policing, crime investigation, and constitutional law. I completed an internship with the Jersey City Police Department, which allowed me to apply my course concepts to the police environment.

My résumé, which is enclosed, contains additional information on my experiences and skills. I will provide references upon request. I would appreciate the opportunity to discuss the special officers' program with you, learn more about the department, and provide further information on my candidacy. Please contact me either by phone or email at your earliest convenience.
Yours truly,
(Your Name Handwritten Clearly)
Peter Smith

(Your Name Typed)

Letter 2: Sample Letter of Interest
John Q. Applicant
Street Address
City, State, Zip Code
E-mail

Phone Number

Date

Contact Person Name and Title
Company Name
Company Address

Position Posting Title and Number
Dear Mr./Ms. (or title):
I am applying for (Position Name) that was advertised or posted in the (Name of Newspaper) or listed at (Name of Website). I am enclosing for your review the completed application, my résumé, copies of certifications/special training, and a list of three references, as were requested in the posting.

My qualifications meet or exceed those listed in the posting, and I would like to emphasize a few of my personal strengths that make me a competitive candidate.

I have successfully completed training, internships, and other special events. My references provide specific examples of the excellence I would bring to the agency. I have a history of outstanding performance in each position I have held and in each assignment that I have undertaken.

I have completed my (Highest Academic Degree) in CJ and have applied that training in my internships and previous employment. I can be reached during the day by e-mail or on my cell phone at (000-000-0000). Thank you for your consideration. I look forward to speaking with you to further explore the assets I would bring to your agency.
Sincerely,
(Your Name Handwritten Clearly)
(Your Name Typed)

Note: End the letter with a simple salutation, space for your written signature, followed by your typed name.

Appendix C

A Guide to Interview Questions

(See chapter 7 for related information.)

A common suggestion to help people prepare for interviews is to tell them to *relax!*—a good commonsense viewpoint. However, as practical as that approach may sound, it must be coupled with preparation, and that means work—hard work.

A good place to begin your interview preparation is to research the agency to which you applied. If you have done this already, perhaps for a letter of inquiry, we suggest that you do it again. Who knows? Something may have changed. Learn as many specifics as possible. Some agencies have specializations or perform unique services. Your research will help you demonstrate your preparedness if the interviewer were to say to you, "We have a responsibility for . . . How do you see yourself fitting in with the other members of the team?" This, of course, is an opportunity for you to say something like, "I saw on your website . . . " You will have demonstrated that you can take initiative and plan ahead.

We have discussed the importance for you to develop an interview script and to utilize what we call "My Ten Points." This is the beginning of your preparation for the all-important job interview. Each *point*, ideally, is a response for many interviewers' questions. Your points will help you present to the interviewer such things as your intellectual (and at times physical) fitness for the job; the fact that you are you a team player; your basic skills, knowledge, and proficiencies for the job; your drive and ambition to be a good employee; and your values, which make you an exemplary employee. Interviewers do not automatically assume you want a job simply because you applied and came to the interview. At the end of this appendix is a chart for you to list "My Ten Points." As you review this list from time to time, you may wish to refine it or even to change items. This list should be in your document portfolio.

Here are some sample questions to help you develop your interview responses. These questions move from simple to more complex. Do not become complacent because the first questions seem easy or commonplace. Your demonstrated proficiency during an interview is only as good as the last question you answered satisfactorily. Your answers are your opportunity to mention something important that may not be presented in a résumé or cover letter.

1. "Tell me a little about yourself."

   The interviewer may be looking to help you relax, get the conversation started, and get you to provide some information about your background and training. Try not to be too casual, keep your comments specific, and focus on your accomplishments as they apply to the job.

2. "What are your main strengths, and can you identify what may be your greatest weakness or two?"

   Identifying your strengths and weaknesses reflect on your self-awareness. You should be prepared to answer questions about your personal and professional development. Your answer to this question, like the other questions that will be asked, needs to help you stand out above the competition. Explaining what you perceive to be a weakness requires some serious thought. You cannot be cavalier about the answer—convey to the interviewer awareness of shortcomings and that you continually work to improve them. Remember, no one is strong in all areas, all of the time. The best answer is that while we rely on our strengths, we do not neglect our less strong points and we seek assistance when it is needed. Seek to turn weaknesses into strengths, or, as Stephen Covey remarks, "Sharpen the sword."

3. "Why are you looking for employment in this agency?"

   This is a somewhat trickier question. The interviewer may be wondering why you are leaving your present job. Some subtexts in the questions are whether there is something wrong with you or your present position. Perhaps the interviewer is determining if you stick with a job once you are employed and whether you are loyal to your employer. You can begin to answer by describing your previous employment, emphasizing the highlights of the position(s), and segue into something that explains the advantages of the position applied for and how this is an opportunity for you to build on what you have already accomplished. You may be able to show that you keep current with changes in the field and help promote the idea that this agency is on the cutting edge of those changes. As you indicated in the earlier question, you have also continued to prepare yourself for change and this position represents a better fit for your career and personal goals.

4. "What makes you stand out from others who may be applying for this position?"

   Caution: Don't fall into the trap of repeating something you have already said!

The preparation for interviews includes a wide array of potential answers. (Prepare your "My Ten Points.") Your ability to be succinct may indicate your awareness about yourself and what drives you—what it is that make you passionate.

5. "Tell me about your relationships with your managers and fellow employees."

   Hopefully, you have had good relationships with managers and fellow employees. You should believe that your interviewer will call former employers for a reference. Be truthful when describing your experiences and the social skills you employed that made your relationships satisfactory and successful for the workplace.

6. "Where do you see yourself in five years?"

   There are at least two perspectives to consider when answering the question. The first is that interviewers may check your level of ambition. A review of the agency prior to the interview should have helped to develop a vision of what you hope to achieve if hired. As you answer this question, you may be describing how you intend to achieve those goals. This also may be an opportunity for you to ask questions now or at the end of the interview. Your conversation may begin with something like this: "I have described for you my goals and the means with which I hope to achieve them in this service. I would like to ask you for your opinion about those goals and my process for success."

The second perspective is that the interviewer may be seeking to discover your intentions about length of service at their agency. If you are not asked what your ten-year plan might be, you could respond with, "In ten years I see myself in _____ position." This shows you have an even bigger picture in mind for the job.

You should also be prepared for general questions. Again, "My Ten Points" will help. One example of a general question is, "How do you define success?"

YOUR PREPARATION FOR THE INTERVIEW

Take each of the sample questions above and prepare a response for them. Do not assume this is a onetime effort. As you prepare for each interview and practice your answers, you may discover that your responses need refinement (especially since you will be applying for jobs with different functions). Each success, each new credential, and each work experience will have the potential to alter your responses. Your answers may also be refined according to specific information you obtain about the agency.

You should practice improving your interview technique. Among the things to consider are how to dress (see appendix E for advice), voice inflection, the use of pauses, how to ask questions of the interviewer for clarification and about the job, hand gestures, body language, and more. As you enhance your self-awareness you will become more conscious about your need to learn about the body language you bring to the interview and your use of verbal language.

A way to learn about yourself in an interview is to *practice*. In the best of worlds, seek the participation of a professional to conduct a practice interview. If no one is available or you are too uncomfortable to ask someone you don't know well, consult a friend. If this is necessary, then you have one example of why you need to practice! You need to be as comfortable as possible in the interview, so that you can focus on what is being asked of you.

If you wish to know how you present yourself, set up a practice interview with a friend and prepare an interview script. Record the practice interview and review the video with someone who will speak honestly. Look how you are dressed, seated, and giving off body language. Listen to your responses. Take notes during the video. Practice making the needed changes and then, as Warner Wolf, the famous sports announcer, has said, "Let's go to the videotape." See if you succeeded and compare notes.

The practice interview setting should be simple—an office. The interviewer sits behind a desk, and you sit in front. A variation is with two chairs on opposite sides of a coffee table or two chairs on the same side of a coffee table. After practicing with one person as the interviewer, have two or more persons interview you at the same time. When more than one person interviews you, the ability to focus is more challenged. By the conclusion of the interview, you should be able to ascertain whether you want the job. Nevertheless, the interview may not answer all questions.

QUESTIONS TO ASK AT THE INTERVIEW

You will almost always be given the opportunity to ask questions at the end of your interview. Even if that opportunity is not put forward, you may suggest that you have a few questions if that is permissible. There are three kinds of questions to ask at this time.

The first questions will have to do with something that came up during the interview and for which you seek clarification. Form these questions carefully. This is not the time to challenge current practices in the organization.

The second questions are similar and concern your research about the agency. These will address your concerns about agency specifics that were apparent from the website, the job posting, or other sources of information. If you have written down the areas you are concerned with, you may wish to produce your notes for accuracy. Prepare your notes in a professional manner—typed.

The third questions are more common and address your personal and career needs. You should be able to address some of the following questions in your research about the agency, but if they are not readily available, then now is your chance to ask. Keep your list short. The following are only examples.

A. When might I expect to hear from you?
B. What is the starting salary?
C. What benefits are offered?
D. What hours/shifts would I be expected to work?
E. Who would be my supervisor?
F. Can you explain the possibilities for advancement in this agency?
G. Will I be working with a team, or will I have independent assignments?
H. Is there any training available for the position?

As was noted above, many of these questions, especially those related to salary, work hours, benefits, and training, may be listed on the websites, and you should attempt to have them answered before the interview.

MY TEN POINTS (DO NOT NEGLECT THIS!)

Point 1—
Point 2—
Point 3—
Point 4—
Point 5—
Point 6—
Point 7—
Point 8—
Point 9—
Point 10—

An interview is not a guarantee of getting a job. Each interview is a learning experience and practice for future interviews. Each interview opportunity will improve your skills responding to employment questions and to make a good impression as you work toward landing the job that starts or advances your career.

Appendix D

Sample Résumé and CV

(Applicants should reread the résumé section of chapter 7 before starting to compile their résumé.)

The résumé opens the door for the recruiter with a glimpse of who you are and your qualifications for the position. Poorly written résumés will not get you an interview (resumeedge.com will prepare a professional resume for a fee). The résumé should be short and to the point, written clearly, with attention paid to honesty and accuracy. There are many types of résumés. Two are provided here as examples: one for general applications, and the other for specific placement with a particular agency. A curriculum vita is a résumé usually intended for academic positions. It requires a list of all courses taught, including workshops and seminars you have presented, and a complete list of your formal and nonformal publications.

Your résumé should be well-written, well-formatted, edited, and above all, professional. Here are some tips for a successful résumé:

1. Have it printed on good quality paper.
2. Place it in a large envelope—not folded.
3. When possible, print the recipient's name on the front of the envelope.
4. When possible, modify the résumé for the recipient or the intended job.
5. Include your basic information: name, address, phone numbers, and e-mail address.
6. List your objective at the top (customize for the desired position whenever possible).
7. List your education, with highest level of education first.
8. Note any honors and awards that you have received (graduating summa cum laude, president of the student association, or having a paper published).
9. List work experience—the most recent work first. List dates of employment and a short list of tasks for each job. List internship in this section.

If you have had the opportunity to travel as part of your education and it was related to CJ, list this under your work experience.

10. List military experience, especially relevant training.
11. List additional skills, including computer skills, foreign language spoken and written, special licenses, or other training.
12. Ensure that all entries are consistent, especially the margins, dates, indentations, etc.
13. Review for word usage. Use a synonym guide or thesaurus to make your résumé more interesting.
14. Use a professional résumé preparer if you lack the computer skills to do the job yourself.
15. State "References provided upon request."
16. Evaluate your social networking sites for content that might be in poor taste.
17. Have your résumé reviewed for excessive length.

Here are some tips for what not to do:

1. *Do not* assume spell check or grammar check is correct.
2. *Do not* refer to social websites unless you are certain that you are represented properly.
3. *Do not* use "cutesy" e-mail names—set up a new e-mail address.
4. *Do not* mislead, such as stating that you have competency in a foreign language when your experience is only limited to a few phrases.
5. *Do not* assume you have thoroughly reviewed and edited the résumé. Have a friend or someone else review it for spelling, grammar, duplications, inconsistencies, and awkward phrasing.
6. *Do not* try to impress using words that are not part of your regular vocabulary.
7. *Do not* include references unless specifically requested.
8. *Do not* use fancy fonts.
9. *Do not* clutter the résumé with irrelevant information.

Resume #1
Amy Student
1609 Forest Avenue, Smalltown, NJ 07001
Telephone (555) 777–1234
E-mail: amystudent12@gmail.com

Objective: To obtain a full-time criminal justice position where I can contribute my knowledge, skills, and passion as a team player

Education: Saint Peter's University, Jersey City, NJ
Bachelor of Arts, criminal justice, anticipated graduation: May 2022
Current cumulative GPA: 3.923; Criminal Justice GPA: 4.0
J.F. Kennedy High School, Smalltown, NJ
Years attended: 2010–2012, graduated in June 2012
Lodi High School, Lodi, NJ
Years attended: 2008–2010

Honors & Awards:
Dean's List, Saint Peter's University
Alpha Phi Sigma, National Criminal Justice Honor Society 2013–2015, Vice President 2015
Criminal Justice Students Association 2011–2015

Work Experience:
Site Coordinator, A.C.E Before/After School Program, Better Place, NJ Oct. 2014–Present

- Worked as a counselor from September 2012–October 2014 until achieving my current promoted position
- Co-manage a before/after school program with a total of 84 children in grades K–5th
- Certified in CPR, EpiPen, and first aid.

GEM Criminal Justice Tutor, Saint Peter's University, Jersey City, NJ Fall 2013 & Fall 2014 semesters

- Worked with a college professor to lead my own interactive class discussion once a week

Sales Assistant, Buttercrust Bakery, Smalltown, NJ May 2009– January 2015
Certified Food Safety Manager by National Registry of Food Safety Professionals on August 9, 2013

Extracurricular Leadership Activities:
Gannon Debating Society

- President, Fall 2015–Spring 2016; Secretary, Fall 2014–Spring 2015
- Worked with partners in developing affirmative and negative cases for team-based National Educational Debate Association tournaments
- Alpha Phi Sigma (Criminal Justice Honor Society)
- Vice President, Fall 2015–Spring 2016; Secretary, Fall 2014–Spring 2015

Additional Skills:

- Bilingual speaker: Spanish and English

References are available upon request.

Resume #2

Brian Santos

1011 Broad Street, Middle Village NY 01001

(555) 333-0001

BrianSan@nt.edu

Objective: To obtain the position of patrolman with the Middle Village Police Department

Education: Bachelor of Arts—Criminal Justice
Anticipated completion: December 2021
Saint Peter's University, Jersey City, NJ
Internship: Jersey City Police Department, Jersey City, NJ August 2014 to January 2015
Academic internship (credit earning) with Jersey City Police Department. Duties include:

- Assist officers in writing reports
- Visit local middle and high schools for crime prevention program
- Assist dispatcher with duties during assigned shift

Experience: All-Town Security, Inc., Jersey City, NJ 07001 September 2014 to Present
Assigned to Newport Mall

- Developed and implemented training for new security guards within the mall
- Co-presented paper on topic of sexual assault awareness for company employees
- Maintained foot patrol of the mall
- Assisted department head with creation and implementation of crime prevention awareness campaign

A & B Lawn Service, Inc. Long Distance, MO 65054 Summers 2013, 2014, 2015

- Handled customer service and landscaping duties

Leadership & Volunteer Experience

- Saint Peters University Criminal Justice Students Association 2012 to Present
- Middle Village Volunteer Fire Department 2010 to 2013
- Big Brothers/Big Sisters of East Jersey 2014 to Present

Computer Experience
Microsoft Word, Excel, Access, PowerPoint, Publisher, Adobe Photoshop
References: Available upon request

Resume #3 Curriculum Vitae
Peter Smith, PhD
123 Broad Street
Middle Village, New Jersey 07701
Home: (555) 123–9999
E-mail address: psmith123@gmail.com

GOAL:

Seeking a full-time teaching position in the field of sociology/CJ, using my professional experience and graduate education for the benefit of students in a higher educational setting.

SUMMARY:
Ten years of experience within an institution of higher education, including eight years of teaching at the College of New Jersey, Department of Law and Justice; at Kean University, Department of Public Administration, Criminal Justice Program, and the Sociology Department; and at Brookdale Community College. Courses include History and Philosophy of Corrections; Criminology; Community-Based Corrections; Probation and Parole; Juvenile Delinquency, Child Protection Agencies, and the Law; Comparative Criminal Justice; Judicial Process; Introduction to Criminal Justice; and others. Member of Alpha Phi Sigma, the Criminal Justice National Honor Society. Faculty Advisor of the Saint Peter's chapter of the National Honor Society. Faculty advisor to the Criminal Justice Students Association.
EDUCATION:
PhD Sociology. Fordham University, Bronx, NY.
MA Counseling. Rider University, Trenton, NJ.
BS Social Sciences. Monmouth University, Long Branch, NJ.

TEACHING EXPERIENCE:
2002–Present: Assistant Professor, Kean College, Department of Criminal Justice

1994–2000: Adjunct Professor, The College of New Jersey, Department of Law and Justice
2001–2003: Adjunct Professor, Public National School of Public Administration and Criminal Justice, Department of Sociology
2001–2006: Adjunct Professor, Brookdale Community College, Department of Sociology
2002–Adjunct Professor: Saint John's University, Graduate School of Professional Studies, Department of Criminal Justice and Legal Studies
Other educational experiences include:

- Supervised student interns for Fordham University, Rutgers University, Monmouth University, The College of New Jersey, and other educational institutions
- Guest-lectured on the subjects of CJ and sociology at various colleges
- Chaired the staff development committee and the regional training programs committee of the National Child Support Enforcement Association
- Instructor for the New Jersey Bar Association, Institute of Legal Continuing Education
- Instructor for U.S. Department of Health and Human Services, Office of Child Support Enforcement

PROFESSIONAL EXPERIENCE:
April 1968 to September 1994: Senior Probation Officer, Monmouth County Probation Department, Freehold, New Jersey
Responsibilities: Prepare pre-sentence reports and supervision of juvenile probationers; staff training officer; director of volunteers; field instructor for Monmouth College.

CONSULTING:

- Served as a consultant, program developer, and seminar participant for the following organizations:
- U.S. Department of Health and Human Services
- U.S. Commission on Interstate Child Support Enforcement
- National Center for State Courts
- Institute of Court Management
- State of Illinois, Administrative Office of Courts
- Several other major private corporations

CONTINUING EDUCATION:

Participated in various seminars and workshops in management, staff development, and social services, including Summer School of Alcohol Studies; Rutgers Youth Institute; AMA Train the Trainer Seminar; Personnel Administration; Criminal Justice Management; and Staffing Pattern Strategies for Child Support Programs.

PUBLISHED ARTICLES AND PRESENTATIONS:

- Child Support and Court Administration, "The Child Support Reporter," U.S. Government, Department of Health and Human Services, Administration for Families and Children, Office of Child Support Enforcement, 1999.
- Academy of Criminal Justice Sciences, 44th Conference, Las Vegas, NV 2004, Paper: "Immigrants and Crime Prevention," in *A Review of Traditional Patterns and Current Trends, Encyclopedia of Police Science*, Third Edition, 2006, "Politics and the Police."
- "Gateway Conference Strategies for Returning Offenders," Education and Employment Opportunities. March 2009.
- Book review, "Who to Release? Parole, Fairness, and Criminal Justice," in the *International Criminal Justice Review*, September 2010.

PROFESSIONAL AFFILIATIONS:

- New Jersey Association of Criminal Justice Educators (2006–2007, Vice President)
- Academy of Criminal Justice Sciences
- American Correctional Association, New Jersey Chapter
- American Parole and Probation Association
- Middle Atlantic States Conference on Corrections
- New Jersey Child Support Council (founding member, first President)
- Eastern Regional Child Support Association (ERICSA)

REFERENCES: Available upon request

Appendix E

The Career Fair Plan

The career/job fair is a valuable resource for finding your entrance into the CJ profession. Look at it as opportunity for networking, career exploration, interview practice, and a job search. Career/job fairs are hosted by colleges, specific industries, and other agencies. You should prepare yourself appropriately for the career/job fair. This appendix is intended to help you with preparation to meet each contingency.

Agencies send representatives to these fairs to provide information, answer questions, collect résumés, and more. Some agencies don't advertise when they are recruiting, while others are always recruiting. Your task is to prepare for all opportunities. Some of the recommendations are rather simple, look at them as a checklist—a checklist that you may wish to review after each career/job fair to ensure that all preparatory activity has been performed and determine what needs to be strengthen. After all, you may encounter something unique at some career/job fair that will benefit you at the next fair.

Each revision of the preparation will help ensure that when you meet agency representatives, you will get their attention and improve the likelihood of a second interview. Be aware that how you present yourself and what you personally display will influence the representatives' perception and the chance of having your résumé receive serious consideration. Leave each fair with the feeling of satisfaction that comes from doing your best to demonstrate your value to those companies in which you are interested. The most important piece of advice for the career/job fair: *Be prepared!*

The following checklist will help you with this preparation for career/job fairs.

MAKE A LIST OF CAREER/JOB FAIRS

The list of career/job fairs needs to be updated regularly. The CJ or career services department at your college will likely have a listing of these fairs.

Career/job fair listings can also be found in publications or on websites; for example, the New Jersey Association of Criminal Justice Educators lists fairs in its newsletter and on its website. Here is another suggestion: Utilize Google Career Fairs! You will discover more than you can imagine. This will be stated later, but for the record let's say it here: After each fair, make notes to yourself about each employer/agency you visited and/or the name of each person who gave you an interview.

Should you receive an interview and engage a representative in conversation, you may be asked whether you have questions. This is the time to ask! Your preliminary review of agencies attending the fair should guide your preparation of questions. Write the questions down. (My Ten Points, appendix C).

OBTAIN A LIST OF EMPLOYERS/AGENCIES/ COMPANIES REPRESENTED AT THE FAIR

Prioritize which companies represent the area(s) in which you would like to be employed. Review each: (a) go to the website and learn as much as possible about the agency/company, or (b) visit www.quintcareers.com/researching_companies.htm. Visit this site to see the wealth of information it offers for your job search. This step is important because it will help to skip agencies that are not relative to your vision and career choice. Obtaining employment, especially for the desired career, takes work—*do not skip this step!* The career/job fair is not a sightseeing tour.

Here are some additional valuable tips about career/job fair representation: First, career/job fairs are attended by companies, corporations, government agencies, private nonprofits, for-profit agencies, and individuals who have their own business. The list will demonstrate the need for a diverse preparation. See all the tips listed below. Second, not all companies or organizations send representatives to every fair. If your needs are not met at the career/job fair, then it may be time to broaden your search, i.e., to the internet and campus career services.

PREREGISTER FOR THE CAREER/ JOB FAIR WHENEVER POSSIBLE

This is an often-ignored step, but it could be a fatal mistake if you choose not to follow through. Generally, you have to submit a résumé (see appendix D for résumé guidance) to preregister. The point is that your résumé will then be screened by employers—and that means a decision about you may be made before you even get to the career/job fair. Of course, if your résumé has attracted the attention of an employer, the agency representative will already have your name on his list when you arrive, and you may get your first interview. If you are in your third year or early in your fourth year of college, your résumé may open the door to an invitation for an internship—some of which are paid.

Upon arrival at the career/job fair, check the listing of organizations and agencies to see if any new ones have been added. While you may not have prepared for them specifically, you will already have a general knowledge of what different organizations/agencies offer. Do not skip them; try to get their literature before seeing a representative so that you will have some familiarity with them when you do approach them. You can be honest with them. If you do not know something, do not be afraid to ask. Because they are late in registering, representatives will not have reviewed résumés ahead of time and you can feel free to offer your résumé and/or the content of the document portfolio.

ALLOW YOUR RÉSUMÉ TO OPEN DOORS FOR YOU

Review your résumé before each career/job fair. Consider having your résumé done professionally and printed on good quality paper. One of the more important things you can do is to have someone else review your résumé and proofread it for the mistakes you cannot see. Your résumé can help sell you. If it is sloppy, wrinkled, and contains bad grammar, poor punctuation, or worse, misspelled words, consider that you have already lost the job. Remember—spell check does not check for the right form of the word, only the correct spelling.

If you have read this book, then you know that we advocate being prepared for different types of careers. You will still have to find the one that best fits you. Some of you will have more than one interest in your choice of profession. Assuming you have more than one interest, prepare different résumés that list different objectives, and have sufficient copies for all the employers you will see. This does not mean that you should hand out a copy of each résumé to every representative. Only distribute the form of your résumé to a prospective employer who has a specific opening that matches that résumé's objective—they will not want all that paper, only the résumé that fits. You have to get your foot in the door to find your niche or career path.

Caution: Some recruiters will not want to keep your résumé; they will simply scan the résumé to take it back to the office. Your résumé should therefore be crisp and clean, ready for a scanner.

PLAN YOUR ATTIRE, AND DRESS PROFESSIONALLY

Everyone likes to think that they understand acceptable or attractive style, and that their personal style is unique. You want to stand out as an applicant, but you do not want your attire to stand out for you. Your attire should not distract the representative's attention. Some career/job fairs have recommended or required attire; find out if they do and dress accordingly. Get someone else's opinion about how you look, including your slacks, suit, colors, tie, shoes, and so on. Nothing may be more important than the first impression you leave with the recruiter. *Never be underdressed!* Try to hit the middle of the road between that and overdressed, but when in doubt, be overdressed.

PREPARE TO MEET REPRESENTATIVES/ INTERVIEWERS

The moment you approach a representative, the evaluation has begun. Your initial preparatory task is your personal introduction. Representatives are impressed by students who can present themselves with self-assurance; "Good morning, my name is _______!" This can be followed by something like this: "I have read about your organization, and I was interested to learn that you _______." Or, "I noticed on your website that you have the _____ project. Could I hear more about it?" And, "I was curious about_____." This is when you mention that "something else" you would like to explore. Representatives are there to answer questions and show off who they are. Don't hesitate to ask the representative what they think are the highlights of working for their company.

In chapter 7, we strongly suggested that you should prepare answers in the form of "My Ten Points." (See appendix C for a guide to interview questions and the "My Ten Points" chart.) These answers should be broad in scope and thus acceptable both to a specific question and other more general questions. The point is that you should be prepared for any questions by the representative/interviewer.

You should practice as many questions and answers as possible with someone else before going to the career/job fair. Do not give your list of questions and answers to them—let them come up with their own questions (in the role of an interviewer) and determine whether the questions are adequately answered. If this is an interview at a career/job fair, you will only be given a few minutes of a representative's time. Your preparation must ensure that you have said what is important quickly, concisely, and with confidence and enthusiasm. Be prepared! The consequence of failing to prepare is that your résumé may be set aside. Try to prepare yourself to ask a few questions at the end of the interview. These questions should be developed to show your interest in the organization. Your key objective for this interview is to do well enough to get a second interview, which is a better time to ask personal questions about salary, benefits, and advancement. (Never ask these questions during an initial interview unless the interviewer brings them up first.) This information may be available in the brochures provided by the representatives, and it is what they use to stimulate interest in their organization. A final concluding question might be, "Should I write a letter to schedule a second interview?"

If this is not an interview, you may only get one question that will require a broader answer. The key in this case is to make a statement, not a speech. The question will probably sound something like, "Why do you want to work for company X?" Your response should be a blend of expressing your interests and explaining how you would meet the company's needs. You will need to anticipate that the representative/interviewer will only have a few minutes with you, as there will be others wanting to see the representative.

Career/job fairs are known for the lines of students waiting to see a representative. This is an opportunity for you. Pay attention to the questions that are being asked by those in front of you, and more importantly, listen to the answers of the representative. Consider this an occasion for you to double up on your interest because you will be learning both from the questions asked and from the answers given.

You have to be ready, and you have to be good to make a lasting first impression. There are some physical things you can do to accomplish this. First, show enthusiasm; put a smile on your face. Second, make and keep good eye contact. Third, give the person a firm, not bone-crushing handshake. And fourth, practice good habits, such as no gum-chewing, no smelling of smoke, and no other things that could be remotely considered in poor taste.

MAKE THE MOST OF YOUR TIME

If a representative on your list has a long line of waiting students, don't just stand there. You can move on to someone else on your list first. You can also go visit someone not on your list who has no one waiting. This is an excellent chance to work on your informal conversation skills. You can assess how you ask questions and then take the next step after you get an answer. Consider this process as interview practice.

The career/job fair is not a social event, and you should take advantage of every opportunity to get your foot in a door. Students will talk among themselves as they stand around waiting. Be cautious of casual conversation.

Never make disparaging remarks—about anyone or anything. You cannot be sure who might overhear you.

BRING THE DOCUMENT PORTFOLIO OF YOUR WORK WITH YOU

The document portfolio (see appendix G) should contain—in addition to copies of your résumé and perhaps a cover letter—copies of papers that you have written that received excellent grades and important remarks from professors, letters from internships, externships, and from volunteering or from specialized training. If you have received any training certificates, copies of them (never the original document) should be in the portfolio. Police departments or other agencies are impressed with students who have earned special skills. Let me provide you with an example. One of my former students had a certification as an underwater welder. I encouraged him to place that certification in his document portfolio. He mentioned it to a police department representative. That department was in need of a diver. Guess who got a job?

Some of this may be more than you will use at a fair. However, if it is an interview and you have attracted someone's attention, you will once more demonstrate your preparedness if you have the documentation to validate your preparation for entrance into a certain career field.

The portfolio is also an organizing tool—representatives like to see students who are prepared. Also, fairs provide students with advertising giveaways—pens, pencils, markers, stress balls, pads of notepaper, candy, and more. You want to have a place to put these things so you are not juggling them around when you pull out your résumé or other documents. Don't burden yourself with items you don't need.

CONSIDER VOLUNTEERING TO HELP ORGANIZE/SET UP THE CAREER/JOB FAIR

This would be a unique time to meet representatives as you help them set up and guide them to their location. You will be the first to meet them, the first to offer your résumé, and then you can ask questions. This is not aggressive—this is proactive.

NETWORK

Network, network, network! Have we said this often enough? Review chapter 7! Unfortunately, or perhaps fortunately, it is not always *what* you know, but *who* you know. Get a business card from everyone you meet. Make notes on the card or on a notepad about each interview or discussion with a representative. Be specific in your notes: List what was important and what was not. Most representatives will tell you what the organization needs in a candidate. This is critical and should be placed in your notes to be included in the follow-up letter and for an interview.

AFTER THE CAREER/JOB FAIR, FOLLOW UP WITH EVERY RECRUITER OR INTERVIEWER

Send letters out immediately. Prepare a generic letter prior to the fair. Tell the company representative or HR person how excited you are, how interested you are, and what you would bring to the organization. Clearly state your qualifications in the letter (see appendix B regarding writing letters) and the fact that you would like a second interview. Include another résumé. Promise that you will make a follow-up call and then do so. Thank the recruiter for attending the fair, for providing information, and for generating excitement about their organization. Send the letter to the address listed on the recruiter's card.

Good luck in your career search!

Appendix F

The Benefits and Downsides of Online Courses

Colleges and universities are including more online courses in their curriculum. Your personal needs and your choice of college may determine how few or how many online courses are required. For example, if you choose a non-traditional college, you will take more or potentially all of your courses online. More traditional colleges offer fewer online courses, but there is a recent trend to increase online courses in the curriculum. Traditional colleges are also developing hybrid versions of courses. Part of the hybrid course is taught online, and the other is taught in the physical classroom. Professors are encouraged, in some cases mandated, to produce online courses or to convert current classroom courses to online courses.

One key to successful utilization of online learning is to make sure that the online college or university is accredited. This is essential to know, because if it is not accredited then either your credits will not be transferred to another college, or your degree may lack validity.

Determine the advantages and disadvantages of online learning. For some it may be a more efficient solution to getting a college degree, while for others it may be the only way to achieve a degree. What follows is a brief discussion of the benefits and disadvantages of online learning to assist the student in finding an objective solution to meet their needs.

THE BENEFITS OF ONLINE COURSES

Online courses are cost-effective, meaning they are less expensive in nontraditional colleges and may be less expensive in traditional colleges, although that is not true in every case.

Online courses are convenient. You can take them from the comfort of your home, and you can study at a time that better fits with your routine. For many students, this can be a tremendous advantage because there is no travel, no competition with time and work, and fewer conflicts establishing a semester schedule of courses. The professor posts the syllabus and course requirements online. The student must then comply with the requirements, which generally have due dates for submission, or online discussions with the professor and/or with other students. In addition, there are fewer requirements of actual time slots when you must be present online. For some students who need special conditions in which to study, a home environment can be established with fewer distractions like classroom noise, questions, or the activity of other students in the classroom. For some students, this equates to less stress.

Online courses are efficient. Not everyone can afford the luxury of enrolling in college and either limiting work or not working at all. Online courses allow the student to both work and go to school. For many, this means a longer time to complete a college degree. However, a degree earned in this fashion may be evidence to an employer of your desire to advance or to be better prepared in your career. One other advantage to online courses is that course sections often have lower limits for the number of students taking the course than would be the standard in a traditional college classroom. In this case, there may be another section that is online or is offered at another college and the credits can then be transferred.

Online courses permit more interactions with the professor. Online courses usually have more work that must be submitted to a professor on a regular schedule. The professor, in this case, responds to your assignments by timely answering your questions, providing critiques, and making suggestions for changes or additional work that will help clarify the learning to be accomplished. Oftentimes, professors are more accessible online (morning, noon, and night) than they are in a physical college campus setting where office hours are posted.

The student develops new proficiencies. When work is done online, the student will sharpen their computer skills. Computers are an essential tool in our daily lives, and the better we learn to navigate the computer and explore its potential, the more effective the computer becomes for us. For example, a student will learn to research course material. The computer is only as valuable as the ability to retrieve information from online search engines. There are other valuable skills utilized in online learning, such as file sharing or incorporating the many audio-visual tools that are accessed through the computer.

Online courses may allow greater specialization. Traditional college campuses have courses designed to fit into curriculums, and there is often a scheme to their availability, that is, what is offered during one's freshman, sophomore, junior, and senior years. Curriculums generally allow some leeway for extra studies called electives, courses that are not required and allow students to expand their field of study. The credits from electives count toward the degree, but some online learning programs do not have electives. Instead, the program is streamlined with only required courses. In some cases, online coursework can result in very specialized degrees that are not found in traditional colleges or that are more difficult to attain because fewer students are available to take those courses. Online education then is a more efficient and effective learning experience.

THE DOWNSIDES OF ONLINE LEARNING

The downsides of online learning are typically the flipsides of the advantages.

The first is a very strong warning to the student: If you are selecting online learning, *make sure* the courses and the school offering the courses are accredited. *Do not* simply accept an online statement from the offering school that either the college or the course is accredited. Check with outside sources about accreditation. Remember, unaccredited schools and courses will result in a worthless degree, which means that you have wasted your time, your tuition money, and any other funds you may have taken out in the form of a student loan.

Online courses mean more reading and more writing assignments. This translates to greater demands on your time—more time completing these assignments than would be required in a traditional course format. It also means greater use of technology—which may not be part of the student's comfort zone.

Online courses mean little or no face-to-face interaction with a professor or other students. The student seeking a CJ career may be less likely to get the practical side of careers than is presented in the classroom. Online learning limits the interaction with the professor for in-depth discussions because the courses are so focused on the assignments listed on the syllabus. As you may imagine, the online environments present more challenges in developing relationships with fellow students and professors. It is possible to communicate, but it will necessarily lack the depth of dialogue found in the physical classroom setting.

Online courses require the self-discipline necessary to schedule yourself and follow through to complete the work. In this case, you may be more responsible for locating the information you need to complete the coursework. Online courses require you to adhere to a strict schedule, and if you fall behind, it may become almost impossible to catch up.

RECOMMENDATIONS

If you decide to pursue your education online, we suggest you consider your ability to take the following steps.

- Assess the accreditation of the schools in which you are interested.
- Compare the costs of online and traditional schools.
- Make a calendar of necessary daily and weekly activities to assess your availability to complete online work.
- Create a space in your home that is designated just for your college work. This will help to minimize distractions. Advise others in your home that when you study, they can help by not interrupting or creating other distractions. Reading, writing, and studying are best accomplished when done at the same time every day. Consistency is the key.
- Once you enroll, make a calendar outlining your study time. Once that is established, stick to it!
- Identify resources to assist you with your online work. This includes persons with special skill sets and local sites of assistance, such as college (and online) libraries. You may also need a go-to space, such as a college library, to which you can retreat to study with fewer distractions.
- Make a post on the forum of the online class you are taking to see whether any other students live close enough to form a study group and with whom you could have face-to-face discussions about coursework.
- If professors do not post real-time office hours, ask whether they will have office hours at some location that is accessible to you. (This may be impossible for many online courses.)
- Internships may or may not be available with online curriculums. Your professors may not be familiar with specific internship opportunities in your area, and you may need to research them. You may not have the advantage of a professor who can visit the site and meet with the supervisor to ensure you are receiving the best possible experience.

SUMMARY

Online learning is good for some students but terrible for others. Each student must carefully consider whether such courses are in their best interest. While the advantages may be very attractive, all disadvantages should be carefully assessed in terms of the individual's personal abilities and style of learning for their success and goal attainment. The wrong decision can have financial repercussions and delay goal attainment, that is, obtaining the degree and beginning a career in CJ.

Appendix G

Document Portfolio Checklist

(See chapter 2 for a full explanation of each of these documents.)

Assemble all "original" documents into a single file, and then use this file to assemble a set of duplicate documents for applications and interviews. Original documents should be maintained in a separate file. Never give away your original documents; if you are required to present them, make sure they are returned to you right away. Review all websites when applying for the required documents. Some important certifications may include lifeguarding, scuba diving, EMT training, CPR, or first aid. Keep your folders updated as you acquire new credentials. Place this document checklist in the front of the document portfolio.

DOCUMENT PORTFOLIO CHECKLIST

_____ Birth Certificate
_____ Social Security Card
_____ High School Diploma
_____ Firearms ID
_____ College or other post-secondary diploma(s)
_____ Skill Certifications
_____ Driver's License
_____ Insurance card(s)
_____ Voter Registration Card
_____ Passport
_____ Military ID
_____ Selective Service Registration ID
_____ Awards
_____ Certificates of Training
_____ CDL License

Appendix H

Civil Service Examinations

Many jobs with local, state, and federal government agencies require civil service examinations. While civil service tests are often very similar, they are specifically designed for the posted position. Prep manuals[1] are available for civil service examinations, and some are available for specific tests for designated positions, such as correctional officer.

However, there are many jobs that are exempt from examination. These positions may be administrative, and the employee serves at the pleasure of the employer. Other positions that are exempt from civil service exams are part-time positions.

An excellent example of the step-by-step process for navigating civil service applications can be found on the New Jersey website for civil service (http://www.nj.gov/csc/). This website defines what an announcement is, and then details a nine-step process that will help the interested person to successfully complete the application process:

Step 1: Identify the job announcement.
Step 2: Review the job requirements.
Step 3: Obtain an application.
Step 4: Pay any application fees.
Step 5: Follow the application checklist.
Step 6: Review the application.
Step 7: Consider the evaluation methods.
Step 8: Review your exam results.
Step 9: Follow up after the exam.

There is a similar process in many states and in the federal government. Pennsylvania also includes a tutorial to help with the process.

CIVIL SERVICE POSTINGS

Generally, a posting for a civil service position will specify whether there is a required examination and what the applicant must do to qualify and then take the examination. Read the posting carefully. Not all postings are for jobs in which there are openings. The posting may exist to set up an examination for future openings. You should take a few examinations for practice, even though they usually require a small fee. Each exam gives you more practice, puts you on a list, and prepares you for future tougher examinations.

The job posting will list the job title and number, the location(s) of the position, the salary range, minimum requirements such as education or years of experience, and other needed skills such as proficiency in certain computer software and credentials such as a driver's license. There should be a description of the job as well as a description of the specific duties the employee would be expected to perform. Prospective employees should read the posting carefully and not immediately discard it if they do not meet the education requirements, as there may be a provision to substitute experience for education or vice versa. In other cases, provisions may be made for the employee, if hired, to complete certain education requirements by a specified date. The posting may also include specific exclusions to the application process, including citizenship, such as citizenship in the United States, in the state, or in the municipality where the position is located. There usually is an application fee or a fee associated with taking the test.

COMPLETING THE APPLICATION FOR THE CIVIL SERVICE EXAMINATION

The application for the position, in some cases, is the civil service examination. The applicant should be advised not to procrastinate completion of the test application. If your application is received after the closing date, it will be rejected. At times, there are points assigned for the date when the application is received; that is, the earlier it is received, the more points are awarded. This does not suggest you should rush and be careless or sloppy. A common mistake of civil service applicants is to attach their résumé with the assumption that it is self-explanatory of personal experience or of education. The application usually has areas for these to be filled in. *Do fill them in* and be sure to provide the details that will allow the reviewer to understand that you have met the education or experience requirements with specificity to the tasks described. If there is insufficient room on the application for all required information then, on the application write *see attached* documentation. Once your application has been accepted, you will be required to provide proof of credentials (education and/or certifications) mentioned in your application. You should bring copies of these documents to your job interview.

The civil service application may be a paper application, or it may be found online. In either case, be accurate, thorough, truthful, and complete. Include copies of all required documents, such as certifications, degrees, or transcripts (and check twice that you have included them—and the right copy of them). Take note—there are specific sites for taking the examination from which you must choose. Be sure to check off the one most convenient for you. The application may list various sites through the state or the nation with position openings. You must specify the places where you will accept employment and check them off as well. Many civil service applications now include a small processing fee. Take this seriously. If you write a check, make sure that there are funds to cover it. If you use a credit card, make sure you enter the correct information—check it twice—and be sure the card is not expired or overextended. Any rejection may nullify your opportunity to be considered a candidate.

CIVIL SERVICE EXAMINATION CENTERS

Whether you are filling out the application online or a paper version thereof, be sure to specify where you will take the examination. You will probably be notified, at a later date, when the examination will be given and where you must report for it. This may seem like simple advice, but here it is anyway: Be sure you know where the center is located. Do not assume you know. Leave plenty of time to get to the examination center—in fact, be early! If you have a mishap, make a wrong turn, get held up in traffic, or something else that causes you to be late, you probably will not be allowed to take the exam and you will have to reapply when a notice is posted again.

THE HIRING PROCESS

One of the purposes of civil service examinations is to increase competitiveness for each position. However, in many cases the employer may simply choose from the top three scores on the test. This is sometimes referred to as the Rule of Three. There is an exception to this rule: If an applicant has a veteran's status—that is, if he or she has served in the U.S. military—then, regardless of test score, they go to the top of the list and must be hired ahead of others. When a list is promulgated, the employer will begin interviewing. If someone does not show up for an interview, they are immediately dropped from the list. Applicants may be found unsuitable for a position because of a criminal record, substance abuse, or other conditions. Eventually, the employer will decide from the top three remaining candidates.

Your name will remain on the list for future vacancies if you are not chosen for the posted position. There is a specified length of time, however, after which a list expires. After a list expires, you must retest for the position to be placed back on the list. Your standing on a list will change over time as some are chosen for positions, some do not respond when called for interviews, or others are found to be ineligible for positions.

If you are selected, the employer will provide you with a start date. At this time, you will be scheduled for an orientation session, which may or may not be followed by training. Training is determined by the specific agency, and some positions only have on-the-job training.

JOB PROTECTION AND DISCIPLINE

Civil service appointments do provide employees with some job protection. If you are selected for a job and you complete the working test period (about one year), then you generally cannot be dismissed from a job without cause, that is, unless you do something wrong. However, disciplinary action may not mean immediate dismissal from employment. There are often steps, or what is referred to as progressive discipline before an employee may be terminated. Progressive discipline includes steps that must be followed, such as warnings, reprimands, suspensions (one or more days), and finally termination. So, learn your job, follow the rules, and if you do, any concerns you have about termination will be moot.

Good luck in your employment search!

Appendix I

U.S. Federal Law Enforcement Agencies and Websites

This appendix covers federal agencies and their websites. There are many, but we have chosen to separate these from the "Important Websites" listed in appendix J. These websites may not seem immediately applicable to your choice of career, but we suggest that you visit some of them to familiarize yourself with other career possibilities. In addition, you may learn something new that can be applied to your chosen profession. Your future is, as yet, undetermined—be prepared!

- U.S. Air Force Office of Special Investigations: http://www.osi.andrews.af.mil/
- U.S. Bureau of Alcohol, Tobacco, and Firearms: http://www.atf.gov/
- U.S. Central Intelligence Agency: www.cia.gov
- U.S. Customs and Border Protection: http://www.cbp.gov/
- U.S. Defense Criminal Investigative Service: http://www.dodig.mil/INV/DCIS/index.html
- U.S. Defense Intelligence Agency: www.dia.mil
- U.S. Department of Homeland Security: http://www.dhs.gov/index.shtm
- U.S. Drug Enforcement Administration: http://www.usdoj.gov/dea/index.htm
- U.S. Federal Bureau of Investigation: http://www.fbi.gov/
- U.S. Federal Protective Service: http://www.ice.gov/graphics/about/organization/org_fps.htm
- U.S. Immigration and Customs Enforcement: http://www.ice.gov/index.htm
- U.S. IRS Criminal Investigations Division: http://www.irs.gov/uac/Criminal-Enforcement-1
- U.S. Marshal Service: http://www.usdoj.gov/marshals/
- U.S. Naval Criminal Investigative Service: http://www.ncis.navy.mil/
- U.S. Postal Inspection Service: http://postalinspectors.uspis.gov/

- U.S. Secret Service: http://www.secretservice.gov/
- U.S. State Department Bureau of Diplomatic Security: http://www.state.gov/m/ds/
- U.S. Secret Service: http://www.secretservice.gov/

OFFICE OF INSPECTOR GENERALS

- U.S. Agency for International Development, Office of Inspector General: http://www.usaid.gov/oig/
- U.S. Department of Agriculture, Office of Inspector General: http://www.usda.gov/oig/invest.htm
- U.S. Department of Commerce, Office of Inspector General: www.oig.doc.gov
- U.S. Department of Defense, Office of Inspector General: www.dodig.osd.mil
- U.S. Department of Education, Office of Inspector General: www.ed.gov/about/offices/list/oig/index.html
- U.S. Department of Energy, Office of Inspector General: www.ig.doe. gov
- U.S. Department of Health and Human Services, Office of Inspector General: http://www.oig.hhs.gov
- U.S. Department of Homeland Security, Office of Inspector General: www.dhs.gov/dhspublic
- U.S. Department of Housing and Urban Development, Office of Inspector General: www.hud.gov/offices/oig
- U.S. Department of Interior, Office of Inspector General: http://www.doioig.gov/
- U.S. Department of Justice, Office of Inspector General: www.usdoj.gov/oig
- U.S. Environmental Protection Agency, Office of Inspector General: http://www.epa.gov/oig/

The Department of Justice uses an online application process. Candidates complete and submit an application electronically through the Office of Attorney Recruitment and Management's website. Read the rules before filling out the application and submitting it. If you make a mistake, you may not be given an opportunity to correct it.

- U.S. Department of Transportation, Office of Inspector General: www.oig.dot.gov
- U.S. Department of the Treasury, Office of Inspector General: www.treas.gov/oig

- U.S. Department of Veterans Affairs, Office of Inspector General: www.va.gov/oig
- U.S. Environmental Protection Agency: ww.epa.gov/oigearth
- U.S. Equal Employment Opportunity Commission, Office of Inspector General: http://www.eeoc.gov/abouteeoc/plan/oig/index.html
- U.S. Postal Service, Office of Inspector General: http://www.uspsoig.gov/investigation.htm
- U.S. National Aeronautics and Space Administration, Office of Inspector General: www.hq.nasa.gov/office/oig/hq
- U.S. Nuclear Regulatory Commission, Office of Inspector General: http://www.nrc.gov/insp-gen/invesprog.html
- U.S. Office of Personnel Management, Office of Inspector General: http://www.opm.gov/oig/html/investigations.asp
- U.S. Postal Service, Office of Inspector General: http://www.uspsoig.gov/investigation.htm
- U.S. Railroad Retirement Board, Office of Inspector General: www.rrb.gov/oig/rrboig.htm
- U.S. Small Business Administration, Office of Inspector General: www.sba.gov/ig
- U.S. Social Security Administration, Office of Inspector General: www.ssa.gov/oig
- U.S. State Department, Office of Inspector General: http://oig.state.gov/isp/
- U.S. Treasury IG for Tax Administration: http://www.treas.gov/tigta/oi.shtml
- U.S. Department of Veterans Affairs, Office of Inspector General: www.va.gov/oig

NATIONAL PARK SERVICE POLICE

- http://www.nps.gov/subjects/uspp/index.htm
- http://www.govtjobs.com (This site publishes job listings and job resource information state by state. Links are included to municipal, city, and county government websites).
- https://www.usajobs.gov/ (This is the federal government's official one-stop source for federal jobs and employment information).
- US Customs and Border Patrol: http://www.cbp.gov/ (This site helps applicants locate careers in Customs and Border Patrol. It also reviews international port and immigration activities).
- http://lawenforcementjobs.com/ (This is a broad-spectrum website for law enforcement jobs).

Appendix J

Important Websites

The following websites are helpful for their job announcements and career and other current information provided in specific areas of CJ. Individual states maintain their own websites for CJ agencies and employment opportunities. A little research will allow you to discover all websites related to a specific state. For example, those interested in a CJ career in New Jersey should review the appropriate websites in the list below. Other states and the federal government maintain similar sites. Make a list of all sites that may provide information about the career of your choice.

- www.paralegals.org. National Federation of Paralegal Association provides legal resources, professional development, and networking opportunities.
- www.lawjobs.com. Post your résumé and investigate legal career opportunities.
- www.rileyguide.com/gov. *The Riley Guide* contains job listings for government, defense, and military service in the United States. Opportunities are provided for service with the U.S. federal government, the U.S. Department of Defense, and the military service.
- www.statejobs.com/mi. The Michigan Job Source: browse employers throughout the state. Government jobs are listed with the Michigan State Civil Service, the Michigan State Police, and Michigan State University. See also www.web1.mdcs.state.mi.us/vacancyweb. To locate job vacancies sorted by job title or pay. www.detroit.lib.mi.us/ceic2/jobs_gov.html. For job opportunities, vacancy announcement numbers, testing dates, and requirements.
- www.911.hotjobs.com. 911 HotJobs provides employment and job information on more than two thousand law enforcement departments and agencies are found at this website, as well as law enforcement job books and online practice tests.

- www.quintcareers.com/researching_companies.htm. Quintcareers includes information about companies that are currently hiring. It covers everything from cover letters to résumés to interviewing skills.
- www.jobbankusa.com. JobBankUSA provides a search of federal government jobs and employment information.
- www.indeed.com.
- www.ezinearticles.com/?Law-Enforcement-exam-strategies-How-To-Pass-the-B-Pad.
- www.interstatecompact.org/: the Interstate Compact is a formal agreement between states that oversees the transfer of parolees from one state's jurisdiction to another.
- www.criminaljusticeusa.com: articles cover recent events in CJ, such as the fastest-growing careers in CJ.
- www.usa.gov/agencies/federal/all_agencies. An A–Z index of U.S. government departments and agencies.
- www.ResumeEdge.com. A professional résumé-writing service.
- www.usdoj.gov/oarm. There are more than ten thousand attorneys working for the Department of Justice due to the diversity of matters it must cover.
- www.collegeanswer.com.
- www.collegeboard.com.
- www.fafsa.ed.gov/.
- https://www.linkedin.com/nhome/. A networking site for professionals who report on their current activities.
- www.Investigations.com. References "Bo" Dietl, a retired New York detective.
- www.sheriffs.org. National Sheriffs Association, concerned with national security/law.
- www.convictcriminology.org. Convict Criminology.
- www.jobfed.com. Federal Jobs Digest.
- www.csrees.usda.gov/about/jobs_faq.html.
- www.opm.gov/oca/payrates/.
- www.nps.gov/uspp/hirproc2.htm.
- www.fws.gov.
- www.reference.com/motif/business/free-ksa-samples.
- www.usajobs.gov. The federal government's official job site. Highlights~@bop.gov: news from the Federal Bureau of Prisons.
- www.resumeedge.com. A résumé service for a fee.
- www.linkedin.com/job/law-enforcement-jobs/?trk=jserp_related_searches. This website lists other websites for employment applications in CJ.

NEW JERSEY

- www.state.nj.us/csc. This website identifies jobs in New Jersey that require the applicant to take a civil service examination. The site details a nine-step process (see appendix H) for successfully completing the application. New Jersey does not have a separate Department of Personnel and this information is found under civil service.
- Corrections: www.state.nj.us/corrections/pages/index.shtml.
- Labor: www.lwd.state.nj.us/labor/index.html.
- Human Services: www.state.nj.us/humanserviceswww.state.nj.us/humanservices.
- Juvenile Justice Commission: www.nj.gov/oag/jjc/offices_hr_opps.htm.
- New Jersey Judiciary: www.njcourts.gov/.
- New Jersey State Police: www.njsp.org/.
- New Jersey Civil Service: www.nj.gov/csc/.
- Physical Efficiency Battery for Federal Law Enforcement: www.nps.gov/uspp/pebstan.htm.

Appendix K

Criminal Justice Jobs

An exhaustive list of CJ jobs would be too numerous to mention or to list every title or specialty. Similarly, it is impossible to describe every position. A review of civil service bulletins for a specific state or for the federal government (found in libraries, government buildings, many college CJ departments, career services offices, and other places, including the internet) will provide a listing of current job opportunities with greater specificity to the duties to be performed. This is a very short list of all possible positions. Remember that there are other lesser titles, such as assistant or deputy, that often accompany the greater titles. There are a great number of positions and a vast number of duties to be performed in each category. The point being that while one position may not be ideal, the training for it may be preparatory for another position that has the characteristics that meet the expectations for a career (The Ten-Year Plan). While some experience a career in a single role, there is usually a broad range of opportunities for advancement and change. Career advancement is best prepared for through education and training.

CORRECTIONS

- Commissioner: in some states referred to as a secretary.
- Director: oversees some aspect of the agency.
- Warden: also referred to as a superintendent or in some cases an administrator.
- Corrections Officer: generally, a law enforcement position, could be state or federal, juvenile, or county.
- Teacher: including special needs titles, such as Reading or Disability Specialist, Vocational Training Specialist.
- Business Manager: could be called an accountant.
- Food Services: a Cook or a Manager.
- Maintenance: includes Supervisors and Specialized Staff.

- Architect
- Grants writer
- Researcher
- Counselor
- Social worker
- Psychologist
- Classification Officer: a non–law enforcement title
- Landscape Manager or Horticulturalist

PAROLE

- Chairman of Parole Board
- Hearing Officer for violations
- Supervisor or officer: usually a law enforcement position

PROBATION

- Supervisor or officer, state or federal: may or may not be a law enforcement position.

LAW ENFORCEMENT

- Police Officer
- Special Officer: resort and summer employment
- Specific types of law enforcement officers: Mounted, Harbor, Juvenile, DARE, Canine, Fraud, Electronic, Vice, Property, Animal, Corporate
- Game Warden
- Public Safety Director
- Campus or Hospital Police
- Sheriff/Deputy
- Trooper/Ranger

FEDERAL LAW ENFORCEMENT

- TSA
- FBI
- CIA
- INS

- DEA
- OSHA
- ATF
- Secret Service
- Border Patrol
- Marshal's Service
- Homeland Security Military Police
- U.S. Postal Service
- Other

COURTS AND LEGAL POSITIONS

- Judge: Federal, State, Juvenile, or County
- Court Clerk
- Prosecutor: Federal or State
- Defense Attorney: there are specialized practices in this category
- Paralegal
- Legal Researcher

ACADEMIC POSITIONS

- Researcher
- Professor
- Forensics expert

PRIVATE EMPLOYMENT AND RISK MANAGEMENT

- Asset Protection Planner
- Computer Fraud
- Cyber Crime Analyst
- Investigator
- Loss Prevention Manager
- Private Investigator

- Risk Analyst

OTHER POSITIONS

- Crime Scene Investigator
- Substance Abuse Therapist

Appendix L

Private and Nonprofit Agencies and Professional Organizations

Private, nonprofit agencies and professional organizations are valuable resources for entrance into the CJ career path. These are not government positions. Private and nonprofit service providers operate through government donations, grants, and contracts. The agencies work independently and in partnership with governments performing such tasks as operating private prisons, halfway houses, community justice centers, and other services for CJ, including offenders and ex-offenders. Private and nonprofit providers are a valuable resource when it comes to changing careers or upon retirement when searching for a second career.

Professional organizations can be wonderful places to obtain career information. Some of this information could include job openings, the latest results from scientific research, changes in policy, news, organizational concerns, and more.

Please review the following private providers' listings and visit their websites for more information. Each description of an organization has been taken from its website.

Behavioral Interventions: BI.Com/

Established in 1978, BI Incorporated (BI) is a wholly owned subsidiary of The GEO Group (NYSE: GEO), a global leader in the delivery of correctional, detention, and residential treatment services to federal, state, and local government agencies. BI provides a full continuum of offender monitoring technologies and community reentry services for parolees, probationers, pretrial defendants, and illegal aliens involved in the U.S. immigration court process. BI also owns and operates an ISO-certified national monitoring center, providing 24/7 expert support supervision services exclusively to governmental agencies.

BI works closely with corrections officials to cost effectively reduce recidivism, promote public safety, and strengthen the communities they serve. BI's solutions help federal, state, and local agencies to supervise a range of individuals—from low-to high-risk offender populations. BI combines the latest in technology, expert technical and customer service, ISO-certified manufacturing practices, and evidence-based treatment and counseling programs to assist agencies to curb future crime and conserve scarce local resources.

Corrections Corporation of America: www.correctionscorp.com/

In 1983, our company became the first to provide privatized prison, jail, and detention services. For more than three decades, we have strived to aid governments by reducing costs, alleviating overcrowding, and providing quality correctional care for inmates and detainees. Our approach to public–private partnership in corrections combines the cost savings and innovation of the private sector with the strict guidelines and consistent oversight of the public sector. This continues to produce proven results.

The GEO Group: www.geogroup.com/

GEO's International Services division provides correctional and detention services for government clients in the United Kingdom, Australia, and South Africa managing seven correctional and detention facilities encompassing approximately 7,000 beds. Through wholly owned subsidiary and joint-venture companies, GEO's International Services division provides correctional solutions that are fully customizable and tailored to each government customer's requirements and standards.

International Community Corrections Association (ICCA): iccalive.org/

The International Community Corrections Association, as a private, nonprofit, membership organization, acts as the representative voice for residential and other community corrections programs. As such, it expects of its members compassion, belief in the dignity and worth of human beings, respect for individual difference and a commitment to quality care for its clients. It requires of its members the professional background, research, and expertise necessary to ensure performance of effective quality services delivered with integrity and competence. ICCA affirms that its primary goal is the successful reintegration of the client into the community.

The Kintock Group: kintock.org/

The Kintock Group is a private nonprofit organization that contracts with federal, state, and county law enforcement agencies to provide cost effective alternatives to incarcerations and reentry services for individuals transitioning from the CJ system to the community.

Kintock Programs provide a wide range of accredited services that encourages self-sufficiency, promotes responsible behavior, and prepares program participants to enter the workforce. Services are provided in residential and non-residential settings.

The New Jersey Association of Criminal Justice Educators (NJACJE): www.njacje.org/

Since 1968, the New Jersey Association of Criminal Justice Educators (NJACJE) has been reaching out to academicians in CJ and related fields in an effort to enhance the quality of undergraduate and graduate education in the discipline. The organization was established during the early years of the Law Enforcement Assistance Administration (LEAA) as the Council of Educational Institutions for Law Enforcement (CEILE). It was formed with the support of the state's Chancellor of Higher Education to develop a Master Plan for Higher Education in Criminal Justice. One of the organizational goals was to function as liaison between the New Jersey Division of Criminal Justice (the major funding agency in the state for LEAA), and the rapidly multiplying Police Science Programs that began to develop. The Council met monthly over the years to discuss issues related to CJ education and to plan and sponsor numerous symposia, seminars, and workshops on various CJ issues. During the 1970s, CEILE affiliated with the Academy of Criminal Justice Sciences and represented the state's CJ educators at their meetings.

The New Jersey Association on Corrections (NJAC): www.njaconline.org/

Mission Statement: To promote social justice and human dignity in the policies and institutions which govern offenders and victims of crime through educational, legislative, and rehabilitative programs.

The New Jersey Chapter of The American Correctional Association: www.njaca.org/

The New Jersey Chapter of the American Correctional Association is a nonprofit professional organization that has served as a forum for corrections in

New Jersey since 1983. Membership includes a wide variety of correctional employees drawing from probation, parole, institutions, community-based facilities, treatments centers, schools, law enforcement, the judiciary, and related governmental and private agencies. We provide CJ practitioners in New Jersey with educational training and networking opportunities.

The American Correctional Association (ACA): www.aca.org/

The American Correctional Association provides a professional organization for all individuals and groups, both public and private that share a common goal of improving the justice system.

Volunteers of America (VOA): www.voa.org/

At Volunteers of America, we are more than a nonprofit organization. We are a ministry of service that includes nearly 16,000 paid, professional employees dedicated to helping those in need rebuild their lives and reach their full potential.

Through our hundreds of human service programs, including housing and healthcare, Volunteers of America touches the lives of more than 2 million people in over 400 communities in 46 states as well as the District of Columbia and Puerto Rico each year. Since 1896, we have supported and empowered America's most vulnerable groups, including veterans, at-risk youth, the frail elderly, men and women returning from prison, homeless individuals and families, people with disabilities, and those recovering from addictions. Our work touches the mind, body, heart—and ultimately the spirit—of those we serve, integrating our deep compassion with highly effective programs and services.

American Society of Criminology (ASC): www.asc41.com/

The American Society of Criminology is an international organization whose members pursue scholarly, scientific, and professional knowledge concerning the measurement, etiology, consequences, prevention, control, and treatment of crime and delinquency.

The society's objectives are to encourage the exchange, in a multidisciplinary setting, of those engaged in research, teaching, and practice so as to foster criminological scholarship, and to serve as a forum for the dissemination of criminological knowledge. Our membership includes students, practitioners, and academicians from the many fields of CJ and criminology.

National Sheriffs' Association (NSA): www.sheriffs.org/

Our primary goal at the National Sheriffs' Association is to preserve and protect the Office of Sheriff, so that the sheriffs of this country can provide quality service to their constituents.

We try to achieve that goal by being a voice for the sheriffs of this nation, and by providing resources to sheriffs all over the country.

The 3,080 sheriffs of the United States are very diverse and have different jurisdictional sizes and challenges of their offices. All sheriffs share the common goal of protecting the citizens that elected them and make the quality of life the best it can be.

National Organization of Black Law Enforcement Executives (NOBLE): www.noblenational.org/

The goal of NOBLE is to be recognized as a highly competent, public service organization that is at the forefront of providing solutions to law enforcement issues and concerns, as well as to the ever-changing needs of our communities.

The objectives that are employed to implement the goal of the organization include:

An emphasis on being a competent learning organization that continuously learns from the collective knowledge of its members, and other sources of CJ research and data, while simultaneously working to rapidly convert this learning into action.

Working to ensure long-term organizational stability by identifying and establishing mutually beneficial relationships with corporations and other funding sources.

Recommending and executing policies, processes, and procedures that recognize and pursue goals common to all segments of the community and law enforcement, with a focus on ensuring strict accountability and uncompromising integrity.

Promoting and encouraging attitudes and characteristics that permit adaptability to the changing demands placed on law enforcement, and the development of professional and communication competencies that help view, comprehend, and shape appropriate responses to an ever-changing environment; and

Increasing the effectiveness and efficiency of NOBLE through a clearly defined and shared sense of purpose and commitment among its members.

International Association of Chiefs of Police (IACP): www.theiacp.org/

The International Association of Chiefs of Police (IACP) is a dynamic organization that serves as the professional voice of law enforcement. Building on our past success, the IACP addresses cutting-edge issues confronting law enforcement though advocacy, programs, and research, as well as training and other professional services. IACP is a comprehensive professional organization that supports the law enforcement leaders of today and develops the leaders of tomorrow.

Police Executive Research Forum (PERF): www.policeforum.org/

The Police Executive Research Forum (PERF) is an independent research organization that focuses on critical issues in policing. Since its founding in 1976, PERF has identified best practices on fundamental issues such as reducing police use of force; developing community policing and problem oriented policing; using technologies to deliver police services to the community; and evaluating crime reduction strategies.

PERF strives to advance professionalism in policing and to improve the delivery of police services through the exercise of strong national leadership; public debate of police and CJ issues; and research and policy development.

Appendix M

Vermont Police Academy Basic Training and Physical Fitness Training

VERMONT POLICE ACADEMY BASIC TRAINING CURRICULUM SUMMARY

	Hours
COMMUNICATION	
Courtroom Demeanor	8
Conflict Resolution	4
Interpersonal Communication	4
Media/Police Relations	2
Report Writing	32
TOTAL	***50***
LAW	
Criminal Law	54
Motor Vehicle Law	44
Occupant Protection Usage & Enforcement	2
Hazardous Material Recognition	8
Introduction to Fish & Wildlife	2
Alcohol Services Education & Alcohol Services Act	10
Introduction to Federal Agencies	2
Juvenile Law & Procedure	8
Police Liability	4
Landlord & Tenant Law	2
Use of Vermont Statutes	2
TOTAL	***138***
INVESTIGATIVE PROCEDURES	
Crash Investigation	40
Case Problems and Evidence Collection	24
Death Investigation	4
Domestic Violence Response	12
Drug Identification & Investigation	8
Interview & Interrogation Techniques	16
Sexual Assault Investigation	12
Sexual/Physical Abuse of Children	12
Hate Crimes Investigation	8
Terrorism	4
NCIC/VCIC	4
Victims Assistance Program	2
Court Diversion	2
NIMS/ICS	4
Vulnerable Adult Abuse	2
Stalking	2
Animal Cruelty	2
TOTAL	***158***
PROFESSIONAL DEMEANOR	
Sexual Harassment Policy	2

Stress Management	8
Core Values & Leadership Training	4
Cultural Diversity	2
Police Ethics	8
History & Principles of Policing	6
Teambuilding & Problem Solving	14
TOTAL	***44***
<u>PHYSICAL FITNESS</u>	
Nutrition Information	2
Physical Assessment	4
Physical Training	95
TOTAL	***102***
<u>POLICE PATROL TECHNIQUES</u>	
Defensive Driving	24
Bloodborne Pathogens	2
Crime Prevention	2
Community Policing	6
Community Policing Project	10
Patrol Procedures Classroom:	
Preparation for Duty	3
Observation & Perception	2
Patrol Techniques	4
Radio Communications	2
Prisoner Transport	2
Scenario Safety Training	1
Arrest Paperwork	1
Unknown Risk MV Stops	4
Crimes in Progress	8
Police K9 Operations	2
Dealing with People with Mental Illness	6
Dealing with the Deaf & Hard of Hearing	2
Dealing with People with Physical Disabilities	2
Traffic Control	2
Patrol Procedures Scenarios:	
Practice Scenarios	54
Final Scenarios	32
Firearms	56
Non-lethal Use of Force	40
Impact Weapon	4
Oleoresin Capsicum Certification	4
Field Experience at Agency	16
TOTAL	***291***
<u>OTHERS</u>	
Administrative/Staff Time	8
Drill and Ceremony	10
FINAL EXAMINATION	2
TOTAL	***20***
TOTAL HOURS FOR BASIC TRAINING	***803***

POST BASIC INSTRUCTION	
D.U.I/DRE Enforcement	40
V.I.N. Verification	4
Basic Fingerprinting Techniques	4
Doppler Radar Operation	8
First Aid	4
C.P.R.	12
Spillman Training (optional)	12
Shotgun Training (optional)	8
LIDAR (Laser) (optional)	8
TOTAL POST-BASIC TRAINING	***100***
TOTAL HOURS FOR BASIC TRAINING	***903***

Source: http://www.vcjtc.state.vt.us/basic.htm

VERMONT PHYSICAL FITNESS TRAINING

Physical Assessment Minimum Standards: 40th Percentile Requirements					
MALE	***Flexibility***	***Bench Press***	***Sit-Ups***	***Push-Ups***	***1.5-mile run***
20–29	16.5	0.99	38	29	12:29
30–39	15.5	0.88	35	24	12:53
40–49	14.3	0.80	29	18	13:50
50–59	13.3	0.71	24	13	15:14
FEMALE	***Flexibility***	***Bench Press***	***Sit-Ups***	***Push-Ups***	***1.5-mile run***
20–29	19.3	0.59	32	15	15:05
30–39	18.3	0.53	25	11	15:56
40–49	17.3	0.50	20	9	17:11
50–59	16.8	0.44	14	n/a	19:10
Physical Assessment Minimum Standards: 50th Percentile Requirements					
MALE	***Flexibility***	***Bench Press***	***Sit-Ups***	***Push-Ups***	***1.5-mile run***
20–29	17.5	1.06	40	33	11:58
30–39	16.5	0.93	36	27	12:25
40–49	15.3	0.84	31	21	13:05
50–59	14.5	0.75	26	15	14:33
FEMALE	***Flexibility***	***Bench Press***	***Sit-Ups***	***Push-Ups***	***1.5-mile run***
20–29	20.0	0.65	35	18	14:15
30–39	19.0	0.57	27	14	15:14

Source: http://www.howstuffworks.com/framed.htm?parent=police-academy.htm&url=http://www.vcjtc.state.vt.us/basic.htm

Appendix N

Paying for College

A college education is expensive, and the costs constantly rise. Public community colleges will cost approximately $7,500 per year, and major private colleges can cost as much as $60,000 per year. Other major costs include fees, books, and room and board (although these costs may be included in the semester billing).

College education for a career requires diligent planning. Debt accumulation for many is unavoidable, but you will want to manage and minimize your debt accumulation from the beginning.

Some considerations for college financial plan include: How much are you willing to pay in cash? How much can you earn? What is your tolerance for loans? And what is your eligibility for scholarships or grants to offset the costs? Loans can take years to pay off, and they may affect your life decisions after graduating with a degree. We urge you to only borrow what is needed to avoid fiscal difficulty and long-term debt that may carry a high interest rate.

Strategies that may seem safe at the time can become a fiscal cliff, such as using credit cards to pay for tuition, books, and other campus activities. The interest rates for credit cards are prohibitive if you cannot pay them off each month. We suggest that if you have a savings account, do not raid it. It represents a safety net in case of unforeseen financial need. Some strategies include saving and earning as you go. To accomplish this, you will need to set up a budget, examine your spending, determine where you can reduce spending, and then keep the savings. There are internet sites to help you with this, including Bankrate.com and Finaid.org.

PART-TIME AND FULL-TIME ATTENDANCE

If you want to finish your degree as quickly as possible, full-time attendance is the surer strategy. Of course, not everyone can attend school full-time, and 120 or more course credits can seem like a very large number. However, remember that each course is about three credits. At three credits a course, you only need to take about forty courses to complete your degree. This may sound more manageable. Nevertheless, part-time attendance will also get you to the goal of a college degree; it will just take a little longer.

Some students may have to change their schedule from full-time to part-time, and others may feel like they need to take a break for personal or financial reasons. We do not advocate taking such breaks under many circumstances, because many students fail to return. However, if a break is necessary, try to return at the earliest possible time, preferably the next semester. If you must change from a full-time schedule, then we suggest other options, including the following:

- Consult with a counselor before you leave.
- Take one or more courses every semester to maintain continuity and enrollment at the college.
- Remember that changing from full-time to part-time status will affect your funding for college. For example, to maintain Pell Grant eligibility, you must be enrolled for a minimum of 12 credits a semester. Part-time students must be enrolled for a minimum of six credits per semester, or federal assistance may be eliminated.
- Enroll in a local college for one or more courses if you are leaving your college campus and returning home. Make sure the course credit will be accepted at the college of your choice and count toward your degree. Do not assume that this is true because a course has the same title as the one taught at your college. Your chosen college will assess the requirements and course content to be sure it is a match with its course.
- Return to the college of your choice at the earliest possible time.

COLLEGE IS NOT FOR EVERYONE

Unfortunately, the *why* you are attending college is not always as clear to everyone as they would like to believe that it is. For some people, college is not an appropriate choice. So why are you attending college?

- Because you want to get a degree?
- Because someone else is paying for it?
- Because someone else is telling you that you should go?
- Because you have always been told that you need to go to college?
- Because you think it is the right thing to do?
- Because you don't want to disappoint someone?

These are all the wrong reasons. You should be attending college because it is what *you* want to do. You should be attending college because it will help you reach a personal goal.

Some students are intimidated by the thought of attending college and by the fear that they will not do well. If this is the case, you do have options. You may take one course to try it out—you can take it at a community college. Community colleges provide wonderful assistance to students, including counseling services, tutors, and labs to assist you with reading, writing, and math problems. These services exist to help you, and you should take advantage of them. Some professors will also extend themselves to help you get over hurdles—seek them out and let them help you.

There is also the consideration that you may discover that college is not for you. This discovery is not failure. This merely indicates a level of self-understanding that can guide you to other satisfying career decisions. We suggest that if this determination is made, find other alternatives to choose from, including technical and vocational schools.

STEPS TO PAY FOR COLLEGE

First, fill out the Free Application for Federal Student Aid (FAFSA) online at www.fafsa.ed.gov/. The FAFSA will establish your eligibility for federal financial aid. (Caution: There are other sites that sometimes come up in place of the FAFSA. These sites charge you a small fee to fill out the form. We suggest that you avoid these sites. They are not the official site.) Among the available programs to assist with funding are Pell Grants, Stafford Loans, and PLUS Loans. The amount you receive from each is determined by the FAFSA. The last two are loans that must be paid back. If you know someone experienced with the FAFSA ask for help but be sure to protect your PIN. The FAFSA is a user-friendly form that allows you to go back and make changes. However, if you misplace your PIN, then the process becomes much more difficult. The FAFSA must be newly completed each year.

Note: Your tax forms or those of your parents will be required.

Second, visit your selected school's financial aid office. The office can advise you of any scholarship opportunities available through a specific school or from other sources.

Third, apply for a scholarship(s). Scholarships are not just for good students or low-income families. There are scholarships for everything, from ones for girls who are over six feet tall, to vegans, to students with unusual last names. It takes time and effort to find them and apply.

There is an expression in football: "Go deep!" Search for scholarships in your hometown (like from the Lions Club or the Elks), college, workplace, and unions. You may spend hours searching, but if you don't quit, you will find financial assistance. Some scholarships only apply to students in their junior or senior year of high school. Some scholarships are for older students. There are scholarships and grants for laid-off workers or for those who are at a midpoint in their careers. Your search will only be limited by your imagination and your ability to describe yourself.

Research has made the recognition of disabilities more common. Any disability (or illness), from attention deficit disorder to classifications such as dysgraphia (a handwriting disability), may qualify for a scholarship or gain assistance at a college or university with test-taking, note-taking, and special permission to use a computer to take tests. Check for scholarships awarded by gender, ethnicity, or religion, and if you have already done something unusual, such as organizing a relief effort, or a charity, or resolved some community issue, then these may qualify you for financial assistance.

This book is about careers in the CJ system, and it seems only appropriate to mention the other side of the coin—those who have offended. Young people for whatever reason may have at some point found themselves on the wrong side of the law. An education has the most potential to help people regain their footing in society. There are exclusions from some specified careers in CJ, such as law enforcement, because the offense eliminates the possibility of carrying a weapon. Nevertheless, there are jobs available in other sectors of the CJ profession for which a weapon is not a requirement. In fact, if the offense was a juvenile offense, the list of precluded forms of employment is considerably shorter. In some cases, there may not be an offense but a documented problem, such as substance abuse. Such cases may be eligible for Pell Grants or even grants from agencies such as the Rehabilitation Commission. A degree is a powerful way to decrease uncertainty in your future. If there is uncertainty about this, we would suggest that the reader visit the Convict Criminology website and read the profiles of some ex-con PhD professors of criminology. (Especially be sure to visit the Convict Criminology website for information about Dr. Richards, who founded the group.)

Any of the ideas mentioned above can be entered into online search engines. Enter them, rephrase them, turn expressions around, and reenter them. Do not be discouraged—*keep searching!*

Check online. Here are some easy sites that are visited regularly by students: www.fastweb.com, www.collegeanswer.com, and www. collegeboard. com. These may or may not help you find a scholarship, but they will provide a guide to what is possible and to the application process. Once you start the process, the answers you develop may apply to many scholarship opportunities.

Federal loans. Realizing you need a loan can surely be an "ouch" moment—they incur debt. Loans are available to both parents and students.

Be cautious of private loans from banks and other lenders. Read carefully for the interest rates and conditions, such as when they must be paid back or when interest starts to accumulate. Federal loan programs generally offer better interest rates and terms for repayment. Many federal loans have loan forgiveness if you elect to do public service after completing your degree or if you go to work for a federal agency. Another piece of good news about federal loans is that there may be deferred payment conditions in the event of a job loss.

State loans. States provide loans and grants. For good students, there may be in-state free tuition if you score in an upper percentile of your class. Some state universities offer free tuition to students who excel during all four years of high school. New Jersey and Georgia, for example, have the STARS program.

Foundation grants. Search foundations, such as those founded by Bill Gates, George Soros, Guggenheim, and others, for special opportunities. These are sites that should be visited frequently because there are deadlines for the completion of the application process. Application guidelines must be followed rigorously. Be thorough and do not assume. If help is needed, contact information is generally provided—use it!

Here is a list of what you should *not* do when seeking scholarships, grants, and other forms of funding:

- *Do not* downplay low income or other forms of personal adversity (some of which are mentioned above). These need to be acknowledged on all applications. If you have a personal hardship, acknowledge it. If something changes at home, or if there is a job loss, medical event, or another sibling who decides to also attend school, contact your financial aid office. You may be eligible for additional financial aid or a work-study program.
- *Do not* discount a work-study program. Colleges offer such programs. Work-study is the opportunity to work on the college campus in exchange for tuition. Some jobs are offered by the college, some are offered through a private company, or some are offered as the result of obtaining a Pell Grant. There are usually more students seeking these jobs than there are positions available. Even if you are advised that all current positions have been filled, you should ask if there is an application for you to complete in case someone else drops out. Once you are on the list, the chances that you will obtain a work-study position the following semester increases greatly. After obtaining a position, you most likely will continue to be eligible in each of the following semesters as long as you participate. Work-study offers should not be ignored. This is

employment that can also be placed on a résumé, and you may be able to use your supervisor as a reference to secure a future job.

- *Do not* ignore other potential sources of funding. Don't forget to compare financial aid packages and use any AP (Advanced Placement) credits, which may help you graduate sooner. Numerous websites provide additional help, including the College Board (https://www.collegeboard.org/) and American Student Assistance (www.asa.org/). Also, use the various tax deductions for which you may be eligible. While paying for college, you may be eligible for some additional tax credits, such as the American Opportunity tax credit (www.irs.gov/uac/American-Opportunity-Tax-Credit) and the Lifetime Learning tax credit (www.finaid.org/otheraid/lifetimelearning.phtm).

A final note on advancing toward the degree. If you have hobbies, interests, or other unique experiences (such as proficiency in a foreign language), you may be able to use it to get college credit. There are CLEP examinations (visit clep.collegeboard.org), and if you successfully complete them, you will be awarded college credit. Please make sure that your college will accept these credits first, and that the course(s) tested for are accepted by your college toward the degree you are seeking.

EMPLOYMENT AFTER COLLEGE

Some public employment opportunities, such as teaching or law enforcement, may offer incentives for accepting employment, such loan forgiveness of federal loans after working for a specified period of time. Completion of specified courses and advanced degrees may result in additional salary incentives.

Military Service, The GI Bill, and Other Sources of Reimbursement

Opportunities for active-duty military personnel stationed stateside or abroad include college credit that may be earned in several ways. First, there are colleges and universities that provide independent study and classroom instruction. Some are offered on U.S. military bases in other countries. Among the colleges and universities that offer such coursework are the University of Maryland, Kaplan University, Central Texas Community College, and Pepperdine University.

Then there is the College Level Examination Program, or CLEP (visit clep.collegeboard.org). CLEP can be valuable if you choose to do self-preparation for your career. You can study on your own, pay a fee for the CLEP test, and if you pass, you will be awarded college credit. Many training programs in the military have been evaluated for college credit by the American Council on Education (ACE). Visit www.acenet.edu for further information. Take advantage of any training operations you complete. Your training officer can probably advise which training opportunities have been approved for college credit. In some cases, the training may only be assessed for a few credits, whereas others may be assessed for many credits. The author evaluated training for ACE at Fort Leonard Wood, the Coast Guard Academy, and the Virginia State Police, and because of the depth of training, the number of hours of instruction, and the content of the course, the evaluators determined that that training was worth college credits in specific course areas. ACE evaluations are paid for by the military (or other vendors), and there is no charge for the men and women in the service for this award of college credit.

Upon leaving the service or terminating active duty and remaining on reserve status, there is also the GI Bill, which can help cover the cost of college. The money from the GI Bill is used to reimburse the student for tuition, books, and even a potential living allowance. The only catch is that the student must pass each course with a grade of C or better. Many colleges and universities provide a tuition discount out of respect for our military personnel's service to their country. Tuition reimbursement for undergraduate credits and for graduate school may be possible if you are already on the job or in an active search of a job. While working you should be able to continue your education.

The number of courses you elect to take will be driven by your work and personal responsibilities. If you are already working, ask whether your company/agency has a reimbursement plan. These are not uncommon in government and private nonprofit agencies, although not all may offer the program. Nevertheless, *ask!*

As a side note, this is a good interview question to ask if a potential employer asks you whether you have any questions. You may discover a little-known benefit to going to work for a particular company, *and* you will demonstrate through your question that you seek to improve yourself. Your questions about tuition reimbursement may even generate more questions from the employer, through which you can share more about yourself, your interests, and your potential skill development that would be valuable to their company/agency. Again, this is an opportunity for you to sell yourself and your value to a particular agency or company—just through this one question.

Appendix O

Criminal Justice and Trade Publications

Publications about CJ fall into several categories, including professional magazines, journals, newsletters, and trade publications. Each publication has value for the person seeking to enter the CJ field, someone looking to change positions within the field, or a CJ employee who simply wishes to remain current in the industry.

JOURNALS

The journals that are listed below are those that the student may find to be helpful when determining a career path. The vast number of journals in the field makes it impossible to list them all. Students often find journals difficult to read because they often include complicated statistics and unfamiliar technical language. This is not meant to discourage or to dissuade students from reading journals—they should, especially since journals contain current research and articles about ideas that influence the field.

- *The Journal of Correctional Education*
- *The Journal of American Probation and Parole*
- *The Journal of Prisons and Prisoners*

MAGAZINES

Magazines differ from journals in that they contain articles of high interest, special projects and their success, notifications of conferences, job openings, book critiques, and much more. Magazines in the area of CJ advise the reader of leaders in the field and how they came to their positions. The descriptions below have been taken from each magazine's website.

Corrections Today magazine, Alexandria, Virginia, American Correctional Association: https://aca.org/

Corrections Today magazine is a professional magazine that addresses current issues, training opportunities, and needs. It is sent to every member of the American Correctional Association and provides lists of new members, associate organizations, job postings, conference listings, and much more.

New Jersey Cops, www.njcopsmagazine.com/

New Jersey Cops magazine is the voice of New Jersey Law Enforcement and the only monthly publication that provides direct access to more than 65,000-plus Law Enforcement professionals across the state of New Jersey.

Now in its 25th year of publishing, we reach every police department, municipality, mayor's office, county sheriff's office, state police facility, correctional facility, federal and state law enforcement office, colleges and universities, and local offices of related organizations.

Each month, we publish industry news and events, profiles of cops and their departments, product and equipment reviews, legislative developments, and updates and advice from experts on and off the job.

Every issue includes important information about lifestyle and leisure pursuits—such as automobiles, financial planning, real estate, education, legal, travel, and especially health and wellness.

New Jersey Cops is recognized by state and national law enforcement groups as a leader in editorial coverage of important topics such as Best Practices for police work; National Police Week; National Law Enforcement Memorial; Special Olympics; the Police Unity Tour; police health issues.

NEWSLETTERS

Newsletters tend to focus on local CJ news or to be regional in scope. That is, they may be specific to an agency, to a state, or to a specific group. Newsletters will contain articles about the group's membership, issues that group members are currently facing, and changes in relevant legislation, as well as advice columns and much more.

"The George Yefchak Quarterly Newsletter of the New Jersey Chapter of the American Correctional Association," www.njaca.org/about_us.htm/

The newsletter is the voice of the membership discussing relevant issues in probation, parole, correctional institutions, community-based correctional facilities, treatments centers, law enforcement, the judiciary, related governmental and private agencies, and the training academies.

"The New Jersey Criminal Justice Educator Newsletter," www. njacje.org/

Since 1968, the New Jersey Association of Criminal Justice Educators (NJACJE) has been reaching out to academicians in CJ and related fields to enhance the quality of undergraduate and graduate education in the discipline. The organization was established during the early years of the Law Enforcement Assistance Administration (LEAA) as the Council of Educational Institutions for Law Enforcement (CEILE). It was formed with the support of the state's Chancellor of Higher Education to develop a Master Plan for Higher Education in CJ. One of the organizational goals was to function as liaison between the New Jersey Division of Criminal Justice (the major funding agency in the state for LEAA), and the rapidly multiplying Police Science Programs. The Council met monthly over the years to discuss issues related to CJ education and to plan and sponsor numerous symposia, seminars, and workshops on various CJ issues. During the 1970s, CEILE affiliated with the Academy of Criminal Justice Sciences (ACJS) and represented the state's CJ educators at their meetings.

"Prison Legal News," www.prisonlegalnews.org/

"Prison Legal News," a project of the Human Rights Defense Center, is an independent 72-page monthly magazine that provides cutting edge review and analysis of prisoners' rights, court rulings and news concerning CJ-related issues. "PLN" has a national (U.S.) focus on both state and federal prison issues, with some international coverage. "PLN" provides information that enables prisoners and other concerned individuals and organizations to gain a better understanding of a broad range of CJ topics, including issues related to the protection and enforcement of prisoners' rights.

"PoliceOne's eNewsletter," www.policeone.com/police-newsletter

"PoliceOne's eNewsletter" brings the latest police news to more law enforcement professionals than any other online. The newsletter is sent out three times per week to more than 150,000 LEOs. What's even better, it's free to sign up.

The "PoliceOne eNewsletter" is designed to keep all members of the law enforcement community, from chiefs to rookies, up to date on the latest news and industry trends. It covers topics such as police technology, safety, and training affecting officers everywhere. Each newsletter contains exclusive columns, secure tactical tips, and videos from BluTube and PoliceOneTV.

TRADE PUBLICATIONS

Trade publications are different in content from other publications listed in this appendix. The trade magazine is usually specific to a CJ profession such as architecture or food service. Trade publications are often ignored by students, professors, and those looking for careers in the CJ field. Their recipients include practitioners who work in a specific specialty, professionals, and administrators who service the CJ profession, and members of CJ organizations or associations. What makes these magazines distinct is that they offer a wide range of information. Sometimes an entire edition is devoted to a specific theme. Their value is immense because they provide information on upcoming conferences, job openings, new construction projects, new products specific to the industry, changes in philosophy, changes in legislation, changes in administration personnel, selected news articles, and so much more. One of the more peculiar and interesting features of these publications is that they will often include articles about more obscure topics that are not found in traditional textbooks or other resources (one example might be the history of food service in prisons). The trade publication is usually controlled by public agencies, unions, or other corporations.

Correctional News: Design, Construction, Operations, San Rafael, CA, Emlen Media Corporation: https://correctionalnews.com/

Correctional News was founded in 1984 and addresses design, maintenance, and operational issues surrounding correctional facilities as well as a wide range of current correctional issues.

Security Magazine, http://www.securitymagazine.com/

Security is uniquely focused on solutions for enterprise security leaders. It is designed and written for business-minded executives who manage enterprise risk and security. *Security* provides management focused features, opinions, and trends for leaders in business, government, and institutional sectors in print, in person, and online.

Appendix P

Codes of Ethics

Codes of ethics have been written to help guide the conduct of group members. We encourage the future CJ professional to review the sample codes for this industry that we have included in this appendix. When you begin your first job and/or move on to other agencies, you will discover that each area of the industry, and each specific agency or department, has its own code of ethics. We refer the reader to chapter 8 of this book, which explores the overall subject of ethics for the CJ employee.

AMERICAN CORRECTIONAL ASSOCIATION CODE OF ETHICS[1]

Preamble

The American Correctional Association expects of its members unfailing honesty, respect for the dignity and individuality of human beings, and a commitment to professional and compassionate service. To this end, we subscribe to the following principles.

- Members shall respect and protect the civil and legal rights of all individuals.
- Members shall treat every professional situation with concern for the welfare of the individuals involved and with no intent to personal gain.
- Members shall maintain relationships with colleagues to promote mutual respect within the profession and improve the quality of service.
- Members shall make public criticism of their colleagues or their agencies only when warranted, verifiable, and constructive.
- Members shall respect the importance of all disciplines within the CJ system and work to improve cooperation with each segment.

- Members shall honor the public's right to information and share information with the public to the extent permitted by law subject to individuals' right to privacy.
- Members shall respect and protect the right of the public to be safeguarded from criminal activity.
- Members shall refrain from using their positions to secure personal privileges or advantages.
- Members shall refrain from allowing personal interest to impair objectivity in the performance of duty while acting in an official capacity.
- Members shall refrain from entering into any formal or informal activity or agreement which presents a conflict of interest or is inconsistent with the conscientious performance of duties.
- Members shall refrain from accepting any gifts, services, or favors that are or appear to be improper or implies an obligation inconsistent with the free and objective exercise of professional duties.
- Members shall clearly differentiate between personal views/statements and views/statements/positions made on behalf of the agency or association.
- Members shall report to appropriate authorities any corrupt or unethical behaviors in which there is sufficient evidence to justify review.
- Members shall refrain from discriminating against any individual because of race, gender, creed, national origin, religious affiliation, age, disability, or any other type of prohibited discrimination.
- Members shall preserve the integrity of private information; they shall refrain from seeking information on individuals beyond that which is necessary to implement responsibilities and perform their duties; members shall refrain from revealing nonpublic information unless expressly authorized to do so.
- Members shall make all appointments, promotions, and dismissals in accordance with established civil service rules, applicable contract agreements, and individual merit, rather than furtherance of personal interests.
- Members shall respect, promote, and contribute to a workplace that is safe, healthy, and free of harassment in any form.

AMERICAN PROBATION AND PAROLE ASSOCIATION CODE OF ETHICS[2]

1. I will render professional service to the justice system and the community at large in effecting the social adjustment of the offender.

2. I will uphold the law with dignity, displaying an awareness of my responsibility to offenders while recognizing the right of the public to be safeguarded from criminal activity.
3. I will strive to be objective in the performance of my duties, recognizing the inalienable right of all persons, appreciating the inherent worth of the individual, and respecting those confidences which can be reposed in me.
4. I will conduct my personal life with decorum, neither accepting nor granting favors in connection with my office.
5. I will cooperate with my co-workers and related agencies and will continually strive to improve my professional competence through the seeking and sharing of knowledge and understanding.
6. I will distinguish clearly, in public, between my statements and actions as an individual and as a representative of my profession.
7. I will encourage policy, procedures and personnel practices, which will enable others to conduct themselves in accordance with the values, goals and objectives of the American Probation and Parole Association.
8. I recognize my office as a symbol of public faith and I accept it as a public trust to be held as long as I am true to the ethics of the American Probation and Parole Association.
9. I will constantly strive to achieve these objectives and ideals, dedicating myself to my chosen profession.

INTERNATIONAL ASSOCIATION OF CHIEFS OF POLICE: LAW ENFORCEMENT CODE OF ETHICS[3]

As A Law Enforcement Officer, my fundamental duty is to serve mankind; to safeguard lives and property; to protect the innocent against deception, the weak against oppression or intimidation, and the peaceful against violence or disorder; and to respect the Constitutional rights of all men to liberty, equality and justice.

I Will keep my private life unsullied as an example to all; maintain courageous calm in the face of danger, scorn, or ridicule; develop self-restraint; and be constantly mindful of the welfare of others. Honest in thought and deed in both my personal and official life, I will be exemplary in obeying the laws of the land and the regulations of my department. Whatever I see or hear of a confidential nature or that is confided to me in my official capacity will be kept ever secret unless revelation is necessary in the performance of my duty.

I Will never act officiously or permit personal feelings, prejudices, animosities, or friendships to influence my decisions. With no compromise for crime and with relentless prosecution of criminals, I will enforce the law courteously and appropriately without fear or favor, malice, or ill will, never employing unnecessary force or violence and never accepting gratuities.

I Recognize the badge of my office as a symbol of public faith, and I accept it as a public trust to be held so long as I am true to the ethics of the police service. I will constantly strive to achieve these objectives and ideals, dedicating myself before God to my chosen profession . . . law enforcement.

Notes

PREFACE

1. https://nypost.com/2020/04/30/over-70-percient-of-inmates-in-federal-prisons-have-covid-19/.
2. https://www.law.cornell.edu/wex/criminal_justice.

INTRODUCTION

1. Butterfield, F. 1998. A newcomer breaks into the liberal arts: Criminal justice. With a little help from the movies and TV, a subject that once got no respect attracts students. New York Times: 87.
2. https://nces.ed.gov/programs/digest/d07/tables/dt07_222.asp.
3. https://datausa.io/profile/cip/criminal-justice-corrections.
4. See https://smartasset.com/insights/the-economics-of-the-american-prisonsystem.
5. See http://www.vera.org/files/price-of-prisons-california-fact-sheet.pdf.
6. Ibid.
7. See http://www.detroitnews.com/article/99999999/POLITICS/80414001.

CHAPTER 1

1. "What works" is a specific term that refers to problem-solving approaches, that is, approaches that have been researched and found to be successful. They are also referred to as "evidence-based approaches."
2. The Pete Rose case is an example of the intersection between criminal law and civil actions. While he has paid his debt and served his time, Major League Baseball has instituted and maintained a lifetime ban from baseball.

3. *Dry-labbing* is the presentation of evidence, i.e., DNA, for which no test has been conducted. The Innocence Project has uncovered several instances of this that resulted in innocent persons being sentenced to prison. Fortunately, through the Innocence Project, they have been exonerated and released from prison.

4. Law enforcement agencies have Employee Assistance Programs (EAP) to help those who are struggling with personal problems. There are peer counseling programs in many states, in which police officers generally trained as clinicians volunteer their time to assist fellow officers. New Jersey's Cop 2 Cop program is the only program that is mandated by state statute.

5. Robert Longworthy and Lawrence Travis, *Policing in America: A Balance of Forces* (Upper Saddle River, NJ: Prentice Hall, 1999)

6. Ted Conover, *Newjack* (New York: Random House, 2000).

7. Len Ward is the Director of the Division of Parole and Community Programs for the New Jersey State Parole Board. He holds a BA from Jersey City State College and a master's degree in public administration from Fairleigh Dickinson University. He began his career in the Department of Transportation and advanced to positions with the Departments of Law and Public Safety and the Department of Corrections. He is a certified instructor by the NJ Police Training Commission and certified by the U.S. Department of Justice in community-oriented policing. He is an adjunct professor of criminal justice at Fairleigh Dickinson University.

8. Dorothy Taylor, *Jump Starting Your Career: An Internship Guide for Criminal Justice*, second ed. (Upper Saddle River, NJ: Pearson Education, Inc., 2005).

9. See *Seven Habits of Highly Successful People* by Stephen Covey. You may be particularly interested in the section titled "Sharpening the Sword."

10. Matthew Sheridan and Stephen Richards, "Collateral Consequences: Felony Convictions," in *The Encyclopedia of Criminal Justice Ethics* (Thousand Oaks, CA: Sage Publications, 2013).

11. Todd Clear, George Cole, and Michael Reisig, *American Corrections*, eighth ed. (Belmont, CA: Thompson Higher Education, 2009)

CHAPTER 2

1. Michael Di Lieto, *How to Become a New Jersey Police Officer or State Trooper* (Maywood, NJ: NJ Law Enforcement Recruit Resources, 2005–2008).

2. Jennifer A. Richeson and Richard J. Nussbaum, "The Impact of Multiculturalism Versus Color-Blindness on Racial Bias," *Journal of Experimental Social Psychology* 40, no. 3 (May 2004): 417–423.

3. https://www.policechiefmagazine.org/creating-a-multicultural-law-enforcement-agency/

4. http://www.goarmy.com/careers-and-jobs/browse-career-and-job-categories/legal-andlawenforcement/military-police.html.

5. http://www.wood.army.mil/usamps/CMDTReadingList.pdf.

4. http://www.wood.army.mil/usamps/CMDTReadingList.pdf.

CHAPTER 3

1. Census of State and Federal Correctional Facilities, 2005, http://www.bjs.gov/content/pub/pdf/csfcf05.pdf.

2. Census of Jail Facilities, 2006, http://www.bjs.gov/content/pub/pdf/cjf06. pdf.

3. Lauren E. Glaze and Danielle Kaeble, "Correctional Populations in the United States," *Bureau of Justice Statistics* (December 19, 2014), 1.

4. Glaze, "Correctional Populations in the United States," 2.

5. Todd Clear and Natasha Frost, *The Punishment Imperative* (New York: New York University Press, 2014).

6. "The Uniform Crime Reporting (UCR) Program has been the starting place for law enforcement executives, students of CJ, researchers, members of the media, and the public at large seeking information on crime in the nation. The program was conceived in 1929 by the International Association of Chiefs of Police to meet the need for reliable uniform crime statistics for the nation. In 1930, the FBI was tasked with collecting, publishing, and archiving those statistics," http://www.fbi.gov/about-us/cjis/ucr/ucr.

7. Recidivism statistics attempt to measure some form of failure after someone has been convicted of a crime and has been incarcerated. The reader should carefully review the definition used by a researcher to ensure the correct usage of the word in that specific piece of research.

8. Bureau of Labor Statistics, *Occupational Outlook Handbook*, BLS.gov.

9. bls.gov/ooh/protective-service/correctional-officers.htm#tab-6.

10. Jeanne Stinchcomb and Vernon Fox, *Introduction to Corrections*, fifth ed. (Upper Saddle River, NJ: Prentice Hall, 1999).

11. https://www.salary.com/research/salary/benchmark/correctional-officer-salary.

12. "Sheriff/Police Chief Salaries," at http://www1.salary.com/SheriffPolice-Chief-Salary.html.

13. http://www.payscale.com/research/US/Job=Deputy_Sheriff/Salary.

14. https://www.salary.com/research/salary/alternate/police-or-sheriffs-patrol-officer-salary.

15. Sheriff Joe Arpaio and Len Sherman, *Joe's Law: America's Toughest Sheriff Takes on Illegal Immigration, Drugs, and Everything Else That Threatens America* (New York: AMACOM, 2008).

16. The Constitutions of New Jersey and Pennsylvania, in 1776, required that the sheriff be elected.

17. http://www.payscale.com/research/US/Job=Parole_Officer/Salary, 2015.

18. http://www.payscale.com/research/US/Job=Probation_Officer/Salary, 2015.

19. Bureau of Labor Statistics, *Occupational Outlook Handbook*, https://usafacts.org/data/topics/economy/jobs-and-income/

20. See Stinchcomb and Fox (1999) for detailed descriptions of the work of parole and probation officers.

21. Ibid.

22. Ibid.

23. http://www.bjs.gov/content/pub/pdf/scefy8210.pdf. Note: This figure does not consider hidden costs, that is, costs that are subsumed by other state departments, such as vehicles, that in some states are located in the treasury department.

24. http://www.bjs.gov/content/pub/pdf/scefy8210.pdf. Note: This figure does not take into account hidden costs, that is, costs that are subsumed by other state departments, such as vehicles, that in some states are located in the treasury department.

25. http://us.wow.com/search?s_it=topsearchbox.search&s_chn=25&s_pt=aolsem&v_t=aolsem&q=American+probation+and+parole+Association+recommends+a+case+load+of+50+cases+per+officer, Summer 1991.

26. http://www.bjs.gov/content/pub/pdf/ppus13.pdf.

27. https://www.salaryexpert.com/salary/job/youth-worker-corrections/united-states.

28. https://www.salary.com/research/salary/posting/correctional-counselor-salary.

29. https://www.salary.com/research/salary/benchmark/administrative-assistant-i-salary.

30. https://www.ziprecruiter.com/Salaries/Correctional-Case-Manager-Salary.

31. https://www.google.com/?gws_rd=ssl#q=Private+prisons%2C+ %2C+2001, February 2001.

CHAPTER 4

1. See http://www.bjs.gov/content/pub/pdf/scefy8210.pdf.

2. Johnnie Cochran, attorney to O. J. Simpson, Abner Louima, Michael Jackson, and Sean Combs, began his law career as a deputy city attorney, went into private practice, and later joined the Los Angeles County District Attorney's office as the first black assistant district attorney. He was inspired by Thurgood Marshall and the *Brown v. Board of Education* case, and later wrote, "I read everything I could about Thurgood Marshall and confirmed that a single dedicated man could use the law to change society."

3. Jeffrey Toobin, *The Run of His Life: The People v. O.J. Simpson* (New York: Random House, 1996).

4. See *Gideon v. Wainright*.

5. Dan T. Carter, *Scottsboro: A Tragedy of the American South* (Baton Rouge: Louisiana State University Press, 1979).

6. John Grisham, *The Innocent Man* (New York: Doubleday, 2006).

7. See innocenceproject.org. The Innocence Projects were created after the first O. J. Simpson prosecution, are found in all 50 states, and to date are responsible for almost 400 exonerations. What is important to remember is that an exoneration means a person did not commit the crime. An exoneration is not a technical error of constitutional rights. There is an estimate by the Innocence Projects that as many as 5 percent (and it may be more) all persons convicted may in fact be innocent of the crimes for which they have been charged.

8. DNA is material contained in chromosomes that is self-replicating. DNA is considered to be unique as a material that can positively distinguish one person from another.

9. James Inciardi, *Criminal Justice*, sixth ed. (Orlando, FL: Harcourt, Brace, and Co., 1999).

10. Courts of limited jurisdiction are federal courts set up to address specific situations (such as bankruptcy and family matters). The courts of limited jurisdiction cannot hear cases that would fall under general or other jurisdictions.

11. *Filibuster* is the use of a speech to obstruct a legislative proceeding.

12. *Cloture* is a motion to bring an end to a debate.

13. See http://learn.org/articles/Judge_Become_a_Judge_in_5_Steps.html.

14. https://www.history.com/news/anita-hill-confirmation-hearings-impact.

15. Abe Fortas stepped down from the Supreme Court because of ethics accusations. He is most famous for his defense before the U.S. Supreme Court in the case of *Gideon v. Wainright*. Gideon was an indigent defendant in a Florida prison who handwrote an appeal in pencil to the Court.

16. *Impeachment* is the formal process of accusation of wrongdoing (illegality) against an elected official that may lead to removal from office. There may also be civil or criminal penalties for the accused acts.

17. See http://www.bloomberg.com/news/articles/2014-01-13/federal-judgesin-u-s-see-25-000-more-as-salary-freeze-falls.

18. https://www.recruiter.com/salaries/coroners-salary/.

19. https://www.indeed.com/career/forensic-scientist/salaries.

20. https://www.salary.com/research/salary/recruiting/bailiff-salary.

21. https://www.salary.com/research/salary/benchmark/court-reporter-salary.

22. https://www.salary.com/research/salary/benchmark/court-clerk-salary.

CHAPTER 5

1. Park police are only assigned to three cities: the District of Columbia, New York City, and San Francisco.

2. This website answers many questions about careers in the federal government, as well as questions about the application process.

3. Go to this website, http://www.nps.gov/uspp/hirproc2.htm, for a step-by-step process to becoming a U.S. Parks police officer. This site provides an explanation of qualifications, disqualifiers, and the Physical Efficiency Battery (PED), as well as other details about the Comprehensive Written and Psychological Examination. The website also provides several sample examinations questions. Visit http://www.fws.gov/ for job descriptions and to view some interesting videos of wardens on the job.

4. Visit www.fws.gov/ for job descriptions and to view some interesting videos of wardens on the job.

5. Visit http://www.secretservice.gov/ for a detailed job description and multiple links that explain the career and hiring process in the Secret Service.

6. Dr. Kenny held several positions as a treasury enforcement agent, including a group manager field investigator, a district director's representative (Monmouth/Ocean Counties, New Jersey), a district quality officer, a chief of advisory, and a chief of review. He earned his PhD at Rutgers University and is a tenured professor at Fairleigh Dickinson University. He is an expert in workplace violence, school violence, and domestic violence, and he has published various papers on these subjects. See his complete biography on the website.

7. See www.opm.gov/oca/payrates/.

8. See http://www.bop.gov/jobs/eligibility/index.jsp.

9. See http://www.bop.gov/about/agency/.

10. Glynco, Georgia, is the location of the Federal Law Enforcement Training Center (FLETC). This facility trains new federal employees in basic skills and other agents with advanced skills instruction. Each year the FLETC prepares more than forty thousand employees for a wide variety of duties, with more than 250 courses of instruction from fingerprinting to interview skills, to high-speed pursuits and defensive driving, to computer crimes, and more.

11. See https://www.fletc.gov/training-catalog.

CHAPTER 6

1. https://www.cre.org/real-estate-issues/we-are-made-wise-not-by-the-recollection-of-our-past-but-by-the-responsibility-for-our-future-george-bernard-shaw/.

2. Work from home became a mainstay for many professions to survive the pandemic. The virtual internship, like the pandemic, may be a learning moment for many. Just as academics had to adjust to all virtual platforms, students might benefit from realizing that events like the pandemic are seldom prepared for. A person in a constant state of preparation, or to put it another way, be engaged in a program of ongoing personal development, is better prepared to meet crises and change as it occurs

3. Dorothy Taylor, *Jump-Starting Your Career: An Internship Guide for Criminal Justice*, 2nd ed. (Upper Saddle River, NJ: Pearson Education, 2005).

4. https://cuny.manifoldapp.org/read/environmental-press-revisiting-the-concept-in-current-research/section/1c4610b6-ebce-47af-b302-e2b05b384dcb.

5. Con Gottfredson and Bob Mosher, *Innovative Performance Support: Strategies and Practices for Learning in the Workflow* (New York: McGraw Hill Companies, 2010).

6. https://investingnewshubb.com/2021/03/17/6-benefits-of-working-part-time-instead-of-full-time.

CHAPTER 7

1. Headhunter: a professional human resource recruiter. They typically recruit for specific upper management positions

2. Stephen Covey, *The Seven Habits of Highly Successful People* (New York: The Free Press, 2004).

3. William Johnson et al., *The Criminal Justice Student Writer's Manual*, third ed. (Upper Saddle River, NJ: Pearson Education, Inc., 2005).

CHAPTER 8

1. https://www.washingtonpost.com/graphics/investigations/police-shootings-database/. The article logs the more than 5,000 fatal shootings by off duty police officers and more than 500 more by on-duty police officers.

2. https://www.policemag.com/536451/report-228-american-police-officers-died-by-suicide-in-2019.

3. https://www.uscourts.gov/educational-resources/educational-activities/facts-and-case-summary-miranda-v-arizona.

4. https://www.rogerebert.com/far-flung-correspondents/serpico-the-cop-who-wouldnt-take-money.

5. https://nypost.com/2020/05/28/everything-we-know-about-the-death-of-george-floyd/.

6. https://www.biography.com/crime-figure/rodney-king.

7. https://nmaahc.si.edu/blog/scottsboro-boys.

8. https://www.cbsnews.com/news/amadou-diallo-kadiatou-protests-george-floyd-police/.

9. https://www.biography.com/crime-figure/trayvon-martin.

10. https://work.chron.com/importance-ethics-criminal-justice-practitioner-6542.html.

11. Jay Albanese, *Professional Ethics in Criminal Justice: Being Ethical When No One Else Is Looking* (Boston: Pearson, 2008).

12. https://www.msn.com/en-us/news/crime/derek-chauvin-pleads-the-fifth-won-t-testify-in-his-own-defense/ar-BB1fGK2I.

13. https://www.nj.gov/oag/newsreleases09/pr20090921a.html.

14. http://digitallibrary.usc.edu/cdm/ref/collection/p15799coll69/id/3986.

15. A Federal Consent Decree is handed down by a federal court upon finding that an agency or some function of state government is in violation of the U.S. Constitution. Upon acceptance by the specific state to be under a federal consent decree, the federal court then appoints a federal master to oversee changes in the state that will bring the state into compliance with the U.S. Constitution. Once the federal court is satisfied that the state or agency is now in full compliance, then it will lift the federal consent decree.

16. https://www.bbc.com/news/world-us-canada-54210448.

17. https://www.fox5atlanta.com/news/gbi-completes-investigation-into-death-of-rayshard-brooks.

18. https://www.cnn.com/2020/10/07/us/jonathan-price-police-shooting-texas-report/index.html.

19. See http://www.prisonexp.org/, 1999–2015.

20. Philip Zimbardo, *The Lucifer Effect* (New York: Random House, Inc., 2008).
21. https://www.simplypsychology.org/milgram.html.
22. http://forejustice.org/zimbardo/p_zimbardo_interview.htm.
23. Matthew J. Sheridan presentation "Ethics," American Correctional Association, Boston, 2016.
24. https://grammarist.com/usage/malfeasance-misfeasance-and-nonfeasance/.
25. Consent decrees have been handed down by the federal courts to reform prisons, law enforcement, and other governmental agencies because of constitutional violations. The court then appoints a federal master who will oversee the changes to become constitutionally compliant.
26. Joycelyn Pollock, *Ethical Dilemmas and Decisions in Criminal Justice*, fifth ed. (Belmont, CA: Thompson Higher Education, 2007).
27. https://www.americanbar.org/.
28. Pollock, *Ethical Dilemmas and Decisions in Criminal Justice*.

CHAPTER 9

1. https://www.hollandcodes.com/riasec-inventory.html.
2. https://www.hollandcodes.com/riasec-inventory.html.
3. ttps://www.themyersbriggs.com/en-us/products-and-services/strong.
4. P. Tontodonato, 2006. Goals, Expectations, and Satisfaction of Criminal Justice Majors: Implications for Faculty, Students, and Programs. *Journal of Criminal Justice Education 17*(1):162–180.
5. https://www.ssa.gov/pubs/EN-05-10377.pdf.

CHAPTER 10

1. https://www.bls.gov/ooh/protective-service/private-detectives-and-investigators.htm.
2. https://www.bls.gov/oes/current/oes339032.htm.
3. https://www.bls.gov/ooh/Protective-Service/Private-detectives-and-investigators.htm.
4. https://www.salary.com/research/salary/posting/private-security-guard-salary#:~:text=The%20base%20salary%20for%20Private%20Security%20Guard%20ranges,with%20the%20average%20total%20cash%20compensation%20of%20%2427%2C222.
5. https://mourelatos.wordpress.com/2010/10/17/five-key-areas-of-risk-management/.
6. https://careers.acfe.com/job/chief-auditor/57726122/.
7. https://www.acfe.com/.
8. https://corporate.lowes.com/careers/search-apply/ft-asset-protection-agent-day-2102704br.

APPENDIX A

1. L. E. Noel, L. E., *Voyages: Canada's Heritage Rivers* (Guilford, CT: Breakwater Books, 1995), 1.

APPENDIX H

1. John Dempsey, *Police (with Criminal Justice CourseMate with eBook Printed Access Card)*, Second Edition (Boston, MA: Cengage Learning, 2012).

Raymond Foster and Tracey Biscontini, *Police Officer Exam for Dummies* (Hoboken, NJ: Wiley Publishing, 2011).

Donald Schroeder and Frank Lombardo, *Barron's Police Officer Exam*, Ninth Edition (New York: Barron's Educational Services, 2013).

Donald Schroeder and Frank Lombardo, *Barron's Correction Officer Exam*, Fourth Edition (New York: Barron's Educational Services, 2014).

APPENDIX P

1. www.aca.org/ACA_Prod_IMIS/ACA_Member/About_Us/Code_of_Ethics/ACA_Member/AboutUs/Code_of_Ethics.aspx?hkey=61577ed2-c0c3-4529-bc01–36a248f79eba.
2. www.appa-net.org/eweb/DynamicPage.aspx?Web Code=IA_CodeEthics.
3. www.theiacp.org/resources/law-enforcement-code-of-ethics.

Glossary

CJ has terms unique to the professions. The terms post-trick and shift differential serve as illustrations. This glossary is limited to terms generally associated with a job search and especially for events such as interviews.

Adjudication: The conclusion or process of a juvenile criminal proceeding resulting in an acquittal, conviction, or dismissal of a case.

Adjunct: A part time professor/instructor at a college or university.

Arraignment: A pretrial hearing during which an accused person is advised of their constitutional rights and pleads guilty or not guilty to criminal charges.

Arrest: The taking into custody of a person by law enforcement agency.

Arrest Warrant: A warrant resulting from a complaint, which is signed by a judge and authorizes law enforcement to arrest a person because believed to have committed a crime.

B-PAD: A part of the hiring process which assesses the applicant's ability to make decisions, communicate, evaluate ethics, and responses to stress. It is a behavior-based test.

Change of Venue: The transfer of a case from one jurisdiction to another because of prejudicial publicity, greater convenience of witnesses, and to obtain a fair and impartial jury.

Charge: An accusation in an indictment, filed by the prosecution, that a crime has been committed by a person.

Child Protective Services: Governmental agencies which investigate charges of child abuse or neglect and seek the remediation of the problems.

Community Supervision: A court order which requires the supervision of a sentenced person, generally by a parole or probation officer. The intention is to ensure that the conditions of the sentence are fulfilled such as those which would ensure victim safety, which may include restraining orders, and that the offender receives employment, job training, education, or counseling.

Commutation: A sentencing change resulting in a less severe punishment which is authorized by a government official such as a president governor, generally preceded by a review of the parole board with a recommendation.

Crime Analyst: Someone trained to examine socioeconomic and spatial patterns of criminal behavior which includes types of crime, time of day, and place(s) of occurrence. The analyses improve effectiveness to prevent crime and mitigate criminal behavior.

Criminalist: A person (often a medical examiner) generally trained in forensics (pathology, medicine, anatomy, psychiatry), with knowledge of criminal law, who draws conclusions after examining evidence, substantiates witness testimony, and offers expert testimony.

Criminal Justice System: Three major governmental and private components (law enforcement, courts, and corrections) comprise the criminal justice system. They provide law enforcement through apprehension, both prosecution and defense, sentencing and punishing of convicted offenders.

Criminal Record: The record of criminal arrests, charges, convictions, and other interactions with the CJ system.

Criminologist: A trained researcher of crime, its causes, consequences, and costs. They are professors in universities, government employees, who assist with policy creation, and propose recommendations with which to respond to or prevent of crime.

Criminology. See *Criminologist*.

Curriculum: A specified college program of courses and activities, noting grade attainment for the award of a degree with a specialty (called a major).

Dismissal: A judicial decision which legally terminates a case, with or without prejudice.

Disposition: The conclusion of criminal proceedings with outcomes such as dismissal, acquittal, or sentencing of a defendant.

District Attorney (DA): The DA is the chief law enforcement officer within a specific jurisdiction who decides whether or not to prosecute criminal offenses.

Docket: The official record of court proceedings which includes the list of cases scheduled to appear before the court.

Due Process: The constitutional protection of legal individual rights, both procedural and substantive.

Equal Employment Opportunity Commission (EEOC): A federal agency charged with enforcing federal laws which provide protections from discrimination because of age, color, disability, national origin, race, religion, sex, and sexual orientation.

Evidence: Physical objects and testimony presented during adjudication (or trial) of a criminal matter which prove or disprove expert testimony, the testimony of the victim, the accused, or other witnesses.

Exoneration: The official clearance of conviction of a criminal act. This is not to be confused with violations of due process. The person did not commit the act and was wrongfully convicted.

Expungement: Records of arrest and conviction which are sealed and generally do not have to be disclosed to potential employers. An exception is for CJ employment.

Externship: An experiential learning opportunity, generally in relation to a college course of study in a specific field with CJ employers and agencies which exposes the participant to practical experiences.

Felony: A state or federal statute which defines what a crime is and the punishment. If confinement is suitable for the offense, then state or federal prison time (usually exceeds one year), and may also include fines, forfeiture, and other stipulated penalties.

Forensic Anthropologists: examine human and other remains (often limited to a few bones or other skeletal features) to acquire information about victims such as age, types of injuries and other distinguishing features such as height and weight, race, and cultural characteristics.

Forensic Computer Investigators: use technology to gather electronic (often computer) evidence from cybercriminals. Private security firms are employed to protect IT systems.

Forensic Psychologists: function as jury consultants for selection, prepare witnesses for testimony, determine competency to stand trial, conduct criminal profiling, and evaluate prisoners for rehabilitation programs.

Forensic Science Careers: A broad category which includes work in a crime lab or with a crime scene investigative unit to collect, preserve, and analyze evidence such as bloodstain pattern analysis, ballistics. They also may help determine the type of person who committed the offence.

Grand Jury: Eligible citizens serve on a jury to examine evidence to determine whether it warrants a subsequent criminal trial.

Indictment: A formal charging document presented by a prosecutor to a grand jury to determine whether there is sufficient evidence for charging someone with a crime.

Internship: A structured experience (also called a practicum or co-op) during which a student observes, participates in, and explores potential careers. This is considered professional development for that career. Virtual Internships became a tool during the pandemic and allow students to explore internships in a virtual context and to investigate opportunities not available because of distance.

Jail: A local or county facility used to hold persons awaiting trial or offenders sentenced to less than one year.

Judicial Officer or Judge: An appointed position, also called an officer of the court, with legal authority to preside over cases brought before the court to determine cause or render decisions.

Landmark Case: A U.S. Supreme Court case which affirms, augments, extends, clarifies significant constitutional issues that will then be followed by the judiciary to decide cases or directs others to proceed in a specific fashion when dealing with that constitutional issue.

Loss Prevention Specialists: Trained to enable retail stores and corporations to minimize or eliminate theft by customers and employees. The position may be a second career for someone trained in law enforcement or who has earned a degree in CJ. The position may be a means to work toward a position in law enforcement or security.

Misdemeanor: An offense which is less serious than a felony according to state or federal statute which may result in any of several forms of punishment including imprisonment (usually less than one year), probation, fines, community service, or other penalties.

Mistrial: A declaration by a judge that a fundamental procedural error or act or wrongdoing occurred during the trial.

Motion: A verbal or written request in writing by the prosecutor or defense attorney for which a judge responds with a ruling.

Notarized: A document is authenticated by a notary (a public officer) who attests to the legitimacy or signature (made in front of the notary) of the holder of the document.

Occupational License: A government issued license which allows a person to perform jobs in a specific context. The license has limitations such as not permitting the holder to possess or carry a weapon, explosives, or to operate a vehicle.

Pardon: A release issued by a governor (or the president of the United States) which relieves a convicted person from the consequences of the offense.

Parole: A release from imprisonment by a parole board. The offender then reports to a parole officer until the sentence is completed or the person is discharged form parole. A parolee has conditions monitored by the parole officer to help ensure public and victim safety.

Parole Revocation: A filing by a parole officer when the parolee has violated parole conditions such as abuse of drugs or alcohol, failure to complete counseling, violating restraint orders, or possession of a weapon, The revocation hearing may result in a return to confinement.

Plea Agreement (Also referred to as a **Plea Bargain**): The accused through the defense attorney and the prosecutor agree to the outcome of a criminal case, subject to court (judge) approval.

Part-Time Lecturers. See *Adjuncts.*

Police Dispatcher: A police department's position in which the person takes calls, records messages, sets up case numbers, and alerts officers who may be dispatched to respond and investigate incidents that require police intervention.

Bibliography and Suggested Readings

A bibliography usually does not contain opening remarks. This bibliography is an exception and contains references and suggested readings to help the reader explore careers. These are the references which guided the development of *Contemporary Criminal Justice Careers: A Comprehensive Guide.* They were informative, and at times, interesting sources of information about the CJ profession. This book is a reference to guide students and for those offering career counseling. We have taken a novel approach to References and Suggested Readings by categorization of topics such as General, Careers, Law Enforcement, Corrections, Law, Private Security, and Ethics. Time is a valuable asset, and we have tried to be selective in our recommendations to provide the reader with material that delivers the maximum benefit to acquire needed information.

GENERAL

Bach, Richard. *Jonathan Livingston Seagull*. New York: Scribner, 1970.

Clear, Todd, and Marsha Frost. *The Punishment Imperative*. New York: New York University Press, 2014.

Hassine, Victor, Robert Johnson, and Ania Dobrzanska. 2005. *The Crying Wall and Other Prison Stories*. West Conshohocken, PA: Infinity Publishing Company.

Inciardi, James. *Criminal Justice*, sixth ed. Orlando, FL: Harcourt, Brace, and Co., 1999.

President's Commission on Law Enforcement and the Administration of Justice. *The Challenge of Crime in a Free Society*. New York: Avon Books/Hearst, 1968.

Sheridan, Matthew, and Stephen Richards. "Collateral Consequences: Felony Convictions." *The Encyclopedia of Criminal Justice Ethics*. Thousand Oaks, CA: Sage, 2013.

Sheridan, Matthew, Raymond R. Rainville, Anna King, Brian Royster, and Giuseppe M. Fazari. *Historical Dictionary of American Criminal Justice*. Lanham, MD: Rowman and Littlefield, 2019.

Silberman, Charles. *Criminal Justice, Criminal Violence*. New York: Vintage, 1968.

Toobin, Jeffrey. *The Run of His Life: The People v. O.J. Simpson*. New York: Random House, 1996.

Weisheit, Ralph, and Frank Morn. *Pursuing Justice*. New York: Anderson, 2015.

CAREERS

The American Correctional Association. *The American Prison: From the Beginning—A Pictorial History*. The American Correctional Association, 1983.

Bartollas, Clemens, and Stuart Miller. *Juvenile Justice in America*, seventh ed. Upper Saddle River, NJ: Prentice Hall, 2001.

Bergman, Larry W. "Corrections as a Wholistic Profession?" *The Keepers' Voice*, vol. 15, no. 1 (Winter 1994): 43.

Bowker, Lee. *Prison Victimization*. New York: Elsevier, 1980.

Carlson, Peter, and Judith Garrett. *Prison and Jail Administration: Practice and Theory*, second ed. Boston: Jones and Bartlett Publishers, 2008.

Clear, Todd, George Cole, and Michael Reisig. *American Correction*, eighth ed. Belmont, CA: Thompson Higher Education, 2009.

Conover, Ted. *Newjack*. New York: Random House, 2000.

Grisham, John. *The Innocent Man*. New York: Doubleday, 2006.

Johnson, Lee. *Experiencing Corrections: From Practitioner to Professor*. Thousand Oaks, CA: Sage, 2012.

Kenny, James F. *Hiding in Plain Sight: Deceptive Tactics and the Criminal Victimization Process*. New York: Palgrave MacMillan, 2020.

Pollock, Joycelan M. *Prisons: Today and Tomorrow*. Burlington, MA: Jones & Bartlett Learning, 1997.

Rafter, Nicole. "Gender, Prisons, and Prison History." *Social Science History*, vol. 9, no. 3 (1985): 233–247.

Schroeder, Donald, and Frank Lombardo. *Barron's Correction Officer Exam*, fourth ed. New York: Barron's Educational Services, 2014.

Stinchcomb, Jeanne, and Vernon Fox. *Introduction to Corrections*, fifth ed. Upper Saddle River, NJ: Prentice Hall, 1999.

LAW ENFORCEMENT

Daly, Robert. *The Prince of the City*. New York: Berkeley, 1984.

Dempsey, John. *Police (with Criminal Justice CourseMate with eBook Printed Access Card)*, second ed. Boston, MA: Cengage Learning, 2012.

DiLieto, Michael. *How to Become a New Jersey Police Officer or State Trooper*. Maywood, NJ: NJ Law Enforcement Recruit Resources, 2005–2008.

Evola, Alley. *So You Want to Be a Cop: What Everyone Should Know Before Entering Law Enforcement*. Lanham, MD: Rowman and Littlefield, 2017.

Foster, Raymond, and Tracey Biscontini. *Police Officer Exam for Dummies*. Hoboken, NJ: Wiley, 2011.

Longworthy, Robert, and Lawrence Travis. *Policing in America: A Balance of Forces*. Upper Saddle River, NJ: Prentice Hall, 1999.

Maas, Peter. *Serpico: The Cop Who Defied the System*. New York: Viking, 1973.

Royster, Brian. *Crossroads: Conflicted Journey of a New Jersey State Trooper*. Bloomington, IN: Xlibris Publishing, 2018.

Rupp, Kelly. *Police Writing: A Guide to the Essentials*. Upper Saddle River, NJ: Pearson Education, 2015.

Schroeder, Donald, and Frank Lombardo. *Barron's Police Officer Exam*, ninth ed. New York: Barron's Educational Services, 2013.

Smalleger, Frank, and John Worrall. *Policing Today*. Upper Saddle River, NJ: Pearson Education, 2010.

Twersky-Glasner, Aviva, and Matthew Sheridan. "Police Psychologist: Gatekeeper and Ally." *New Jersey Criminal Justice Educator*, 10–11, 2005.

Walker, Samuel, and Charles Katz. *The Police in America: An Introduction*, fifth ed. New York: McGraw-Hill, 2005.

CORRECTIONS

The American Correctional Association. *The American Prison: From the Beginning—A Pictorial History*. The American Correctional Association, 1983.

Bartollas, Clemens, and Stuart Miller. *Juvenile Justice in America*, seventh ed. Upper Saddle River, NJ: Prentice Hall, 2001.

Bergman, Larry W. "Corrections as a Wholistic Profession?" *The Keepers' Voice*, vol. 15, no. 1 (Winter 1994): 43.

Bowker, Lee. *Prison Victimization*. New York: Elsevier, 1980.

Carlson, Peter, and Judith Garrett. *Prison and Jail Administration: Practice and Theory*, second ed. Boston: Jones and Bartlett Publishers, 2008.

Clear, Todd, George Cole, and Michael Reisig. *American Correction*, eighth ed. Belmont, CA: Thompson Higher Education, 2009.

Conover, Ted. *Newjack*. New York: Random House, 2000.

Grisham, John. *The Innocent Man*. New York: Doubleday, 2006.

Johnson, Lee. *Experiencing Corrections: From Practitioner to Professor*. Thousand Oaks, CA: Sage, 2012.

Rafter, Nicole. "Gender, Prisons, and Prison History." *Social Science History*, vol. 9, no. 3 (1985): 233–247.

Schroeder, Donald, and Frank Lombardo. *Barron's Correction Officer Exam*, fourth ed. New York: Barron's Educational Services, 2014.

Stinchcomb, Jeanne, and Vernon Fox. *Introduction to Corrections*, fifth ed. Upper Saddle River, NJ: Prentice Hall, 1999.

LAW

Brotman, Ellen. *Careers in Criminal Law*. Washington, DC: American Bar Association Criminal Justice Section, 2010.

Camenson, Blythe. *Careers for Legal Eagles and Other Law-and-Order Types*, second ed. New York: McGraw-Hill, 2005.

Campbell, Charles F. *The Intolerable Hulks: British Shipboard Confinement*. Tucson, AZ: Fenestar Books, 2001.

McClurg, Andrew. *1L of a Ride: A Well-Traveled Professor's Roadmap to Success in the First Year of Law School*, fourth ed. West Academic Publishing, 2021.

Miller, Robert H. *Law School Confidential: A Complete Guide to the Law School Experience: By Students, for Students.* Kindle Edition. New York: St. Martin's Griffin, 2021.

Paterson, Anne. *Careers in Focus: Law*. Chicago, IL: Ferguson Pub. Co., 2001.

Raz, Manda, Erwin Loh, and John Devereux, eds. *Careers in Law: A Guide for Students, Graduates, and Professionals.* Kindle Edition. New York: Springer, 2020.

Tuttle, Cliff. "Juris Doctor: The Versatile Degree." *Pennsylvania Law Weekly* 18 (December 11, 1995).

Susskind, Richard. *Tomorrow's Lawyers: An Introduction to Your Future*, second ed. Kindle Edition. Oxford: Oxford University Press, 2017.

PRIVATE SECURITY

Churchill, David, Doloris Janiewski, and Peter Leloup. Eds. *Private Security and the Modern State: Historical and Comparative Perspectives*. New York: Routledge, 2020.

Hucklesby, Anthea, and Stuart Lister, eds. *The Private Sector and Criminal Justice*. London: Palgrave Macmillan, 2018.

Miller, Wilbur R. *A History of Private Policing in the United States*. London: Bloomsbury Publishing, 2018.

O'Hara, Stephen P. *Inventing the Pinkertons; Or, Spies, Sleuths, Mercenaries, and Thugs: Being a Story of the Nation's Most Famous (and Infamous) Detective Agency*. Baltimore: Johns Hopkins University Press, 2018.

Schmalleger, Frank, Larry Siegel, and Carter Smith. *Private Security Today*. New York: Pearson, 2017.

Sparrow, Malcolm K. *Managing the Boundary between Public and Private Policing: New Perspectives in Policing*. Washington, DC: National Institute of Justice, 2014.

Tripp, Tara, and Sutham Cobkit. "Unexpected Pathways: Criminal Justice Career Options in the Private Sector." *Journal of Criminal Justice Education, vol. 24, no. 4 (2013): 478–494.*

ETHICS

Albanese, Jay. *Professional Ethics in Criminal Justice: Being Ethical When No One Else Is Looking*. Boston: Pearson, 2008.

Arrigo, Bruce A., and Christopher R. Williams. *Ethics, Crime, and Criminal Justice*, third ed. New York: Pearson, 2022.

Cape, Ed, and Julian Webb. "The Ethics of Criminal Justice Professionals in an Era of Change." *Legal Ethics*, vol. 9, no. 1 (2006): 1–5.

Pollock, Joycelyn. *Ethical Dilemmas and Decisions in Criminal Justice*, fifth ed. Belmont, CA: Thompson Higher Education, 2007.

Sherman, Lawrence. "Learning Police Ethics." *Justice, Crime, and Ethics*, third ed. Cincinnati: Anderson, 1998.

Williams, Christopher, and Bruce Arrigo. *Ethics, Crime, and Criminal Justice*. Boston: Pearson, 2008.

Zimbardo, Philip. *The Lucifer Effect*. New York: Random House, 2008.

MULTICULTURALISM

Hanser, Robert, and Michael Gomila. *Multiculturalism and the Criminal Justice System*. New York: Pearson (2014).

McNamara, Robert, and Ronald Burns. *Multiculturalism, Crime, and Criminal Justice*. New York: Oxford University Press (2020).

Richeson, Jennifer A., and Richard J. Nussbaum, "The Impact of Multiculturalism Versus Color-Blindness on Racial Bias," *Journal of Experimental Social Psychology* 40, no. 3 (May 2004): 417–423.

LEARNING STYLES

Sheridan, M., and Steele-Dadzie. "Structure of Intellect and Learning Styles of Incarcerated Youth Assessment: A Means to Providing a Continuum of Educational Service in Juvenile Justice." *The Journal of Correctional Education, vol. 56 (2005): 347–376.*

Subject Index

Name Index

About the Authors

Matthew J. Sheridan, EdD Professional Profile: Over 30 years of progressively responsible experience in the CJ field as both practitioner and academic. Convict criminologist, frequent presenter of papers on corrections and criminology issues. Frequent lecturer at New Jersey colleges and universities, professional and other interested organizations. Core areas of expertise include correctional and parole operations, correctional administration, Juvenile Justice, correctional education, and the courts. CJ management including institutions, community residential, day treatment, and private organizations for effective responses to need. Private consultant for improving operational proficiency for compliance with state and federal standards. Conducting and reviewing. For questions, please contact at msheridan@georgian.edu.

Thomas J. Lalka, DBA, MBA. Professional Profile: A corporate leader with demonstrated experience in communicating real-world initiatives and the ability to manage large groups. Skilled at mentoring and advising individuals at both the corporate and student level. Highly involved with academic issues of students with career issues, hiring, and training new associate faculty in the U.S. and Asia. Proficient in facilitating classes in mathematics, statistics, economics, finance, and logistics at both the graduate and undergraduate levels. Five years of experience with the largest credit card corporation (Total Systems) in the fraud division. Executive for 19 years with the Kroger Company which included market level and corporate responsibilities supervising distribution and transportation. Former board of director on the Universal Pricing Code council. Tom's career has taken him from the corporate world to academia through advanced degrees. His academic career followed his corporate career and enables him to utilize his corporate experience. His academic success took him to Japan for five years in the Graduate Business/Management and Education Military Programs Asia Pacific. Dr. Lalka can be contacted via tlalka@email.phoenix.edu.